Unemployment After Keynes

By the same author

Inflation: A Theoretical Survey and Synthesis
(George Allen & Unwin, 1982)

Unemployment After Keynes

Towards a New General Theory

John Hudson
Lecturer in Econometrics
University of Bath

HARVESTER · WHEATSHEAF · ENGLAND

ST. MARTIN'S PRESS · NEW YORK

First published 1988 by
Harvester · Wheatsheaf
66 Wood Lane End, Hemel Hempstead
Hertfordshire HP2 4RG
A division of
Simon & Schuster International Group

and in the USA by
St. Martin's Press, Inc.
175 Fifth Avenue, New York, NY 10010

Printed and bound in Great Britain by
Billing & Sons Limited, Worcester

British Library Cataloguing in Publication Data

Hudson, John, 1947–
Unemployment after Keynes: towards a
new general theory.
1. Unemployment
I. Title
331.13′7 HD5707.5
ISBN 0-7450-0094-0
ISBN 0-7450-0293-5 Pbk

Library of Congress Cataloging-in-Publication Data

Hudson, John (John R.)
Unemployment after Keynes: towards a new general
theory/John Hudson.
p.   cm.
Bibliography: p.
Includes index.
ISBN 0-312-02388-X
1. Unemployment. I. Title.
HD5707.5.H84 1988
331.13′7—dc19   88-17442
                                                    CIP

1   2   3   4   5   92   91   90   89   88

for Alex and Chris

Contents

Preface   ix

1: Theories of Unemployment   1

2: Towards a New General Theory   39

3: Retaining Supply-Side Capacity   76

4: A New Empirical Approach   119

5: An Agent-Based Applied General Disequilibrium
   Model   140

6: Model Simulations   164

7: Policy and Other Conclusions   175

Appendix 1: Program Listing   189

Appendix 2: Nag Library Subroutines   234

References   236

Index   245

Simular for Mevier?

Preface

Economics is in some disarray. The problem of unemployment, which many of the OECD countries are experiencing, has presented a challenge which economists have apparently been unable to meet. Keynesian policies are no longer thought to be sufficient to allow economic recovery, whilst monetarist alternatives seem even more barren of hope. In the thirties similar problems provided the stimulus for the development of radical new approaches in economics. To date there is relatively little evidence of any such advances being made today. One of the few areas of development which does offer some hope of offering new insights into economic problems is that of the disequilibrium theorists, and it is this approach which will form the basis of the analysis in this book.

The General Theory provided radical new theoretical insights, which stimulated economics and economists for nearly half a century. Yet it has its shortcomings in ignoring the supply side of the economy. Central to Keynes' analysis was his critique of classical economics' belief in Say's law that supply creates its own demand. Yet implicit in Keynesian analysis is an equal oversimplification in the parallel belief that demand creates its own supply. Keynes' law, as this might be termed, has led to the assumption that unemployment can always be cured by a simple expansion of demand. Recent experience, however has shown that this is not always the case. It is partly to explain the patchy performance of Keynesian demand management policies in recent years that the theoretical part of this book is aimed. Building on the work of those who have examined economics in disequilibrium I look at the impact on the supply side of the economy of the birth and death of firms. These are subjects which are almost never covered in textbooks and are at the very periphery of macro-analysis, whereas they should be at the centre. Policies should aim at retaining existing supply side capacity, for example by establishing an appropriate framework to deal with bankruptcies as well as providing the optimal climate for the survival of new firms, thereby expanding new capacity. There is an important role for governments to play in, for example, saving firms the market would let die and ensuring that new entrepreneurs have an appropriate degree of training. This first half of the book contains detailed analysis of both the American and British economies, and the picture which consistently emerges is that the former is much more flexible in adapting to changing conditions.

One of the reasons disequilibrium theories have had a relatively limited impact is that current modes of analysis are not sophisticated enough to analyse them. Small wonder the economist can tell us little about the real world when he uses models characterised by perfectly competitive firms, constant returns to scale and homogeneous labour and capital with the latter in the form of malleable jelly. I argue that current computer techniques offer the opportunity of overcoming the limitations imposed by mathematical tractability, and present two examples of how this might be done. The most ambitious of these attempts to model individual agents within an economy, and by summing the outcomes of their actions arrive at macroeconomic variables. This technique of agent-base modelling, as I have called it, therefore allows us to attempt to replicate the real world in our models, rather than proxy it.

The first half of the book was written in stages, beginning with the realisation, that when a factory is demolished it cannot suddenly start producing again if demand for its products revives. But the second half was physically much more onerous, due to the difficulty of constructing such a model, difficulties I had not really understood when commencing the book. In addition, as the model steadily increased in size it ate its way through three mainframe computers. Because of this its completion was continually delayed, and I would like to acknowledge the patience of Wheatsheaf Books and their former editor, Romesh Vaitilingham, without which the book would never have seen the light of day. I should also acknowledge the help of Michael Ashworth, Dixie Harvey and Neil Howitt whose comments on the program vastly improved it, an anonymous reviewer and David Collard who commented on parts of the typescript. Finally I would thank my wife for her patience and support, and now I think I will go walking across the hills with my two sons again and watch some cricket.

John Hudson

1 Theories of Unemployment

The past decade has seen unemployment return to the centre of the economic stage. To someone who learnt their economics prior to this period it is sometimes puzzling as to why this should have happened. It seemed in the 'halcyon days' of the early 1970s that mass unemployment had been permanently banished as a major economic problem. Depressions of the kind witnessed in the 1930s were the problem of another era, of possible interest to the economic historian and the odd theorist found occupying an ivory tower, but to those of us interested in real world problems this was not a matter of major interest. The speed with which this belief has had to be abandoned should serve as a salutary lesson not just to this generation of economists, but to future ones as well.

The period of the 1930s, of course, saw a major advance in economic theory with the publication of the *General Theory*. This can justifiably be classified as a revolution because it started economists onto a new line of thinking which led to a solution of the problems of the time. To date there are few signs that the traumas of the present crisis are about to result in a similar development. Advances in economic theory have been seen in the last decade. Some of them are currently regarded as being important, and some may even stand the test of time. But most of these are merely a new twist to an old tale, having come within the existing strand of thought, and offering few new insights and still fewer solutions. This strand of thought is based on the Walrasian market clearing paradigm, which cannot and never has been able to explain mass unemployment, and it is only in the work of those who reject this approach that there can be seen any solutions emerging to restore full employment. This disequilibrium approach to macroeconomics is still in its infancy and the number of insights arising from it have not been that great. None the less it is this approach that I shall be adopting and hope to develop further.

Many would argue that a new approach is not necessary, that the existing theory which they happen to favour is capable of, with a few extensions, both explaining and removing the problem of mass unemployment. It is my belief that this somewhat complacent view is wrong for several reasons. Firstly the continuing failure of governments in Western Europe to reduce unemployment after several years suggests a lack of understanding about how the economy works. Current theories are, to differing degrees, too aggregative, and either too demand or supply biased. In analysing macro problems a firm micro foundation is lacking. Where individual agents are found in macro-theories they are 'representative', no allowance is made for differences in attitudes, circumstances or abilities which underlie many of the problems in the real world. Output and employment in such models are largely determined either by demand or supply factors separately, rather than both together as appears to be the case in the real world. Moreover supply side economics has concentrated on only a very limited aspect of this side of the economy, namely the effects of taxes on labour and investment. There has been no genuine attempt to develop a full theory of the supply side.

But not only is there a need for a new theoretical approach; there is also a need for a new analytical approach. Current techniques, based on building tractable mathematical models, oversimplify the economy to the point where their usefulness in answering many questions is severely limited. This is reflected in Drazen (1980) who notes the difficulty of analysing even the basic Arrow-Debreu model, a difficulty which is magnified many times over when analysing disequilibria where economies, or parts of economies, may switch from being in excess demand to excess supply. This is one reason why the results of the disequilibrium theorists have been so tentative. There is an overriding empirical need for a new approach founded on a greater degree of realism, which can supplement the standard mathematical approach. Again there are hints in the literature of how this can be done by making use of developments in computing. I hope to extend these to show how economists can use both small and large scale computer models to analyse theoretical questions. The former can be used to examine by stimulation the dynamic properties of aggregated macroeconomic systems of the type theorists are trying to get to grips with. As for the latter, the rapid increase in computer power provides us with the opportunity to build a computer model in much greater detail and with a much greater degree of reality then can be achieved by traditional methods of analysis. We can model an economy, its institutions, individual agents, firms and government in minute detail, and by summing the results of individual decisions we can obtain macroeconomic variables. Thus, for example, the impact of a tax change can be traced through from the reactions of individual firms and consumers to its impact upon unemployment, the balance of trade and other macro-variables. This will represent a significant methodological breakthrough, and in its train will follow new theoretical insights.

UNEMPLOYMENT IN THE USA AND THE UK.

The trends of unemployment in the UK and the USA are shown in Figure 1.1. It can be seen that for much of the postwar period the rate in the USA was much higher than in the UK. This was generally taken as signalling that the economy was running at a much higher level in the UK, but it is also worth bearing in mind that the statistics relate to different concepts in the two countries. In the UK the figures come from those claiming unemployment benefit at employment exchanges. In the USA they are derived from sample surveys asking whether the respondent is looking for work. This will almost certainly give higher estimates than the other method. In any case, since the mid 1970s this picture has changed. The recession which hit both countries in the wake of the 1973–74

Table 1.1: Statistics on the UK and the US economies

UK	1970	1971	1972	1973	1974	1975	1976	1977	1978	1979	1980	1981	1982	1983	1984
Imports	5.3	5.2	10.0	11.9	1.2	-7.1	4.2	1.2	3.9	10.4	-3.9	-3.4	3.9	5.5	8.5
Exports	1.6	3.0	4.2	4.9	1.5	5.5	1.3	-1.7	2.3	2.1	1.5	0.2	0.9	3.0	1.0
Investment	2.6	1.9	-0.3	7.2	-4.1	0.2	1.5	-2.6	3.9	2.3	-5.2	-8.5	6.7	4.0	6.5
Consumption	2.7	3.1	6.1	5.1	-1.4	-0.7	0.3	-0.5	5.5	4.5	-0.3	-0.1	1.0	4.0	1.5
Unemployment	3.1	3.9	4.3	3.3	3.1	4.6	6.0	6.4	6.3	5.6	6.9	10.6	12.3	13.1	13.2
GDP	2.2	2.7	2.3	7.9	-1.1	-0.7	3.9	1.0	3.6	2.1	-2.2	-1.1	1.9	3.0	2.5
Gov. def.[a]	0.0	0.0	3.1	3.9	5.6	11.0	8.1	4.1	6.5	7.3	6.4	5.3	3.4	5.7	2.8
Mfg emp.[b]	8.3	8.1	7.8	7.8	7.9	7.5	7.3	7.3	7.3	7.2	6.8	6.1	5.8	5.5	5.4

USA	1970	1971	1972	1973	1974	1975	1976	1977	1978	1979	1980	1981	1982	1983	1984
Imports	3.9	4.1	10.7	6.5	-1.2	-11.5	18.6	7.3	13.0	6.1	-0.2	7.0	1.4	7.5	27.1
Exports	8.5	0.7	9.2	25.5	11.5	-4.5	6.3	2.5	12.2	15.4	8.8	0.7	-7.9	-5.5	4.5
Investment	-3.5	7.1	11.5	8.4	-8.2	-12.2	9.5	13.6	9.9	3.8	-7.1	3.1	-6.8	9.7	18.2
Consumption	2.2	3.7	5.8	4.3	-0.6	2.2	5.6	4.9	4.5	2.7	0.5	2.0	1.3	4.8	5.3
Unemployment	4.8	5.8	5.5	4.8	5.5	8.3	7.6	6.9	6.0	5.8	7.0	7.5	9.5	9.5	7.4
GDP	-0.2	3.4	5.7	5.8	-0.6	-1.1	5.4	5.3	5.0	2.8	-0.3	2.5	-2.1	3.7	6.8
Gov. def.[a]	1.2	2.3	1.5	0.6	0.8	4.9	3.3	2.7	2.1	1.2	2.7	2.5	4.3	5.9	5.1
Mfg emp.[b]	19.4	18.6	19.2	20.2	20.1	18.3	19.0	19.7	20.5	21.0	20.3	20.2	18.9	18.7	19.7

Sources: International Financial Statistics (1985), *Economic Trends Annual Abstract, Business Statistics* (1982) (Supplement to the *Survey of Current Business*), *Economic Statistics* (1900–83).

Notes:

a. Gov. def. the ratio of the government deficit to GDP.
b. Mfg emp. employment (in millions) in the manufacturing industries.
All other variables are annual percentage changes, except the rate of unemployment.

OPEC oil price increases lifted unemployment to record levels in both countries. But in the USA it then fell to levels almost, but not quite, comparable with the troughs in previous cycles. In the UK the subsequent decline was minimal, so that between 1978 and 1980 the two series virtually coincided. This is the first and perhaps most important difference in the recent experience of the two countries. The second lies in the subsequent increase in unemployment from 1979 onwards, which may be linked both to the second major OPEC price hitch, and to the entrance of the Thatcher and Reagan governments in the two countries. Unemployment in the UK rose much more sharply than in the USA, where it stood at just over 9 per cent, some 3 per cent lower than the UK figure in 1982. The third major difference lies in events since then. Unemployment has continued to rise in the UK, although at a much slower rate than previously, and there is no indication or expectation that it will fall in the near future. In the USA it did fall, and fall very rapidly. Following the large lay offs of 1982 there was a rapid rehiring of production workers in the automobile and other durable industries, although there has been a marked slow down in the growth of manufacturing employment since mid-1984, and the signs are that unemployment may soon be on the increase again. None the less, to date the continued contraction of employment in old decaying industries, such as steel, has been offset by rapid employment growth in the new, high-tech industries, especially electrical and electronic equipment, which has not been the case in the UK.

Thus unemployment in the USA is a problem, the trough of every cycle since 1969 has been higher than the previous one, and the following peak has been higher than its predecessor. Opinion polls indicate that this is a major political issue, and it is probably, along with the deficit, the main economic problem of the decade. But in the UK it is more than that, it has divided the country into those who have jobs and those who do not, into the rich and the new poor, into the South and the North, with the North having shifted to include the industrial Midlands of the country. It is not a problem which threatens to get out of hand, it already has and the repercussions whether on the football terraces of Europe or the streets of the inner cities have already irreparably damaged British society.

The labour force in the UK has experienced low growth over the past decade relative to other OECD countries, growing annually by 0.6 per cent in 1973–9 and only 0.2 per cent in 1979–82. Since then it has been rising again due to demographic trends and increases in female participation rates, backed up by an encouraged worker effect. In the USA, however, growth rates in the same periods were 2.6 per cent and 1.6 per cent respectively. Thus the poorer employment performance of the UK economy over this period cannot be blamed on demographic factors. But there are other differences between the two countries' labour markets, which may go some way to explaining the different paths unemployment followed in the two economies. First, the US has far fewer legal, regulatory and financial restrictions on the hiring and firing of labour than the UK and most other West

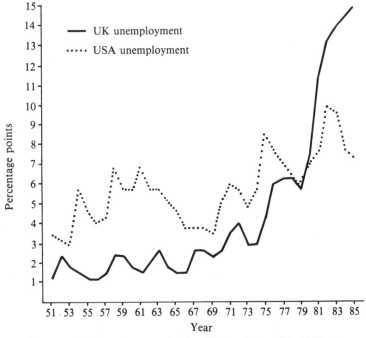

Figure 1.1: Unemployment in the USA and the UK, 1951–85

European countries. The practice of laying off workers during the downswing of the business cycle, to rehire them in the upturn, which is widespread in the US, is practically unknown in the UK and much of Europe. Partly because of this the average spell out of work has over the years been consistently longer in the UK than in the USA. Thus in August 1984 out of the 3.1 million unemployed in the UK, 61 per cent had been out of work for more than six months, in the USA the corresponding figure was just 18 per cent. Collective bargaining is, of course much more important and widespread in the UK than in the USA, where union members accounted for 16 per cent of the private workforce in 1982. This compares with 25 per cent in 1966, and the number of workers covered by major collective bargaining contracts is less than 5 per cent of the workforce. Perhaps because of this there has been a much greater degree of real wage flexibility in the face of demand and supply side shocks, and also greater regional differences in wage inflation in the USA than in the UK.

However, perhaps the most important difference between the two countries in recent years has been in their differing policy stances. In the UK, and much of Europe, the emphasis has been in cutting budget deficits, by deflationary fiscal policies. Since 1979 the UK government has been almost solely preoccupied with reducing inflation, and a stringent budgetary regime has been accompanied by an equally stringent monetary regime. Real interest rates have been exceptionally high during the period 1979–86. This together with North Sea oil has been responsible for the high value of sterling on the international exchange markets, which in turn has led to a sharp drop in exports and investment coupled with rising imports. Large tracts of British industry have been decimated and, as we shall see, record numbers of insolvencies quickly followed. This decline is somewhat disguised by the influence of North Sea oil, and, as can be seen from Table 1, gross domestic product shows some decline but by no means a catastrophic one. However this Table also shows the massive decline in employment in manufacturing industries since 1979 which has left output in this sector at its lowest level since 1967. The decline in individual sectors has been even more dramatic. Production of crude steel, for example, fell from 21.46 million tons in 1979 to 13.70 million tons in 1982, this being the lowest level since 1947. Such rapid declines are unusual, the only comparable period this century being that of the Depression of the early 1930s.

In the US the supply-side strategy has given precedence to lower tax rates. The effective rate of household tax has fallen by about 1.5 per cent since 1980. More spectacular have been the cuts in corporate taxation. These have had three main strands to them:

1. They increased depreciation rates by shortening the depreciation lives of assets and allowing accelerated depreciation.
2. They extended the investment tax credit (ITC) to short term assets not previously covered.
3. They introduced 'lease back' provisions which permitted firms with insufficient profits to transfer profits tax depreciation allowances.

Some of these provisions, e.g. accelerated depreciation, were later reversed. As a result, in the 1985 fiscal year the net impact on revenues was put at $11.2 billion, or 4.5 per cent of corporate profits. Because of this, and also because of the fall in the rate of inflation, the average rate of tax on corporate profits has been halved from 44 per cent in 1980 to 22 per cent in 1984.

At the same time, largely because of rising defence expenditure, public expenditure has increased, with the share of federal spending in GNP rising by one percentage point since 1980. Thus by the 1984 fiscal year the budget deficit had risen to $175 billion or 5 per cent of GNP. There has been widespread concern at this rise, which led to both Senate and the House adopting balanced budget bills which require spending cuts in 'controllable items' in order to balance the budget by 1991. This seems unlikely to happen and is probably an overreaction to the rapid rise in the budget deficit since 1979, but this deficit is still 1 per cent below that of the other major economies. In any case these policies must take a large proportion of the credit for the sharp turnaround in the unemployment figures. Moreover this was accomplished despite a tight monetary policy which saw short-term interest rates touch 20 per cent in 1978/9. Real interest rates, were still quite low, but have since risen steadily and the long-term rate on AAA commercial borrowing has been hovering at about 9 per cent since 1983. In historical terms this is one of the most unusual features of the recent recovery.

Partly because of these high interest rates, and partly because the reduction in corporate taxation has attracted venture capital from abroad, the dollar reached record levels in early 1985. On average it rose by 58 per cent against other currencies during the period 1980(3)–1985(1), although it has since fallen back. This had led to both a deteriorating trade position with both a sharp drop in exports and a sharp rise in imports. Because of this the growth of US industrial production has been much less than that of total final demand, leading to increased calls for protectionism. The high dollar has also been partly responsible for the relatively low rate of inflation which has accompanied the boom, and for the first time in many years the Phillips curve is shifting inwards. However, overall it would have been better if the dollar had not been allowed to rise so high, allowing a more sustainable boom without such adverse effects and possibly a smaller budget deficit.

MAINSTREAM THEORIES OF UNEMPLOYMENT

Neoclassical Theories

Neoclassical thought evolved in Europe around 1870, with the publication of major works by Walras, Menger and Jevons, as a reaction against the dominant classical tradition, as represented by Ricardo and John Stuart Mill. This moved neoclassical economists away from the classical's concern with the long-term problems of accumulation and growth. None the less they retained their faith in Say's law that supply creates its own demand. Most pre-Keynesian economists also appeared to believe in the efficiency of the free market system. Their analysis of the labour market was conducted within a partial equilibrium framework just as any other market, and as with any other good changes in price would bring about equilibrium between supply and demand. This is shown in Figure 1.2, which although simple and well known has been included as it is central to much of what follows. The market clearing wage is currently $(W/P)_0$. If the demand curve for labour were to fall, to D_1-D_1, e.g., then a fall in the real wage to $(W/P)_1$ would clear the market. This partial adjustment approach being justified by the assumption that the labour market is independent of what happens in the money markets, an assumption known as the classical dichotomy. Thus the neoclassical model is one where unemployment is simply not a matter of concern for economists and policy makers. At worst it is only a problem of temporary disequilibria which can be solved by a reduction in wages. This was a difficult position to hold in the face of the Depression which then engulfed both Europe and the USA in the 1930s. However, as Casson (1983) has shown, the economists of the period argued that if large-scale unemployment persisted then it must be because something was preventing wages from falling. This 'something' was generally either unemployment insurance or trade unions, as can be seen by examining the reactions of leading neoclassical economists to the Depression.

Cannan (1930) argued that the main impact of unemployment benefit was on job search by reducing the necessity for the unemployed worker to take the first job that was offered. Clay's (1929b) argument followed a different path, but led to the same conclusion. He argued that unemployment insurance allowed a reserve army of labour from which employers could hire at need and just as easily return unwanted labour. He also argued that trade union control of wages might simply be regarded as an application of monopoly pricing to labour. This allowed them to fix the wage rate instead of allowing competition to force wages down to the point at which the labour market clears. Pigou (1924) used a sophisticated two-sector model, one unionised the other not. If wages are held above the competitive rate in the former then workers will be attracted into this sector, provided there is a possibility of their gaining employment, until the expectation of earnings is equal in the two industries. However, this will result in a permanent increase in unemployment.

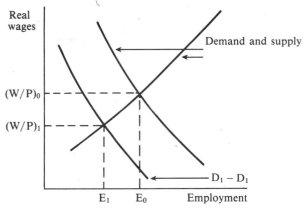

Figure 1.2: Demand and supply in the labour market

Keynesian Theories of Unemployment

Keynes' theory was in direct response to the neoclassical theories discussed above—not so much from theoretical dissatisfaction, but from a revulsion against their failure to restore full employment. Keynes' (1936) contribution centred on his attack on Say's law, that supply creates its down demand. His theoretical position was that unemployment arose because of a lack of effective demand for the goods and services workers produce. This is generally caused by a sudden collapse in the marginal efficiency of capital, leading to a sharp drop in investment. The basic source of this volatility is the uncertainty of entrepreneurial expectations about future profitability. Keynes' analysis is thus far removed from the neoclassical one of calculable and insurable risk (see Knight, 1921). The initial impact of this decline in investment would be magnified by the multiplier causing the economy to spiral downwards into recession.

Keynes argued that there was no short-term tendency for the economy to move to full employment. Wages would not fall in such a way as to equate demand and supply in the labour market. Exactly why Keynes thought this would not happen is a question which has detained economists for many years. For the moment we shall take it as given, although returning to it later. In this case full employment can only be restored following a fall in the demand for labour curve, as

shown in Figure 1.2, by action to shift the curve back to its
original position. As the demand for labour is a derived
demand, this can only be achieved by increasing the demand
for goods and services. Without this, long periods of underfull-employment equilibrium might be expected to prevail.
Thus the central plank of Keynesian theory is the concept of
effective demand, as opposed to the nominal quantities
which would be observed in equilibrium. He was thus also
quite deliberately dealing with disequilibrium states.
Governments can achieve this increase in one of three
ways. First, by increasing their own direct input into the
economy; second, by cutting taxes and thus increasing consumer spending power; and finally, the government could,
via its control of the money markets, cause interest rates to
fall, thus providing a boost to investment. Each of these
methods would be supplemented by multiplier effects. The
first two would involve an increase in public borrowing
(which Keynes did not think important), whilst the third was
uncertain due to the animal-like intelligence of entrepreneurs. Keynesian policies were probably followed in the
United Kingdom during the period 1945–76, although some
might argue about the exact dates. What is beyond argument
is that by 1979 with the election of the Thatcher government
they had been abandoned, as was any commitment to full
employment. The problem with Keynesian policies was not
so much that they failed to control unemployment, rather
that the policies as followed were unable to secure low
unemployment together with relative price stability. As
governments became increasingly worried about inflation
from the mid-1960s onwards, so successive deflationary
policies pushed unemployment upwards, which relatively
short periods of boom failed to reverse to any significant extent. By 1979 inflation was not merely a major policy target,
but almost the only one.

This reaction to high inflation is somewhat puzzling. It was
never part of Keynes' theory to achieve price stability; rather,
it was aimed at achieving and then maintaining full employment. I have argued elsewhere (Hudson, 1982) that in the UK
the increase in inflation was not so much a result of Keynesian policies *per se*, but of the success they experienced in

achieving full employment. Workers and trade unions grew used to an ever-increasing standard of living and were able to push for this when the economy was not growing sufficiently fast to provide it. The result was that wages and inflation became locked in an upward spiral, which the OPEC oil price pushed even higher. Thus the rational reaction to this inflation should have been to search for ways in which to control wage increases, rather than abandon policies which had been relatively successful in maintaining full employment. Possible strategies would include: a prices and incomes policy, and seeking to expand the economy faster in an attempt to accommodate increased money wages without the need for price rises. At the same time, governments should have sought to reduce the harmful effects of inflation by, for example, a widespread policy of linking contracts, wages, pensions, etc. to the price level.

Taking the period 1945–76 as a whole, the United Kingdom enjoyed extraordinarily low unemployment and, in historical terms, rapid growth in output and living standards. This would appear to reflect successful management of the economy, although some economists have, of course, argued that this had nothing to do with the 'coincidence' that governments were committed to full employment using Keynesian methods. Matthews (1968), for example, has argued that it was buoyancy of private investment rather than government policies which sustained the post-war boom in the UK. However, it is not easy to criticise success and it is a fact that periods of neoclassical/monetarist policies such as the 1930s and 1980s have been characterised by high unemployment and the single period of Keynesian dominance by rapid growth and prosperity. One must also ask why investment was so high. Entrepreneurs invest because of expectations about the future. Could it be that governments committed to full employment engender confidence in the future? If so the high investment of the post-war years could be attributed to the government's readiness to apply Keynesian policies rather than their application *per se*. Equally, current high unemployment in the UK could stem, at least in part, from the absence of any belief in the government's ability, or willingness, to control the economy.

The lessons of the 1930s were also a major factor in the conversion of US policy-makers to Keynesianism. Unemployment stood at more than 25 per cent in the US in 1933; five years later it had fallen by just 6 per cent. By 1944, with the stimulus of the Second World War, it was down to 1.2 per cent. The experience of the 1930s had shown that the market would return to equilibrium, if at all, extremely slowly. The experience of wartime intervention had also shown that governments could do better. Faced with this example, Congress passed the Employment Act of 1946. This committed the federal government 'to promote maximum employment, production and purchasing power', and in so doing provide 'useful opportunities for those able, willing and seeking to work'. Like the UK government, the US administration had taken on board responsibility for maintaining employment, which neoclassical economists then and now say is both unnecessary and impossible. A target rate of 4 per cent was provisionally set for unemployment by the Council of Economic Advisors, and this was approximately achieved during the period 1947–57, without the need for any active government interference. There was then a sharp rise in unemployment. Thus in the 1960 presidential election campaign Kennedy spoke of the need to get the country moving again. However, recovery was slow and in response, he proposed to cut taxes at the beginning of 1963, but this, due to congressional opposition, was not enacted until early 1964. At the time of this tax cut unemployment stood at 5.5 per cent. By the following year it had fallen to 4 per cent. Then for the period 1966–69 the rate averaged 3.7 per cent. After this, unemployment once more began to rise, and since then it has fallen below 5 per cent in only one year, 1973. As we have seen it increased steadily through the 1970s and into the 1980s, until by 1982 it was in double figures. However, Reagan's curious mixture of monetary rectitude coupled with fiscal looseness—a sort of shotgun marriage of monetarism and Keynesianism—worked for a time at least to bring about a near dramatic fall in the unemployment rate. Thus unlike the United Kingdom and the majority of Western European countries, the United States has in practice not renounced Keynesian-style intervention.

However, it must be admitted that not all attempts to apply Keynesian policies have met with the same degree of success as their recent application in America. The 1978/79 expansionary fiscal policy in the UK resulted in a large increase in consumer's expenditure but a much smaller increase in domestic output. The difference was met by imports, and as a result unemployment fell back marginally from 6.4 per cent in 1977 to 5.6 per cent in 1979. Given the size of the government injection such a result was disappointing. A similar fate met the attempts of the newly-elected French government to expand the economy in 1981. In the first quarter of that year real GDP was 1½ per cent lower than it had been a year earlier, with unemployment nearly a quarter of a million higher and rising fast. A supplementary budget was introduced increasing the deficit by nearly 1 per cent of GDP and also levying some new forms of taxation. The overall expansionary impact of these new measures on GDP was estimated at between 1 and 2 per cent. The policy stimulus was concentrated mainly on personal disposable income, and consumer spending did rise by 3½ per cent in 1982, but this mainly went on durables, which again were mainly imported. The current account worsened by 2.2 per cent of GDP, whilst unemployment continued to increase from 7.3 per cent in 1981 to 8 per cent in 1982. These events seemed to take most observers by surprise. The initial forecasts accompanying the new policies foresaw some weakening of the trade balance, but not the sharp deterioration which occurred. The OECD forecast made in the second half of 1981 foresaw no change in the trade balance. Even retrospectively the National Institute in the UK had difficulty in finding equations to explain what happened.

Monetarist Theories
Neoclassical ideas on how the economy works were kept alive during the period of Keynesian dominance by a small group of enthusiasts at Chicago led by Milton Friedman. In a brilliant series of publications Friedman sought first to weaken the foundations of Keynesian thought (1957) and then re-establish the respectability of a 'neoclassical alternative' (1968). By the time of his retirement from his Chair

in Chicago he had fundamentally succeeded in both these objectives. With respect to unemployment Friedman made only one amendment to the neoclassical ideas: the real wage in Figure 1.2 was specified in terms of expected prices, rather than current prices, as the wage contract typically extends for some time into the future. His ideas developed considerably over the years but by 1977 they had hardened into what was to become one of the twin pillars of modern monetarism. The essence of the argument is as follows. Let (W_0/P_0) be the equilibrium market clearing wage. Now let something produce a widespread increase in nominal demand which leads employers to attempt to hire more workers at higher nominal wages. As the workers have no reason to anticipate a change in the price level they will interpret the increased wage offer as an increase in real wages and move along their supply curve. The result will be an increase in employment which will, however, only be temporary as employees come to recognise that prices in general have risen and slide back down their supply curve towards their original position. Unemployment can only deviate below its natural rate if workers are surprised or fooled into thinking their wages to be worth more over the contract period than they actually are. Similarly, increases in unemployment can only occur if workers are fooled in the other direction. The 'price surprise' function therefore turned the Phillips curve on its head. Instead of inflation being a function of unemployment, unemployment was a function of unanticipated inflation. One of the consequences of this is that as people cannot be fooled indefinitely there is only one possible long-run level of unemployment, that which prevails when inflation is correctly anticipated. This concept of a natural rate of unemployment was originally controversial but has now become widely accepted, although Friedman's rationale for it has not.

One serious defect with the theory is that the labour market clearing approach can tell us little about unemployment. The whole basis of the theory is that when demand equals supply there are no unsatisfied buyers or sellers and prices will remain stable. Yet we know that the market has never cleared in this way, that there have always been some unemployed workers and some unfilled vacancies, the technique seems inappropriate to the use to which it has been put. Friedman argues that such unemployment will result from market imperfections, information costs relating to job vacancies and labour immobility. Yet he does not provide a theoretical framework for such a result nor explain what further modifications to the market clearing mythology these will entail. Surely this is totally invalid. If one is going to explain unemployment by reference to search costs in the labour market, then the whole of the analysis needs to be conducted within this framework.

The New Classical Economics
To an extent the monetarist banner has been taken on by Friedman's successor at Chicago, Robert Lucas. His main contribution (1972a, 1972b, 1975), made together with Sargent (1973), and indeed arguably the only contribution of any importance in the last decade, lay in taking an idea originally put forward by Muth (1961), who was in turn building upon ideas originally put forward by Modigliani and Grunberg (1954). Muth proposed that expectations are not adaptive but rational, i.e. they are based on the relevant economic theory. However, the idea lay dormant until Lucas and Sargent applied it to the labour market decision described above. Therefore, to the concept of a natural rate of unemployment was added the further hypothesis that deviations from this natural rate would be short-lived. The rational expectations revolution admitted that people did not possess perfect information, at least with respect to future events. But this would not produce lengthy cycles in unemployment and production, because they were in possession of the full and correct economic theory which allowed them to act as if they were in fact in possession of this full information. Thus any errors workers make in forecasting inflation will be random and short-lived. There will be no lengthy adjustment of expectations to reality as in the adaptive expectations hypothesis, nor will there be any lengthy spells of unemployment. Moreover the government is powerless systematically to influence the level of unemployment as any policy initiatives it takes can be correctly forecast

and allowed for. The government can only affect the rate of unemployment if it acts unpredictably. This result has played a fundamental role in the development of modern monetarist thinking, and justifies the much publicised conclusion that government policy is essentially impotent.

A major problem with the original rational expectations hypothesis is that unemployment is clearly not a random variable, but subject to major cyclical variations. Partly in response to the presence of autocorrelation in unemployment Lucas (1975) and Sargent (1976a) have argued that the price surprise function should be modified to include lagged unemployment. This preserves government neutrality, but their results imply a somewhat lengthy time lag of between three and seven years. The theoretical justification for such lags put forward by Lucas rested on information lags and serially correlated movements in capital stock. The information lags arise when an initial shock to the system causes economic agents to underestimate the true stock of money, which in turn causes them to underestimate the price level. Agents catch on to the true stock of money at an exponential rate through time, but during the catch up period both sets of expectations lag behind. Then through a somewhat complex chain of events the rate of interest, the demand for money and the price level itself are all affected. The net effect is that the price level will be below its equilibrium level, and government spending, which in money terms equals the increase in the money supply, will be above its equilibrium real level, thus causing an increase in output and a reduction in unemployment away from their equilibrium levels. An alternative approach, pursued separately by Fischer (1977), and Phelps and Taylor (1977) attributes the autocorrelation to sticky prices. According to Fischer, non-indexed labour contracts set wages in relation to expected future prices over the duration of the contract. If prices turn out to be lower than expected, real wages rise and employers may lay off workers and reduce output.

Relatively weak evidence is provided for the price surprise term in the unemployment equation in Sargent (1976), but disputed by Fair (1979). There are also simultaneity problems as Barro (1980) has pointed out. The econometric problems involved in testing the price surprise function with rational expectations are immense, and all the above stress the tentative nature of their work. However, other tests by Clark and Summers (1982), for example, which are concerned with more manageable aspects of the problem, have tended to produce unfavourable results. This coupled with the obvious fact that unemployment has fallen very rapidly in the upswing of the most recent business cycle in the US has put the new classicals on the retreat. This fall resulted from government fiscal policies, which stimulated both the demand and supply sides of the economy. Thus Barro (1981) expresses doubts about the explanatory value for business cycles of currently available equilibrium theories. Whilst McCallum (1982) argues that the evidence requires the abandonment of flexible-price equilibrium models *but not of the equilibrium approach to macroeconomic analysis* which can rationalise sticky or slowly adjusting wages and prices. Townsend (in Klamer, 1984) admits that his failure to understand the recent recession in the US indicates that something is missing from his model. He has also disowned the policy neutrality hypothesis claiming that this was never an integral part of new classical economics anyway.

Despite these recent misgivings the position of the modern day new classical economist is very similar to that of his neoclassical predecessor. There are two main differences. First, the old classical dichotomy between the real world and the money markets has been abandoned. The macroeconomy is now seen as an interdependent market-clearing system, rather than as a set of aggregate markets clearing independently via flexible prices. Thus, for example, unexpected changes in the money supply have an impact upon both unemployment and output. The second difference represents a somewhat lagged response to the problems raised by Arrow (1959). He argued that because every economic agent is assumed to be a price taker nobody actually knows the market clearing vector of prices and hence no mechanism for changing prices exists. As a result considerable emphasis is now placed upon incomplete information, uncertainty and the formation of expectations, whereas the classical model assumed perfect knowledge. A further result of this has been the shift from a single to a multi-period analysis, where expectations of the future affect the present. The recent work on search theory and expectation formation is a reflection of this, as well as that on implicit contracts.

None the less, in both the classical and the new classical models unemployment is not a problem, because unemployment cannot exist. Faith in the perfect working of the market implies that the only way unemployment can arise is if wages are above their market clearing rate. In a free market this cannot happen, so if unemployment persists something must be preventing wages from falling. As with the neoclassicals this something is invariably identified as either (1) unemployment insurance or (2) the activities of trade unions, (see Minford, 1983). But why should either of these have led to a sudden and dramatic increase in unemployment in the UK from 1979 onwards, just when both union power and the replacement ratio were falling? This similarity with their neoclassical predecessors is acknowledged by the new classicals. Townsend for instance admitted to the wealth of ideas in Pigou (1927b), who talks about forecast errors, waves of optimism and pessimism and about people getting confused in the sense that they see what other people are doing but are not sure what it means. The main difference according to Townsend is in the sophistication of the techniques open to the modern-day economist, which allow him to do the things which Pigou suggested. Indeed the techniques such as dynamic programing and statistical decision theory, are sophisticated and the wizardry with which the new classical economists apply them awesome. This has led many economists to criticise them purely on the grounds that they have replaced economics with mathematics. In many cases this is probably fair comment. An impressive array of equations often hides a paucity of economic originality. But it ignores the fact that a thorough analytical approach to a problem can often yield valuable insights.

No, the real objection to the new classical approach cannot be that it uses too sophisticated tools, but that it uses them to poor profit. The assumption of market clearing or equilibrium is at odds with everything we know about the world. The suggestion that there are nearly 3½ million people unemployed in the UK because they are all incorrectly forecasting the rate of inflation is close to being absurd. The assumption of rational expectations is quite absurd in many cases to which it has been applied. This is not the same as saying that there are no valid areas of application, but the decisions made by steelworkers in Pittsburgh or Sheffield are not examples of them. It therefore reflects considerable discredit on the profession that so many economists of all persuasions have been so gullible as to use it when analysing the labour market. To Lucas, Sargent and the other new classical economists the ends justify the means in the sense that they do not care about the reality of assumptions as long as the results derived from those assumptions are consistent with the world as they see it. They argue that this 'as if' approach is common to much of microeconomics. Take, for example, the consumers' problem: does anyone seriously believe that individuals actually do complicated utility calculations or even have the information needed to do them? Yet this approach is accepted with little introspection by the bulk of the profession. So why balk when this optimising approach is extended to expectation-formation? However, the former is built on the premiss that people act in their own best interests, perhaps with limited knowledge and a fair degree of randomness. But because agents are acting in their own interests, it can reasonably be argued that any deviations from optimal behaviour when aggregated cancel out, providing a net result reasonably close to what the theory predicts. Rational expectations, on the other hand, requires economic agents to have a sophisticated knowledge of the world and a sophisticated mathematical mind. They clearly do not. They must therefore calculate expectations in another manner. There is no reason at all why expectations formed in this other way should approximate the predictions of an economic model. It is therefore the job of economists to identify what this alternative technique is.

To a large extent however this concern over rational expectations is a false trail. The key assumption behind the new classical economics, is the same as that made by the neoclassical economists. Markets, including the labour market, clear. Unemployment in excess of the natural rate then arises only when workers make forecasting errors in the rate of inflation, leading them to reject jobs they would otherwise accept. Add rational expectations to this and one gets the results that there should be no systematic fluctuations in unemployment and output, and also that governments cannot have any impact upon unemployment because economic agents will always anticipate any systematic government policy. Leave rational expectations aside and we get the result that there will be short-lived cycles whilst expectations adapt to reality. In either case there is no call for government interference with the labour market, the problem is temporary and will right itself. It is this assumption which is at the heart of the difference between the protagonists in the debate.

It is clear that these theories have had an enormous influence, not just on the way economists think, but also on government policy, particularly in the UK and Western Europe. Indeed so great has been their influence that in some respects they represent the most important work since Keynes. Their appeal lies partly in the eloquence, the fervour and the ability of those who have been propounding them, partly in the backlash by economists and politicians disillusioned at the failures of governments in the 1970s, and partly in their appeal to rationality and a natural order. But I believe that this approach has been counter-constructive. It has led economists out of the real world, back into the ivory towers they inhabited before Keynes.

SEARCH THEORIES OF UNEMPLOYMENT

An important accompaniment to both the original monetarist and the new classical analysis has been the developments which have taken place in search theory, which, when originally made, represented the beginning of macroeconomists' search for microeconomic foundations. It also forms the basis of the analysis of the labour market which we shall adopt later, and hence some time will be devoted to considering these theories here.

Interest in search theories began with a study by Stigler (1962), which emphasised the fact that labour markets are not characterised by perfect information, and that individuals needed to undertake search activities in order to gain such information. Using this as a base, Phelps (1968), Mortenson (1970), Holt (1970) and others produced a remarkable series of essays, which gave birth to what has become known as the 'new microeconomic approach to macroeconomics'. Much of this work is aimed at providing a theory consistent with the simultaneous occurrence of unemployed workers and unfilled vacancies, as well as a negative relationship between wage changes and unemployment.

The gist of Phelps' theory is that, given a constant differential between a firm's wage rate and wages paid by other firms, a fall in the unemployment rate will tend to increase quits. At a sufficiently high quit rate the firm will want to increase this differential. Thus one role of unemployment in this model stems from its effects on quits rather than any supposed underbidding for jobs by unemployed workers as often seems implicit in many market-clearing analyses. The number of vacancies will also be relevant as the more vacancies the firm has the more anxious it will be to fill them; in addition vacancies may affect quits. Hence the desired differential will be a function of the level of unemployment and the number of vacancies. The actual rate of wage change is then a constant proportion of the average desired differential.

Holt was also concerned with providing a theoretical basis for the Phillips curve. In doing this he payed slightly more attention to the specific problems of search than Phelps. Important in this context is the concept of a reservation wage which declines with the length of search. If the wage at which a job is offered to a specific worker is above his acceptance wage then he will accept the job, if not, he will refuse it. Thus for an individual worker the longer he is unemployed the lower his acceptance wage will be. Holt then assumes that the wage the worker is hired at will vary directly with his acceptance wage, and hence inversely with the time he has been unemployed. Holt assumes that the wage from his last job is the initial reference for setting the acceptance wage, but that this is adjusted to take account of the worker's initial perception of his job opportunities. For example, when the labour market is tight, workers may reasonably raise their initial aspirations, information on the job market being conveyed by such factors as the number of vacancies, the duration of unemployment that other workers have experienced and the wages that are being offered.

Although more than a decade and a half has passed since the appearance of these papers, they still contain many of the most fundamental insights which search theory has given us into the behaviour of the labour market. This may, in part, account for the limited impact such theories have had, for although many economists mention the importance of search in explaining unemployment, few go on to develop the arguments in any detail. Much of the work that has been done concentrates on the job searchers' reservation wage, and the possible reasons for its decline over time. Important here is the view developed by Telser (1973) that if the individual does not know the true distribution of wage offers, then search provides additional information which can be used to update perceptions of that distribution in a Bayesian-type adjustment process. If the individual rejects a wage offer, then it must have been below the acceptance wage when, if prior expectations about wage offers had been correct, there would have existed the possibility that it might have exceeded it. This will lead to an adjustment of those perceptions, with a probable reduction in the acceptance wage, after each period of unsuccessful search. There are two possibilities which have been developed within the literature, whereby this adjustment process can take place either before or after the offer has been considered. A rather different reason for declining acceptance wages has been proposed by Salop (1973) who abandoned the assumption that individuals sample randomly from a uniform distribution of wage offers. He argued that in fact, job searchers usually have some information about job opportunities in different firms and that they use this to rank them. They then search systematically, starting with those firms with the best opportunities but as the unsuccessful searcher proceeds down the list to the less likely firms, so the expected benefits from search fall and thus his acceptance wage also falls.

Although most of the research has concentrated on the unemployed workers' side of the problem, recent work has considered the employers' side of the problem. For example, Mellow (1982) and Oi (1983) have argued that large employers incur higher costs in monitoring employees. This implies that such firms have more to gain from hiring high-ability workers to minimise monitoring costs. Thus it is argued that larger employers search more, both extensively and intensively. Whilst Barron *et al.* (1985) suggest that search is more a process whereby employers obtain signals concerning capabilities of different applicants. They argue that the fact that employers interview on average eight individuals prior to making an employment offer suggests that the current concentration on reservation wages is misplaced.

A frequent criticism of such models is that they limit search to the unemployed, thus ignoring the fact that a considerable number of people change jobs without ever being unemployed. Although most search models do make this assumption the choice between on-the-job and full-time search has been analysed by Holt, and later by Lippman and McCall (1976). In general it can be concluded that full-time search can be undertaken more intensively than on-the-job search, but that the costs of full-time search, including forgone income, are greater per period than on-the-job search. The individual will quit his job and undertaken full-time search if the benefits outweigh the costs.

Much of the empirical work aimed at testing job search theories has been concerned with the implications of the theory. In particular a lot of work has been done on the effects of unemployment insurance or benefits on the duration of job search. As this reduces the cost of search in terms of income forgone, it should lead to an increase in the average time spent searching and also to the wage offer eventually being accepted. Most of the empirical work supports these conclusions. In the USA Ehrenberg and Oaxaca (1976), Classen (1977) and Moffitt (1985) all find a small, but positive, effect of the size of weekly benefit on unemployment duration. Similar results are obtained for the UK by Nickell (1979) and Narendranathan and Nickell (1985).

A more direct, but more difficult, approach is to attempt

to quantify the effect on the reservation wage of continuing unemployment. Both Kasper (1967) and Stephenson (1976) find only a small effect on reservation wages which decline at the rate of between 0.06 and 0.4 percentage point per month. However, both of these studies, which were for the USA, are subject to selection bias, as they are based on samples of unemployed workers. Those individuals whose acceptance wages decline slowly will, other things being equal, be less successful in search and be over-represented in the sample. Kiefer and Neumann (1979) have avoided this source of bias (although others remain in the opposite direction) and found reservation wages to decline at a rate of 2.5 percentage points per month. Another problem which has, as yet, not been fully appreciated is that if the reservation wage is revised after each unsuccessful interview, then its rate of decline in a specific time-period such as a month will depend upon how many interviews typically take place during that time. In periods or areas of high unemployment and few vacancies one would expect the reservation wage to decline more slowly than in more prosperous times or locations.

None the less, in general, the empirical evidence is favourable to search theories. However, as mentioned earlier, there remains a certain degree of reticence amongst economists in accepting the validity or usefulness of this approach. This is so for a number of reasons. First, in most models all unemployment is treated as voluntary. Secondly, as in Friedman's model, variations in the unemployment rate only occur because someone is being fooled, or lacks all the relevant information. Further criticisms are that all unemployment is regarded as search unemployment and that such models typically exclude on-the-job search. These last two points are relatively unimportant: the latter simply requires a fairly straightforward modification to the theories, while the former requires us to recognise that there are other reasons for becoming unemployed than voluntary quits. Search theories have little relevance in explaining unemployment caused by a lack of demand for the product the unemployed worker's previous firm produced. But they can help to explain that person's behaviour on becoming unemployed. As for the problem with voluntary or involuntary unemployment, one cannot but agree with Lucas (1978) that this is a distinction best forgotten.

The remaining point that variations in unemployment only occur because someone is being fooled stems from one vital assumption—that search productivity is constant. Thus in each period of search there is typically one interview regardless of economic conditions. This assumption, it should be noted, was not in Phelps. He quite explicitly noted that a higher vacancy rate will increase the probability that any unemployed person contacting a firm will find a job vacancy. However, Phelps' successors, driven by the need to state the individual's maximisation problem more explicitly than Phelps, made this simplifying assumption which has rarely been dropped, notable exceptions to this being Parsons (1973) and Hudson (1982). This is clearly unsatisfactory as, during a recession, job interviews obviously decline and we can expect search productivity, defined in terms of the number of job interviews obtained in a given period, to decline too. Thus this assumption must be abandoned. None the less, it is also my view that the search theoretic approach comes closer to describing how the unemployed behave in attempting to find employment, and as such is crucial to any theory of unemployment and the labour market.

STRUCTURALIST AND SCHUMPETERIAN THEORIES OF UNEMPLOYMENT

Monetarists and Keynesians form the two major groupings in the unemployment debate. However, a third group has also emerged which identifies structural change as an important additional ingredient in mass unemployment. Structural unemployment arises out of such structural changes in the pattern of labour demand caused by changes in demand or production techniques, resulting in some skills becoming redundant. Workers with these skills will remain unemployed until they can be retrained, have moved to other areas of the country where their skills are in demand, or industries which require their skills have transferred into their area. This concern with structural unemployment has strong neoclassical roots, as Casson (1983) has observed. Clay (1929a), for example, pointed to labour immobility as an important reason for the failure of labour markets to clear. He argued that there would always be some unemployment due to the impossibility of fitting workers with limited skills and geographical mobility to the kinds of work available. Pigou (1927a) appeared to reject the existence of structural unemployment, arguing that had this been important one would have expected to find shortages of labour in some industries, as well as an excess in others, and that this was not the case. Pool (1938) explained this with the argument that vacancies in prosperous industries had been eliminated by high wages pushed up by union power.

This discussion on structural unemployment was, and is, in many respects simply a special case of the more general neoclassical/monetarist analysis. Both are caused by wage inflexibility and both would be removed by a fall in wages to their equilibrium level. Thus Clay (1928) thought that wage rates in declining industries were too high, thereby causing the unemployment in those industries. Pool, on the other hand, suggested that the source of disequilibrium lay in the more prosperous industries. He argued that workers will only fail to transfer to more prosperous occupations if there are no vacancies and this will only be the case if wages are kept at too high a level in these alternative occupations.

This is somewhat disappointing, the term 'structural' seems to imply physical obstructions to full employment rather than merely price inflexibility. Some of their suggested policies, however, were not always consistent with this view. For example, Cannan (1930) argued for policies to encourage the transfer of workers between industries. This apparently rested on a view which identified the problem as one of market failure, in the form of lack of information on vacancies, barriers to change of residence and so on. Nearly all neoclassicals were uneasy about rigidities in the labour market and therefore about unemployment insurance. Beveridge (1931) argued for the non-payment of benefits to workers who refused to consider taking employment outside their usual trade or district. Other policies such as employment subsidies paid to employers, which was advocated by

Pigou (1927a) and picked up by Layard (1981), were done so only with considerable reservations due to concern that such measures would slow down the adjustment process to a new equilibrium. Suggestions for protection against imports were met with even less enthusiasm, although here there was also concern about the danger of reciprocal action by other countries.

Developments in business-cycle theory, centring on the work of Kondratief (1925) and Schumpeter (1939), offer more fundamental differences with neoclassical theory, as well as the promise of a different approach in the future. Kondratief analysed the development of long-term trends in selected economic indicators, most of which concerned prices and interest rates. He concluded that there exist half-century-long cycles. The upswing of the first long wave covered the period from 1789–1814, that is the 25 years beginning with the French Revolution and ending with Waterloo. The decline lasted for 35 years, ending in 1849. Thus the whole cycle lasted for some 60 years. The upswing of the second cycle lasted for 24 years ending in 1873 whilst the downswing continued until 1896, the whole period lasting for 47 years. The third long wave moves upwards until 1920, once more a period of 24 years. Kondratief thought that these cycles were an essential factor in economic development. The causes of them were inherent in the capitalist system, but beyond this he declined to be more specific. Thus to an extent his work is little more than a set of statistics in search of theory, and because of this he has frequently been ignored. But there is considerable current interest in the cycle, principally because he would appear to have predicted the current depression from a distance of more than half a century. If there is anything beyond coincidence in the Kondratief cycle, then it would indicate that there are more fundamental factors at work in determining booms and depressions, and it is these we must understand and come to grips with if we are to devise appropriate policies.

Schumpeter offered an explanation of the Kondratief cycle in terms of clusters of major innovations attracting imitators and minor improvements causing a wave of new investment and a boom. Gradually this would erode the initial innovative profits. This could lead to stagnation and recession, if a new wave of innovations did not compensate, leading to the whole process starting again with the destabilising effects of this new wave of innovations. Thus technical innovation was highly discontinuous, more like a series of explosions, than occurring continually and imperceptibly over time. There are gaps in Schumpeter's work: he failed to explain, for example, why major innovations occur every 50 years or so. Perhaps his major achievement lay in his disequilibrium approach. The basis of economic development lies in competition over time between entrepreneurs. The emphasis is on the supply side, that is in autonomous investments rather than on demand-induced accelerator investments or multiplier processes as driving forces in economic development (Giersch, 1979). In such a framework development will be viewed primarily as a process of reallocation of resources between industries, that leads automatically to structural changes and disequilibria.

Schumpeter's explanation of the business-cycle is therefore relatively straightforward. It centres on the concept of innovation, a change of first magnitude in either the process of production or on the product side. Prior to this process of innovation the economy must be in a state of near-equilibrium, so that prices have been stable long enough for completely new projects to be undertaken, and also that the recent lack of innovations will have put some pressure on entrepreneurs. This primary wave is then succeeded by a secondary one brought about by induced purchases of inputs and consumer goods. The upswing ends as the potential for exploiting the new innovations is used up, and also possibly because many enterprises begun in the second wave of development may not be viable in the long run. The downswing may simply take the economy back to a new Walrasian equilibrium, in which old patterns of production have been replaced by the new ones. This process is what Schumpeter called 'creative destruction', which he regarded as essential for the performance of capitalism. He was therefore against government action to stop the contraction of old techniques or industries, such as subsidies, tariffs or cheap loans. Alternatively it might overshoot the equilibrium and go into a depression.

Following this, however, there will be an automatic tendency for the market to return to equilibrium, as the remaining firms take advantage of opportunities vacated by failed enterprises. Thus the first part of the cycle is a wave of entreprenurial activity built on a cluster of new innovations. New firms attracted by the high profits being earned by the innovators are attracted into the industry. But there is soon overproduction and capacity. Many entrepreneurs will have borrowed heavily, and as the excess capacity drives prices and profits down they will experience difficulties, perhaps even becoming bankrupt. The main difference between this and conventional business-cycle theories lies in this concept of the bunching of innovations.

In later work, Schumpeter (1943) placed more emphasis upon R & D occurring within firms. So that new innovations occurred within existing large and successful firms through research they finance themselves, either directly or indirectly by providing support for the universities. In his earlier work he had placed more emphasis upon individual entrepreneurs successfully bringing forth new innovations and thus developing into the large corporations of the future. Academic opinion is divided between these two views. Scherer (1965) argued that the statistical evidence shows no clear link between relative scale of research and inventive activities and firm size, thus supporting the earlier Schumpeter view. However, more recent work by Soete (1979a), after analysing US data, concluded in favour of Schumpeter's revised opinion.

The recent development of the microcomputer industry also provides conflicting evidence. The first microprocessor device, the four-bit 4004, appeared from the California semiconductor company Intel in 1971, followed quickly by eight-bit processors from Intel and others. However, the first true business micro was not launched until 1977, when the calculator maker Commodore marketed the Pet and Apple, set up in a garage the previous year, launched the Apple II. In the wake of these early successes many imitators, both new firms and established firms from other fields, were attracted to the market, including Tandy and Texas Instruments in the US and Acorn, ACT and Sinclair in the UK. Despite initial successes many of these companies have met with problems.

In the US, Texas Instruments, Atari and Coleco lost billions of dollars in the home computer market and drastically reduced the size of their operations; whilst in the UK the three major British firms have all met with problems. A major reason for the difficulties all these companies have faced has been the emergence of IBM as the leading microcomputer firm following the launch of its PC in 1981. A survey in *Datamation* in 1985 showed 1985 63.3 per cent of new microcomputer sites were choosing IBM machines. IBM was also used in over half the micro installations surveyed, compared to Apple's 10 per cent. Five years earlier Apple's share was 42 per cent. Thus in less than a decade Apple has grown from a garage into a major corporation. However, the most successful microcomputer company is IBM, which joined the bandwagon somewhat late in the day. The initial breakthrough was made by individuals, but this has not led to the demise of the large corporations.

Mensch (1975) argued that basic innovations have tended to increase at a time of recession, rather than being continuously made over time. This is because they tend to get crowded out at other times by pseudo-innovations or product differentiation, which are of course less risky. These basic innovations then provide the impetus for the next boom. But again recent analysis on the UK by Freeman, Clarke and Soete (1982) rejects Mensch's arguments, which they suggest were based on an incomplete consideration of the data. Instead they find that there is a tendency for basic inventions to cluster together at different times, but these clusters are not systematically related to depressions. Nor do they find any evidence that new innovations are more readily accepted during such times. However, they did find, in support of Schumpeter, technical change to be extremely uneven over time, both between industries and geographically. They have also argued that clusters of innovations are capable of giving a substantial impetus to the economy and that as 'technological systems' mature employment opportunities from new investment diminish and profitability declines.

Schumpeter had little to say about unemployment and wages as such. But his policy recommendations to deal with business-cycles can be found in *The Theory of Economic*

Development. The most important remedy in the long run was the greater familiarity of businessmen with the working of the cycle. Foreseeing what is likely to happen in the future helps them take steps which neutralise cycles. In the short run he also favoured Keynesian-type government expenditure policies, whereby new construction by government enterprises or by great combines is postponed to periods of depression. This is interesting given that it was written in 1911. Even more interesting perhaps are his thoughts on monetary policy. He was against an indiscriminate and general increase in credit facilities which he linked with inflation. But it also hindered the 'rubbish disposal' purpose of a recession, i.e. it prevented the closure of firms in declining industries. However, he did favour a selective monetary policy aimed at differentiating between those firms made technically or commercially obsolete by the preceding boom from those which appeared to be endangered by secondary circumstances, reactions and accidents; it would leave the former alone, and support the latter by granting credit. Schumpeter admitted that such discrimination was not technically possible at the time he wrote. But surely today it is not beyond government's ability, acting through the central bank, to give such directives on lending. These might be in broad terms, either distinguishing certain industries as prime candidates for credit, or more contentiously signalling out other industries not to receive credit.

Whether Schumpeter's mechanism offered a satisfactory explanation of the business-cycle depends, as Kuznets (1940) pointed out, on whether some innovations are so large and discontinuous, or alternatively are bunched together, as to provide a sustained impetus to the economy. There are also other problems with his theory. First, it is an explanation for all cycles, not simply the Kondratief, but shorter ones as well. There is little real indication of what distinguishes these shorter cycles from the Kondratief. Secondly, it is still married to the concept of Walrasian equilibrium. This is the norm, the economy may depart from it in the boom and recession stages of the cycle, but it can be expected to return of its own accord to an equilibrium position. Schumpeter therefore believed that the capitalist system would adjust to equilibrium, although disturbed by the lack of consideration economics and economists gave to the adjustment path. Schumpeter also argued that there is relatively little that can be done to lift the economy out of recession. Any recovery will only be sound if it grows of itself. But for our purposes the main criticism is that it does not explain the current recession gripping the UK in particular and Western Europe in general. This did not happen after a wave of new innovations had been exhausted. It was caused, as we have seen, partly by these economies' need to adjust to a new equilibrium position following the OPEC price rises of 1974 and 1979, and partly by the deflationary, monetarist-inspired policies pursued by governments worried about inflation. Those countries, such as the US, which have not pursued deflationary policies have not been plunged into recession. None the less Schumpeter is still of immense current relevance, because recovery from this recession will depend in part upon how these economies react to the current new wave of innovations, and the relationship between different industries at different stages of development. Schumpeter was the first economist to consider this type of problem, and one of the few economists to place the entrepreneur at the centre of the macroeconomic stage.

CONCLUSIONS

We have seen that there are three main approaches to the problem of unemployment. Keynesians argue that it is basically due to a lack of demand, if government policies increase demand unemployment will disappear. Such policies appear to have been used with success in the past in the UK, and recently in the US, but there are counter examples of when they have been used with less success. One of the tasks of this book is to provide an answer as to why these policies have met with variable success. The new classical position is even simpler, it is to argue that because the market works perfectly, unemployment cannot exist. If, however, it does exist, then it is argued that it must be due to something interfering with the free working of the market place. This something is nearly always either unemployment benefit/

insurance, or trade unions. Corrective policy then amounts to either doing nothing, or at the most, freeing the market from restrictions. The new classical position is therefore little different to the neoclassical position of more than fifty years ago, and it is of some interest as to how a theory which was then so discredited could have been revived in recent years. Finally, we have the Schumpeterian type structuralist position, which argues that unemployment is caused by the reaction of dynamic economies to technical change, which occurs not smoothly over time, but in sudden discrete jumps. Policies here concern the need to ensure that firms in new industries do not go bankrupt in the reaction which follows the boom, although he doubted whether monetary policies could be that selective and by and large he too was prepared to leave recovery to market forces.

Perhaps the key difference between the neoclassical and Keynesian theorists a half a century ago and the monetarist/new classicals and Keynesians now, centres on the market clearing role of wages. Left to itself would the labour market automatically gravitate towards an equilibrium thus removing unemployment and would this happen within an acceptably short enough period of time? Classical and monetarist theorists treat this as a theoretical question and argue yes, thus there is no need for government intervention which could only be harmful. Keynesian theorists believe that this is an empirical question and that in the real world there is little evidence to suggest that this will happen, and therefore in time of recession there is an overwhelming need for governments to intervene with expansionary policies. The reality of the situation is that regardless of theoretical considerations labour markets do not clear instantaneously, nor is there any obvious tendency for them to clear. This is a fact of the real world and one which the theorist has yet to come to grips with. The monetarist theorist now and the classical theorist earlier tend to lay the blame for this either on the actions of trade unions or the existence of unemployment insurance. The Keynesian theorist tends to know that the market does not clear, but is not exactly sure why, although recent developments in search and implicit contract theory may help provide him with some answers.

Keynes himself took an ambiguous stance arguing that in the real world real wages did not fall but that even if they did the effects on unemployment would be ambiguous. The reason for this is simply that workers are also consumers. Cutting their wages will cut their spending, thus although the costs of production may fall for producers, there will be less demand for their products and hence they must cut prices. The net effect of this is uncertain, and the pro-wage cut lobby are left to call on devices such as the Pigou effect in order for unemployment to fall. The only other possibility is that falling prices might improve the economy's trading position with the rest of the world. But if that is out of balance could not a shift in the exchange rate, automatic or managed, achieve the same end?

The fact that the debate has raged over more than half a century is partly due to the paucity of tools, both theoretical and empirical, the economist has in his armoury to analyse the real world. Theoretical general equilibrium models, although mathematically ingenious make too many sacrifices in terms of reality. The standard empirical approach, almost obligatory in any journal, is to model the world in a small number of equations and estimate this world by maximum likelihood techniques; sophisticated statistics applied to theoretical molehills. On the other hand large-scale macroeconomic models are too aggregated, short-run, demand orientated and most importantly of all too far removed from microeconomic principles. Applied general equilibrium models offer some hope, but have had limited application and as we shall argue later, in reality suffer from the defects of both general equilibrium analysis and macroeconomic models. It is not surprising then that given such inadequate tools, the economist has made little progress in recent decades in analysing the economy. Until the economist can break away from a mode of analysis which at the outset imposes simplifying assumptions which distort the real world, there seems little hope of a genuine breakthrough in the subject. Advances in economic theory will simply revolve around the use of more and more sophisticated mathematics in a bid to break free of these limitations, and it is not clear where this will lead.

One of Keynes' main targets in attacking classical and neoclassical ideas was Say's law, that supply creates its own demand. This attack was then, and is now, fundamentally valid, and in general I have much more sympathy with the Keynesian position than the neoclassical one. *Equally, however, one can argue that implicit in Keynesian analysis is another law, which states with equal simplicity that demand creates its own supply.* If there is unemployment then increasing demand will remove it. That was Keynes' position then, and by and large it is Keynesian's position now. There has been relatively little consideration as to whether the economy has the supply-side capacity to meet this demand, perhaps with mass unemployment this is deemed an irrelevant question.

However, in recent years there has begun to emerge a school of thought which seeks to model economies in disequilibrium, looking at both the demand and supply sides of the economy. This argues that at any one time it is unlikely that the economy will be in equilibrium and will be effectively constrained by either demand or supply. The impact of policies then depends upon which regime the economy is in. We shall explore this in the next chapter, but to an extent much of this work is still in its infancy and although perhaps recognised as being important has had little impact on the mainstreams of the subject and still less in policy circles. Korliras (1980) has argued that this is because the non-market clearing theorists have failed to produce a large volume of easily digestible evidence. None the less, I will be arguing that this approach is one which is best suited to explaining real world economies as well as presenting some of the sort of evidence that Korliras wanted. In addition, I will be extending the non-market clearing paradigm into an important new dimension. To date it, along with the rest of economics, has largely ignored the impact of firm and plant closures and the setting up of new firms on the supply side of the economy. This is an omission I shall be seeking to correct.

Thus the purpose of this book is twofold. First, on the theoretical side to expand the theory of the firm in determining the supply side capacity of the economy, and to examine the processes by which, new firms are incorporated and existing firms close down— subjects which have been largely ignored in economics. We shall then examine the impact this has on non-market clearing theories. It is hoped that by doing this we shall be able to explain why Keynesian policies have worked in some periods, but not others. Secondly, on the empirical side it is to suggest a method of analysis which will, for example, enable us to model the equilibrium properties of dynamic, non-market clearing economies characterised by oligopolistic markets, something which has been almost impossible using current modes of analysis. It will also help in the analysis of economies in disequilibrium as they switch between being demand and supply constrained. At its most ambitious this new tool will enable us to model an economy as closely as we can. The limit on this process will not then be provided by mathematics, but by our knowledge of economics and economies.

By doing this it is hoped first to provide a set of policies which will allow that part of the world caught in the grips of a recession to move out of it, and help that part of the world which is not in a recession to stay out of one. Such policies will, must, contain both supply and demand side elements. Secondly, it is hoped that it will prove a catalyst in unifying economics, removing the uncomfortable distinctions between micro and macro and help formulate policies with a view to their impact on the whole economy both in the short and the long terms. Finally, we hope to undermine the position of general equilibrium, tattonement and kindred mythology in economics, and in so doing to remove the platform for any further resurrection of monetarist/neoclassical ideas to plague future generations.

2 Towards a New General Theory

Keynes' *General Theory* was revolutionary in two respects. On a theoretical level it broadened the economist's perspective from the individual or micro level to that of the macro or aggregate level. Quite simply he created macroeconomics, and that achievement places him as arguably the most important economist of his, or any other, generation. Prior to Keynes economists thought of the individual firm or consumer. Unemployment was simply analysed as a good like any other good, within a partial equilibrium framework. If there is excess supply let the price fall and this will remove the unemployment. Keynes' approach focused our minds away from individual markets taken in isolation towards a general equilibrium framework where the demand for labour is determined along with the demands for all other goods. This, however, differed from previous analyses of general equilibrium in that it allowed for a persistent disequilibrium or alternatively an underfull-employment equilibrium. Secondly, on an empirical level he provided a method, that of national income accounting, by which economists could both understand more thoroughly the interactions in the economy and use fiscal policy as an instrument of fine tuning rather than a clumsy hit or miss device to be used only in periods of severe recession. The task here is to both transfer economists' attention towards the non-Walrasian dimension and, as well as extending that dimension, to suggest an empirical methodology which will allow them to analyse economies in a rigorous and realistic manner.

In putting the case for a non-Walrasian approach to

unemployment it is perhaps necessary to consider the major weaknesses of the existing mainstream approaches. These have already been discussed in the previous chapter where it was argued that they are too aggregated, they in general omit supply-side considerations, they are static equilibrium rather than dynamic disequilibrium theories, and they tend to be limited to what can be described in a few, relatively simply equations. The initial push towards an overly aggregative theory was perhaps due to Keynes. His theory is clearly aggregative, working in terms of consumer demand, investment demand and so on. The monetarists have, recently at least, been more concerned with developing a strong microeconomic foundation to their theories, developing 'the microeconomic approach to macroeconomics', which began with the search theoretic approach of Phelps *et al.* (1970). This suggests looking at the problem of unemployment from the perspective of a single unemployed worker or firm with an unfilled vacancy. The individual is then assumed to maximise some utility function defined mainly on current and expected future income. His actions are then assumed to be representative of the unemployed as a whole. Yet this misses out a great deal. In what sense can the actions of a firm making profits of £1 million be summed to represent those of two firms one with a £4 million profit and the other with a £2 million loss? This literature has been interesting, but arguably the only significant impact it has had on economic policy-making is to provide some justification for the neoclassical view that the major obstacle to full employment is unemployment insurance.

The microeconomic approach has also spawned an interesting literature on the possibility of modelling an economy not by looking at the aggregate expenditure of consumers and firms, but by looking at the demands of individual socio-economic groups of consumers and the production of different industries within a general equilibrium framework. This work, known under the general heading of applied general equilibrium analysis, forms a link between part of what will eventually be proposed in this book and existing work. However, from our perspective it suffers from two main defects. First, the approach is almost always a general equilibrium one, whereas I believe that large scale unemployment is essentially a problem of disequilibrium, in which the speed with which equilibria are approached is all important. Secondly, although obviously less aggregated than a macroeconomic model, the disaggregation only goes down to industry level on the one hand and consumer groups on the other. I shall be taking criticisms of this approach further in chapter 4, as well as suggesting an alternative which will enable us to analyse macro problems from a genuinely micro perspective, and to take on board many of the developments which have taken place in economics in recent years. The approach I am taking will also enable us to incorporate supply-side factors into the framework which is being developed. The term 'supply-side economics' has become common coinage since first used by Stein (1981) to describe a new way of looking at fiscal policy which economists such as Feldstein (1983a and 1983b) were beginning to discuss. These were concerned with the impact of taxes on investment and saving, corporate behaviour and portfolio decisions. The empirical evidence on this is ambiguous. For example following the Tax Reform Act of 1969 which virtually doubled capital gains tax, venture capital in the US declined drastically. In 1969 there were 1026 initial stock offerings, by 1975 this had fell to 15, whilst by 1983 after the Reagan tax cuts they had increased to 875. According to Sinai, Lin and Robins (1983) these tax cuts increased fixed investment by at least $9 billion per annum in the period 1983–85. However, Bosworth (1984) found the increase in investment to be very uneven, with more than 90 per cent being due to a rise in outlays for office equipment, business automobiles and commercial structures, despite there being no significant tax reduction for either automobiles or computers. Overall he found there to be virtually no correlation between the growth in specific categories of investment and their associated tax reductions. The disincentive effect of tax on labour supply has been even more difficult to find. Hausman (1981) has recently found a significant impact of taxes on the labour supply of married males. Whilst Glaister, McGlone and Ulph (1979) found a negative price elasticity of labour supply thus supporting the theoretical possibility that a cut in the direct tax rate might increase labour supply. However, as Brown (1983) has argued, all these studies are seriously flawed and there is little than can safely be said about labour-supply elasticities, and therefore the incentive or disincentive effects of taxes.

It can be seen that the supply-side debate has concentrated largely on the effects of taxation. These are potentially important, but can hardly be said to encompass the main features of the supply side of the economy. A truly general theory needs to explain the determinants of labour productivity and potential output such as education, health, the ability of those in executive positions, capital stock, and the vintage structure of this capital stock. The product cycle, innovation and technical change also play crucial roles in the real economy. Central to all of these is the firm. Supply-side capacity or potential output will be determined by the number of firms in the economy and their size structure. Let us suppose that some great natural disaster or act of war were to destroy large numbers of firms. Is it to be supposed that Keynesian policies of increasing demand would be of any relevance in reducing the resulting unemployment? Of course not, and yet I will be arguing that something very close to this destruction can, and does, occur during the business cycle, and thus Keynesian policies might not always be relevant or successful. This quickly becomes apparent to anyone travelling through any of the major industrial cities in the UK. They will see environments which are devastated, a high proportion of factories either empty or demolished, not just small factories, but large ones which had previously played a central role in manufacturing. It will also become clear that it will take more than a revival of demand to restore full employment, because the supply-side potential is no longer there. The factories in which the workers used to work, the machines they used to work with are gone. Much of the capacity it has taken decades to build has disappeared within the space of a few years.

The firm, and decisions taken by the firm, have several features which we would wish to incorporate into a general theory. Firstly, it is constrained in what it can produce with its existing workforce and capital stock by a specific production function. Capital stock can be increased, but there are constraints on the speed with which this can be done. These are partly financial, partly physical and partly administrative. On the financial side the firm will need finance or access to credit, yet at the same time it will not wish to become too highly geared, for instance, to possess a high debt to equity ratio. On the administrative side, as it grows it will need to develop more sophisticated management control methods, or risk becoming inefficient. Finally some types of capital may take considerable time to obtain, due to bottlenecks in the supplier firms or natural lags in construction. In addition to these lags, the firm may not want to expand too quickly, due to uncertainty about potential markets as it expands its products. The labour constraint also operates on several levels. First, there is the number of workers the firm employs and their occupational mix. Secondly there is the quality of this workforce. This depends upon each individual worker's natural ability, health, the amount of formal education he received in the state/private school system as well as any on-the-job training. Of particular importance is the ability of management, particularly senior management, who organise and control the firm. It is not simply the level of potential output in equilibrium which is determined by the ability these relatively few people bring to their job. It is also the ability of an economy to withstand a recession or to recover from a depression which depends to a significant degree on the ability of those controlling major or rapidly growing firms. This, in part, may explain the high salaries such individuals frequently command.

NON-WALRASIAN THEORIES

Disillusionment with the Walrasian market clearing approach has resulted in some interest in non-market clearing approaches. Drazen (1980) attributes Patinkin (1965) with the first fully worked out model which distinguishes Walrasian demand and supply functions from those which would appear if agents perceived quantity constraints. Firms' expectations of future sales determine the demand for labour, involuntary unemployment results from constraints on how much labour can be sold. Clower (1965) followed this by arguing that Keynesian theories of unemployment should be couched within a general equilibrium framework. A key distinction lies in the notional demands household would make in an unconstrainted Walrasian equilibrium, and their effective demands they make when constrained. This distinction plays an important role in countering the influence of Walras law, according to which the sum of the value of excess demands, both positive and negative, in all markets is zero. If one market has excess supply this must be accompanied by excess demand in some other market. Thus unemployment existing in the labour market must be accompanied by unsatisfied demand in some other market. All that is, therefore, needed to clear all markets simultaneously is for prices to adjust to the equilibrium price vector, which presumably in this example means a reduction in wage rates. Using Clower's distinction between nominal and effective demand it can be shown that Walras law only holds for notional demands. Unemployment results in effective demand being less than notional demand and there is no reason why it should be accompanied by unsatisfied effective demand in some other market.

Barro and Grossman (1971 and 1976), expanding on the work of Patinkin and Clower, looked at individual behaviour and non-market clearing under parametric price and quantity constraints. They were concerned with the equilibrium which would prevail if the time period were so short that prices were fixed and equilibrium were brought about through quantity adjustments. They show that the fixed level of nominal wages and prices determine in which market quantity constraints appear. Also important is the work of Muellbauer and Portes (1978) who argue that conventional macroeconomic models had been mis-specified by the omission of a systematic kind of structural change which can be represented by indicators of excess demand. This would result in economies or parts of economies to pass through distinct regimes, in each of which rule different but stable behavioural relationships.

In another important contribution Malinvaud (1982) assumes a putty-clay technology where the productive equipment is characterised by both its capacity $\bar{y}$ and its capital intensity k which is the ratio between the volume of capital (K) and $\bar{y}$. Within this framework investment has two dimensions relating to variations in productive capacity and capital intensity, i.e.

$$I = \bar{y}\dot{k} + k\dot{\bar{y}} \qquad (2.1)$$

where $\dot{k}$ and $\dot{\bar{y}}$ are time derivatives. This equation implies that investment occurs both to increase the capital intensity of capacity output and to increase capacity output at a given level of capital intensity. Unemployment in the model can arise because of too high a level of capital intensity, just as in the Harrod-Domar model. This tends to arise because wages are too high. Thus the resultant unemployment can appropriately be labelled as classical. The difference with the classical school results from the long-run persistence of unemployment in a non-market clearing model, as a result of shortage of capacity. This is shown in the equation determining the growth of capacity.

$$\dot{\bar{y}} = [a(\pi^e/r) - b(1 - V^e)]\bar{y} \qquad (2.2)$$

where V^e is the expected level of capacity utilisation, π^e the expected profit rate, which depends on wage rates and r the rate of interest. If expected profits are low $\dot{\bar{y}}$ will be negative, capacity output will fall resulting in what might be termed a capital depression. An incomes policy should then be employed to reduce real wages and increase expected profitability. But as in the short term this will also reduce demand then it also needs to be accompanied by policies aimed at expanding demand.

Perhaps the most interesting contribution, at least from the perspective I am taking, comes from Hahn (1976) who takes a preliminary look at the role of bankruptcy. He argues that the deflation necessary to eliminate unemployment may bring with it bankruptcy for a number of debtors, which may lead to discontinuities in behavioural functions. Thus the existence of an equilibrium becomes problematical. He also argues that the bankruptcy problem implies that adjusting government spending or money supply to the given money wage may more plausibly eliminate unemployment than letting money wages fall and fixing government policy variables. In the former case prices will then be higher than in the latter, thus avoiding bankruptcy. Drazen (1980) picks this up, and argues that although it may prove a false scent it appears worth pursuing. To a large extent this pursuit will form one of the central themes of this book. These contributions, apart from Hahn's, although interesting do not seem to take us very far forward. They tell us what will happen if prices do not move to clear markets, but in what sense is this any different from early Keynesian analysis which seems to have been predicated on sticky wages. All rest on the assumption of downward rigidity in the wage rate and this would be sufficient to result in unemployment even under the classical system. However, it appears to me that this approach is none the less important. The labour market does not appear to clear in the real world, or at least in Europe now and in Europe and the United States in the 1930s. To build an entire theoretical framework which assumes that it does clear seems less than fruitful. There are two questions of importance. First, why do prices not adjust to maintain equilibrium. Secondly, what are the dynamics of a system where adjustment is brought about, at least partly, by quantity adjustments. Disequilibrium theorists have been mainly concerned with the latter question, and their work should be looked upon as an important beginning.

TOWARDS A NEW GENERAL THEORY

In this section we shall attempt to build upon the work of the disequilibrium economists discussed above, building a model where industries can either be constrained by demand- or supply-side factors. Two things in particular will distinguish it from these other theories. Firstly, we will be crucially concerned with the possibility of capital scrapping and bankruptcy, and the implications of these for unemployment and output. Secondly, it will be more disaggregated than most analyses, examining how some industries can be constrained by demand and others by supply.

As has been seen in Keynesian theories the level of output

is determined by the level of demand. Whilst, in neoclassical, monetarist and new classical theories it is even simpler than that. It is, apart from short-term deviations, always at its full-employment level. Supply-side constraints are ignored in both types of model, despite the claims of the latter to be supply-oriented. In reality the picture is likely to be considerably more complicated than either of these possibilities. In recent years this has begun to be realised and some macroeconomic models are being constructed which include both supply and demand constraints. The response of such a model to macroeconomic stimuli is then very different depending upon whether we are in a supply- or demand-constrained regime. One example of this can be found in METRIC (1981) and Helliwell *et al.* (1985), but these are tentative and their full implications have not yet been explored.

More generally, and abstracting from any potential mismatches between the structure of demand and supply, output (Y) will be constrained by effective demand (Y^d) and what might be termed effective supply (Y^s).

$$Y = \min(Y^d, Y^s) \qquad (2.3)$$

Effective supply can be thought of as consisting of what the economy is capable of producing at any one time, and is the sum of what each individual firm is capable of producing. Firms are in turn constrained in the production process by their existing level of capital stock and workforce. The capital constraint is formed by both the amount of capital, the number of machines for example, and its vintage structure. It is possible that for the production of some goods only capital of a given vintage can be used. However, this is not a possibility we shall go into here and assume that the only difference between vintages lies in efficiency and not in product possibilities.

Let us now look at what will happen in a recession, assuming that the economy begins from a position of equilibrium. The recession might be caused by a variety of causes, for example a fall in demand for export goods, a reduction in the propensity to consume, or a supply-side shock such as the rises in OPEC prices in 1974 and 1979. The recession is likely to be accompanied by a reduction in supply-side capacity.

This will be so for several reasons. First, there will be an increase in company failures. These are closely associated with the business-cycle (as can be seen from Figures 3.1 and 3.2 in the next chapter). Firms will close down, and in many cases their employees become redundant and capital stock is scrapped. Once this has happened, once a factory has been demolished, its capital scrapped and its workforce disbanded, it cannot suddenly begin production again if demand for its product were to increase. In addition, many other firms which do not fail will none the less reduce their production capabilities by cutting back on expenditure and failing to replace worn-out capital. Some large firms may even close plants, again scrapping capital and making their workers redundant. *Thus the reduction in effective demand will be followed by a reduction in effective supply.* Suppose now that there is an increase in demand, possibly caused by an expansionary fiscal policy. What will be the impact of this on unemployment? There are four possibilities which depend upon whether wages are flexible and *whether capital is of the putty-putty type or the putty-clay type.* This latter qualification on the effectiveness of Keynesian policy has not previously been fully realised.

The traditional assumption is of putty-putty capital and it is with this which we shall begin. The term 'putty' stands for capital in a malleable state which can be made into equipment requiring capital : labour ratios of various magnitudes. Thus the putty-putty model is one where capital can be combined with labour in variable proportions both before and after the investment decision is made. It might be something of a puzzle how in the perfectly competitive world of neoclassical mythology firms could ever become bankrupt. But clearly they do, and we shall ignore this problem. It is also something of a puzzle why capital should ever be scrapped if it is perfectly adaptable to other uses and with other combinations of labour. But again, this clearly happens and is also something we shall ignore. If wages are flexible downwards then, ignoring for the time being any considerations of what happens to effective demand, there should be few impediments to full employment. More workers can be employed with the existing level of capital stock, and unemployment should not be a long- or even a short-term problem. This is similar to the standard classical position: equilibrium will be restored, albeit at a lower level of output, productivity and living standards. If wages are inflexible downwards, then there will be unemployment which standard Keynesian policies should be effective in removing. Once again the full-employment equilibrium so reached will be one with lower output, productivity and living standards than previously.

If, however, capital is of the putty-clay mould then these rather familiar and comfortable conclusions will no longer hold. Johansen (1959) was the first to develop a putty-clay model, where the term 'clay' stands for capital in a hardened state its use requiring one unique capital : labour ratio. In the case where wages fall, then in the short run there will be unemployment due to a shortage of capital. In this case reduced labour costs will not increase employment. There are no factories for the unemployed to work in, nor the capital for them to work with. In the longer run, it is possible that this reduction in labour costs will stimulate entreprenurial activity in labour-intensive industries, encouraging the growth of new firms and extra investment by existing firms. This increased output might then find a market replacing foreign competitors, either at home or abroad. Thus there might be a return to full employment in the long run. However, the problem with this is that the possible fall in unemployment would be at the cost of locking the economy into a low-wage, low-productivity state more characteristic of developing countries. This may be a solution to the problem of unemployment, but it is not a solution without costs. In the case where wages are not flexible downwards, then Keynesian policies to increase demand will not increase employment, as again there are not the factories nor the capital to employ the unemployed and hence meet this demand. Instead there will simply be an increase in imports and possibly inflation. The only solution which will reduce unemployment in this case is a simultaneous expansion of both the demand and the supply side. It is this model, with a putty-clay capital stock, which we shall now explore in more detail. I regard a putty-clay model with different types of labour and capital as being one which more closely resembles the economies of the USA and the UK than the traditional putty-putty, single homogeneous capital and labour model. As this has never been seriously considered, we shall do so now.

A PUTTY-CLAY MODEL

Many different assumptions could be made about the nature of capital. However, I do not believe that the world is characterised by capital of the putty-putty variety. Instead a fixed proportion of capital in any one firm is likely to have relatively inflexible *ex-post* capital:output and capital:labour ratios. In addition much of capital is industry-specific and cannot be transferred to other firms. Thus if that industry contracts, much of its capital shock must be scrapped. The labour force of a firm can be divided into a number of separate groupings defined by skill and occupation, e.g. skilled, unskilled, white-collar, managerial, etc. Similarly capital stock is equally non-homogeneous, with a simple division into machines and building structures. We shall assume that there are n different types of labour which might be employed in a single firm, and m types of capital, although not all need be. Thus, omitting for the moment a superscript to denote the individual firm, its production function, which determines that firm's effective supply, may be written as:

$$Y^s = f(K_1, K_2, \ldots, K_m, L_1, L_2, \ldots, L_n) \qquad (2.4)$$

where K_i represents the amount of the ith type of capital, e.g. buildings or machines of different types at the firm's disposal, and L_j the amount of labour of type j it currently employs. The possibilities for substitution between different grades of workers in a modern factory is also limited. Frequently the ratio of workers with different skills in any given factory is sharply limited by the production technology the firm has at that instant of time. In the polar case where there are no *ex-post* substitution possibilities between different types of labour and capital the production function may be written as:

$$Y^s = \min(a_1 K_1, a_2 K_2, \ldots, a_m K_m, b_1 L_1, b_2 L_2, \ldots, b_n L_n)$$
$$(2.5)$$

where a_i represents the fixed ratio of output to the ith type of capital, and b_j the fixed ratio of output to the jth type of labour.

Let us suppose that it is the stock of buildings (K_1) which forms the binding constraint and therefore part of all other factors are either surplus or exactly equal to current production needs. In this case potential output will be given by $a_1 K_1$. The firm's excess of factors will then be given by:

Firm's excess of $K_i = K_i - a_1 K_1 / a_i$ for $i = 2, \ldots, m$ (2.6)

Firm's excess of $L_j = L_j - a_1 K_1 / b_j$ for $j = 1, \ldots, n$ (2.7)

There are similar equations when other factors, including labour, are binding. I shall assume that the demand for any factor in short supply is determined by the level of demand for the firm's product (Y^d). In this case, when it is the first type of labour (L_1) which is constraining output, excess demand for L_1 will be equal to:

Firm's excess demand for $L_1 = (Y^d_t / b_1) - L_1)$ (2.8)

where Y^d is the level of (unsatisfied) demand for the firm's products. Firms are unlikely in this case immediately to dispose of factors of production as soon as they are in excess supply. There are costs in doing so. In addition, as the problem is caused by a binding factor constraint we might also expect the firm to attempt to increase the constraining factor, i.e. obtain more of the factor which is in short supply. Thus we might assume some form of partial adjustment mechanism to be at work.

When effective supply is greater than effective demand for the firm's product then all factors are surplus to the firm's current production needs, and it is more likely that all will be reduced, but again not fully and immediately. Instead we might once more suppose there to be some form of partial adjustment mechanism at work. Thus for such a firm, omitting any stochastic factors, labour demand in period t will be given by:

$$L^d_{jt} = \lambda L^*_{jt} + (1 - \lambda) L_{jt-1}$$
$$= \lambda Y^d_t / b_j - (1 - \lambda) L_{jt-1} \qquad (2.9)$$

where these equations now include time subscripts. L^*_j is the quantity of the jth type of labour required to produce the current level of demand for the firm's products (Y^d). Similar equations will apply for capital, although we might find the adjustment mechanism to be very different. There are two ways a firm can reduce its capital stock. First, by not replacing worn-out equipment, which is likely to be a gradual and continuous process. Secondly, by actually scrapping or selling off existing capital stock. This is likely to be highly discontinuous, and will generally involve the closure of a set of related processes. An example would be when a large company decides to close down a particular plant.

The total demand for the jth factor of production can be found by summing the demand for all F firms whether constrained by demand, labour or capital:

$$L_{jt}^d = \sum_{i=1}^{F} \lambda^i [(Y^{di}/b_j)\delta^i + \sum_{k=1}^{m} (a_k K_k/b_j)\gamma^{ki}$$

$$+ \sum_{l=1}^{n} (b_l L_l/b_j)\mu^{li}] + (1 - \lambda^i)L_{jt-1}^i \qquad (2.10)$$

where $\delta^i = 1$ if the ith firm is constrained by demand, and zero otherwise.

$\gamma^{ki} = 1$ if the ith firm is constrained by K_k and zero otherwise.

$\mu^{li} = 1$ if the ith firm is constrained by L_l and zero otherwise.

where the final term in square brackets reflects the demand from firms where the jth labour factor is in short supply. For simplicity I have assumed that firms have the same partial adjustment process regardless of whether they are constrained by demand- or supply-side factors, although this can differ between firms. Ignoring voluntary quits, the difference between this and the total supply of labour represents the level of unemployment or alternatively the amount of excess demand for this factor. It is probable that at any one time some types of labour will be in excess demand whilst others will be in excess supply. One could further complicate the picture (although we shall not) by introducing regional labour markets. What might then emerge is a shortage for a given type of labour in some regions coupled with excess supply in others.

It is now possible to begin to define the different types of unemployment.

Pure Demand Deficient Unemployment: This is equal to the unemployment in demand deficient industries which could be removed by an increase in demand which is specifically targeted at these industries. This may not equal all the unemployed in the demand-deficient industries as firms might run into supply constraints which would then limit the impact of any further increases in demand. The appropriate policy response to this type of unemployment is a Keynesian-type reflation of the economy. There is also the possibility of distinguishing what might be termed *demand balance unemployment*. This occurs not through a generalised lack of demand, but through a mismatch between effective demand and supply across industries. Thus, for example, there might be unsatisfied demand for some industries simultaneously with a lack of demand in others. Some of the resulting unemployment could be reduced by re-targeting demand to match the pattern of effective supply more closely.

Pure Supply-Deficient Unemployment: Supply-deficient unemployment is almost a new concept to the literature, although there are suggestions of it in Scott (1978), for example. It is equal to the unemployment in the supply-deficient industries which could be removed by increasing all the factors of production as needed. One could further subdivide this type of unemployment into capital-deficient unemployment and skill-deficient unemployment, depending upon the limiting factor. The appropriate policy response to this type of unemployment is therefore to increase the limiting factors. For labour this means training, or retraining, workers with the skills which are in short supply. For capital, policies to encourage investment would be needed.

Joint Demand- and Supply-Deficient Unemployment: This is that unemployment which is due to both a lack of demand for the goods firms produce *and binding factor constraints*.

Only in some form of equilibrium will firms be simultaneously constrained by both factors at its current level of production. In such cases the firm's potential supply will equal the current demand for its product. However, as discussed above, firms currently constrained by demand will eventually meet supply constraints if demand for their product increases. At such a level of output it is correct to think of the firm as being constrained by both demand- and supply-side factors. Similarly if firms currently constrained by factors of production were able to increase them, they would eventually meet a demand constraint. Once more it would be correct to think of that firm as being limited by both supply- and demand-side factors.

At some level of output all firms will eventually be constrained by both demand and supply. But for the economy as a whole this does not mean that there will always be *joint demand- and supply-deficient unemployment*. If employment is at the full-employment level, then by definition there can be no unemployment other than frictional. Joint demand- and supply-deficient unemployment is equal to the difference between full-employment output and the greater of Y^d and Y^s. For this type of unemployment to be tackled *both* effective demand *and* effective supply need to be increased. Simply raising effective demand above the level of effective supply will leave that demand unsatisfied by the domestic market and probably lead to an increase in imports. Similarly, to increase effective supply above effective demand will only lead to a greater degree of unused capacity. The two go hand in hand and policies to increase the one without the other would be ineffective and even damaging. However, if effective demand is actually less than effective supply, then an increase in demand if correctly targeted at the demand-deficient industries will by itself reduce unemployment up to the point at which effective demand equals effective supply. Similarly, if effective demand exceeds effective supply then expansionary supply-side policies would also have some success in reducing unemployment, provided once more that they were correctly targeted at the supply-deficient industries.

Frictional Unemployment: In addition to these categories of unemployment there is also frictional and seasonal unemployment. Frictional unemployment is a difficult concept to define with any precision. It is related to job-search activities in the labour market, and is determined by a series of socio-economic variables, although economists have tended to focus their attention on the real wage and social security payments. These are important in determining the optimal length of search an unemployed worker will contemplate when searching for a new job. However, attitudes to work are also important not just in the job-search decision, but also in determining the likelihood of mismatches, i.e. workers taking unsuitable jobs which they shortly leave to enter the job market again.

I have made no direct mention of structural unemployment. This is generally defined as the existence of unemployment for some factors, coexisting with excess demand for others. To an extent the concept of structural unemployment coincides with that of skill-deficient unemployment together with demand balance unemployment. The definitions I have chosen however emphasise the importance of the structure of demand and places more emphasis on adjusting this structure to reduce demand balance unemployment, rather than on adjustments to the supply side of the economy. This is something which will be explored in more depth later. These definitions also link skill-deficient unemployment with capital-deficient unemployment, thus placing more emphasis on all the factors of production than the more traditional concept of structural unemployment.

THE IMPACT OF A RECESSION

Assume an economy at full employment and in equilibrium, with no demand-deficient or supply-deficient unemployment. What will be the impact of a large drop in demand? Effective demand will, of course, fall, output will fall, the multiplier will operate, and unemployment will increase along the lines suggested by the standard Keynesian analysis. But that will not be the end of the story. This reduction in demand will lead to an increase in insolvencies and bankruptcies, which

Table 2.1: The distribution of insolvencies by industry

United States	1983 number	1983 liability	1978 number	1978 liability
Mining and Manufacturing	4433	6371	1013	879
Wholesale Trade	3598	2784	740	346
Retail Trade	11429	2329	2889	777
Construction	5247	1548	1204	328
Commercial Service	6627	3039	773	326

Source: Dun & Bradstreet, liabilities refer to total current liabilities in (current) $million.

Great Britian	1984 total	1984 comp	1984 cvl	1978 total	1978 comp	1978 cvl
Agriculture & Horticulture	84	25	59	31	10	21
Total manufacturing	4599	1255	3344	1156	270	886
Food, Drink & Tobacco	136	34	102	47	10	37
Chemicals	116	32	84	26	8	18
Metals & Engineering	1420	418	1002	328	30	298
Textiles & Clothes	1348	229	1119	245	56	189
Timber & Furniture	393	107	286	136	20	116
Paper, printing & publish	492	161	331	114	27	87
Other manufacturing	694	274	420	260	119	141
Construction	1913	911	1002	989	434	555
Transport & communication	754	348	406	241	157	84
Wholesaling	1252	405	847	330	102	228
Retailing & food	218	81	137	119	31	88
Motor vehicles & garages	378	169	209	129	50	79
Other retailing	1587	621	966	702	394	308
Financial institutions	196	82	114 }	796	320	476
Business services	970	382	588 }			
Hotels and catering	397	156	241	167	79	88
All other industries	1896	1097	799	700	496	204
Total	14244	5532	8712	5360	2343	3017

Source: Companies in . . ., various issues.
Note: 1. The figures for 1984 and 1978 are not strictly comparable, the former are based on the 1980 standard industrial classification (SIC), and the latter on the 1968 SIC. This appears to have had most impact upon the figures for wholesaling and retailing. 2. Comp = compulsory liquidations, CVL = creditors' voluntary liquidations.

will not be limited to firms in decaying industries, but will be felt right across the economy. This is what happened in both the UK and the USA in the recent recession, as can be seen from Figures 3.1 and 3.2 in the next chapter, and Table 2.1, which shows the industrial distribution of insolvencies during and prior to the recent recession. It is important to emphasise that firms in all types of industries will close down. Those in declining, low-profit industries will be in a poor position to withstand further reductions in profits and a large number of them will fail. Similarly, newly incorporated firms in growing industries may well have borrowed substantially in the process of expanding their productive potential in the expectation of a rapidly growing market for their product. When such expectations are not realised, these firms may not be able to repay their debt, there will be short-term overcapacity in the market and many may be forced to close. Probably, the safest industries will be those in mature, established areas of the economy which are not yet in a state of decline.

One will have great difficulty in finding references to any of this in economics, perhaps as a reflection of the continuing influence of 'Keynes' law' that demand creates its own supply. But this reduction in the number of firms will mean that effective supply will also be reduced. There will be fewer firms in the economy, fewer entrepreneurs and less capital. Therefore the potential productive capacity of the economy will decline, and the ability of the economy to respond to an increase in demand will also decline. It will also decline because many firms which do not close down will reduce potential supply by cutting back on the labour force, failing to replace worn out capital stock or even scrapping capital stock. Some large firms may close down whole plants, whilst others will scale down the operations at establishments which will then run at a lower capacity. Redundant capital may be sold off to other firms. This is likely to be the case for non-industry-specific equipment such as typewriters. But other capital will be more industry-specific such as welding equipment. This will not be easy to sell and will be either mothballed or scrapped. To an extent this may be countered by the birth of new firms. In normal times this process of creative destruction might well be sufficient to maintain the supply-side capacity. But in a recession, or a depression, this will not be the case, for, as we shall see in the next chapter, many of these new firms will be doomed to speedy liquidation, and even those which are eventually to succeed will need several years of rapid growth to fill the gap to bring effective supply back up to its full employment level.

The impact of the recession will not be limited to non-human capital, it will spill over into the labour force. Unemployment will reduce the productive potential of human capital in two ways. First, the health of the long-term unemployed will deteriorate. They become more susceptible to physical and mental illness, violence and early death, for example from heart disease (Brenner, 1979). Secondly, the attitude of the unemployed to work is also likely to change. Work discipline and habits need to be learned. For the person who has been continually employed for 20 years a lengthy spell of unemployment may have little impact on these habits. But for a younger person just entering the labour force prolonged unemployment may have a more formative impact on his attitudes. Finally, there is the fact that the nature of work skills are continually changing. On-the-job training does not end after an initial period, but is a continual process. Extended unemployment is likely to leave a worker with out-of-date skills, not just for the new high-technology industries, but also for the one which previously employed him. All of these factors will tend to reduce effective supply, although as they will also tend to reduce full-employment output as well, the impact on the dynamics of a return to full unemployment may be limited. None the less, this is of concern to the economist because of the efficiency implications, and because the natural rate of unemployment may itself be pushed up.

Now assume a boost to demand, perhaps due to expansionary government policies which increased effective demand. In the short term, provided the increase in demand is targeted at industries with demand-deficient unemployment, output will increase, but only by the gap between effective demand and effective supply. Once effective demand exceeds effective supply there will be no further expansion in output because there is not the industrial capacity to meet it. It is then likely that the degree of unsatisfied demand will be met by imports, and accompanied by inflation. In the long run increased demand may result in an expansion of effective supply more rapidly than would otherwise have been the case. Existing firms are likely, perhaps after some lag, to increase their investment. New firms will find it easier to survive the initial years and also to expand. Both of these effects will result in an increase in effective supply which may in time be sufficient to restore full employment. But in the intervening period imports will be higher than previously which could result in a large deficit on the balance of trade. Moreover, it is also possible that the increase in the propensity to import might not be temporary. Once an individual buys a particular foreign car or washing machine, he may well continue with this choice later, even though domestic products are then available. Thus, by itself, an expansionary fiscal policy in a recession might do no more than create a mild increase in output, coupled with a sharp deterioration in the trade balance continuing into the longer term. If this is the case, could it be persevered with over the period of years it might take to restore full employment? Fiscal policy may be sufficient for fine tuning of the economy, but by itself is unlikely to be a suitable instrument to tackle unemployment in a large-scale depression of the kind faced by Western Europe in the 1980s.

Table 1.1 suggested that this is what happened in the most recent two periods of expansion in the UK. In 1972–73 the 'Barber boom' saw consumers' expenditure increase by nearly 12 per cent in two years. This did appear to provide an incentive to firms to increase capacity as the rapid growth in investment in 1973 shows. The unemployment rate also began to fall quite sharply by 1973. More marked still, however, was the increase in import volume of over 20 per cent in the two-year period. The expansion of 1978–79 saw an even smaller reduction in unemployment, and a marked increase in imports. The USA has proved more resilient in recovering from recessions. In part at least, this is due to the greater flexibility of the US labour market and the greater ability of a firm's productive capacity to survive a recession in the US.

This is something we shall expand upon in the next chapter. None of these recessions corresponded even remotely to that which currently grips the UK and much of Western Europe. The reduction in effective supply that this must have brought in its wake must be far greater than anything experienced since the 1930s, and the likely impact on the balance of trade from any attempted expansion would, in the absence of any other measures, almost certainly lead to the attempt being abandoned.

TARGETING FISCAL STIMULI

The application of Keynesian policies will be most effective if it is done prior to a recession developing which results in a contraction of effective supply. Prevention in this case is better and easier than cure. However, the traditional Keynesian response to a recession of expanding demand may be ineffective if the expansion is targeted at the wrong industries. As an example, assume the recession to be triggered by a drop in demand for a specific group of industries such as that which affected the car industry and its suppliers following the 1974 and 1979 OPEC oil price increases. In the normal way this will have Keynesian-type multiplier effects on other industries so that there will follow a generalised lack of demand. If the government were to respond to this by large-scale construction projects in different regions from that in which the car industry is centred, then the probable effect would be excess demand and inflation in the construction industry. If the construction industry was previously working at full capacity, then there will be relatively little slack for this increased demand to take up, few extra workers employed and the initial multiplier effects of the project will be virtually nil. If the project is a long-term one, then unemployed car workers may eventually switch regions and jobs. But the long-term effect of this will be an over-expanded construction industry for normal needs, and when the projects are completed there will be fresh problems of readjustment.

More beneficial would be a cut in taxes, to stimulate consumer demand. This would do relatively little to help the car industry, but it would help with the original multiplier effects. However, even here care is needed to target the tax cuts at consumers in such a way that spending is increased in a similar pattern to that of the original car workers. Cutting the taxes of the high income groups would, for example, probably be a relatively unsuccessful way of increasing demand as their expenditure patterns are likely to be very different from those of the car workers. The increase in consumer demand will be for products for which again there will be relatively little slack. This time, the main effect is likely to be on imports.

The most successful way of tackling the recession by Keynesian policies will be to attempt to direct the fiscal stimulus in such a way as to increase the demand for cars thereby leading to an increase in the derived demand for labour in the car industry, possibly by the selective use of indirect taxes or even subsidies. However, care is needed, as the drop in the demand for cars may, as in 1974, imply the need for both the economy and the industry to adjust to a new equilibrium situation. It is not possible to pretend that this has not occurred, and it will not be possible for the car industry to remain unchanged indefinitely. In this case what is required will be a limited policy initiative designed to give the car industry time to adjust to the new equilibrium, without laying off workers, without letting imports take an increased share of the market, and most importantly without having car plants closing altogether. Such an initiative should come with a specific date, at which it is to end. Failure of the car manufacturers to adjust to this new situation by that time would then lead to their liquidation and shareholder losses, *although not the subsequent loss of the production capacity.* In this interim period of adjustment it may also be that specific import restrictions, relating to cars only, would need to be agreed internationally.

In other cases the trigger to the recession may be of a more temporary nature, such as a drop in demand for capital goods. This was the industry Keynes thought most subject to arbitrary fluctuations. The appropriate action in this case would be to attempt to restimulate the demand for investment goods, perhaps by cutting interest rates or increasing incentives to firms to invest, as well as policies designed to increase demand in general. Thus the government in applying Keynesian demand management policies should bear in mind the initial causes of the recession, and adopt the most appropriate set of policies to deal with those causes, rather than the automatic reaction, applied too often in the past, of a random increase in demand. They should also consider the long-term impact of their policies, and the need to preserve balance in the supply side of the economy, by avoiding large-scale projects which temporarily alter that balance. The Channel tunnel linking England to France seems to be just such a project. If it is being undertaken mainly to boost employment, then it is misguided. There are more urgent construction programmes, such as inner city and infrastructure reconstruction which can be undertaken, which will have an impact in the areas of highest unemployment, and which can be continued in one form or another in the future. Once the Channel tunnel has been built, there will be a large-scale readjustment problem as the construction industry in the south-east contracts to its equilibrium size, and as other cross-Channel industries also have to readjust. Thus this project will merely transfer present problems into the future, rather than provide a long-term solution.

SUPPLY-SIDE MULTIPLIERS

One of the central concepts to emerge from the *General Theory* was that of the investment or government expenditure multiplier. An increase in government spending, for example, will increase output directly of course, but also indirectly. Part of the extra income at workers' disposal as a result of this increase in government spending will itself be spent on goods and services, giving rise to further increases in output. We can also think of multipliers on the supply side of the economy. Take the example where the ith firm is constrained by the kth type of labour, due to there being a shortage of this type of labour in the economy as a whole or the region of the economy in which the firm operates. A current example are computer specialists. If one more such specialist were to become available to the economy, possibly as a result of a retraining programme, and was employed by this firm, then the demand for other labour would also increase. Specifically the total number of extra workers taken on by the firm would be:

$$\Delta L^i = \sum_{j=1}^{n} (b_k/b_j) \qquad (2.11)$$

Similar multipliers may also be calculated for various types of capital stock. Because all firms will not be faced with the same production function these factor supply multipliers will not be the same for all firms in all industries. In general it is to be supposed that it will be greater in relatively labour-intensive industries. Thus for retraining to have the greatest impact upon unemployment, it should not necessarily be concentrated upon those skills which are in shortest supply, but on those skills with the greatest supply-side multipliers; that is, upon skills constraining output in labour-intensive industries.

In practice supply- and demand-side multipliers will interact with one another in several ways. First, the extra workers employed will increase their spending and thus expand effective demand, reducing unemployment in those industries previously constrained by a lack of demand. Secondly, the employment of one more computer programmer will also produce an increase in the desired capital stock equal to:

$$\delta K^i = \sum_{j=1}^{m} (b_k/a_j) \qquad (2.12)$$

If the firm does not have an excess of capital, because it cannot usefully use it in the absence of skilled personnel, this will need to be accompanied by an increase in investment. Provided capital-producing firms are not themselves constrained by some scarce resource but by demand, these firms will increase output and employ more labour.

SCHUMPETERIAN DYNAMICS

Following a Schumpeterian line of thought it is interesting to consider the consequences of different industries being in different stages of development. At any one time some are likely to be young and dynamic, some will have reached a state of maturity and some be in decline. In today's world, in both Western Europe and the USA, these could be computers, cars and steel, respectively. In normal times a gradual pattern of change may result in some regionalised problems of unemployment, but it will not threaten the whole economy. For example, in the UK the decline of the textile industry in the 1950s was matched by the growth of other employment opportunities. In the USA as Table 2.2 shows, there has been a *gradual shift* in the last two decades away from labour- and resource-intensive industries towards high-technology ones.

The appearance of a cluster of new products/processes might be expected to change this normal pattern of evolution. Indeed the process of change would probably speed up, but there is no reason to suppose that this would lead to a reduction in demand for existing products until new products are available as substitutes. Take the invention of word-processors, which we shall assume to have superseded typewriters. An individual firm's demand for typists will not fall until it is able to purchase wordprocessors. The mere fact that wordprocessors have been invented, or that some are now available in a rationed market, will not by itself make typists redundant. Immediate problems for typewriter manufacturers, however, might arise if firms stop investing in new typewriters in anticipation of the newly-invented wordprocessors shortly becoming available. Although even here it would be expected that the waiting period must not be too long or firms would have no choice but to carry on

Table 2.2: US shares of value-added and employment by industry group

Group	Value-added			Employment		
	1960	1970	1980	1960	1970	1980
High-technology	27	31	38	27	30	33
Capital-intensive	32	30	27	29	30	28
Labour-intensive	13	13	12	21	20	19
Resource-intensive	28	25	23	23	21	20

Source: R. Z. Lawrence, Brookings Papers on Economic Activity 1:1983

replacing worn-out typewriters. In the longer run, of course, typewriter firms will have serious problems, but this is a normal part of Schumpeter's process of creative destruction. More serious adjustment problems, however, might occur if the new wordprocessors were three times as efficient as old-style typewriters, leading to a substantial reduction in the demand for typists, even supposing that they can satisfactorily be retrained as wordprocessor operators. The number of typists will now exceed the demand for them and many will need to be retrained for other occupations, although if the economy were previously in equilibrium there will, in the short term, be no immediate demand for them elsewhere. Once they become unemployed, the Keynesian demand multiplier will reduce demand in the economy. But to counter this the increased efficiency of firms should lead to a general increase in living standards, which can be expected to expand demand. Because the firms will save all the costs of employing the typists including any non-wage costs, but the typists are unlikely to lose all their income due to unemployment insurance, it might be hoped that the net effect will be expansionary. Thus it would appear likely that the unemployment will initially be localised to specific occupations, and there will follow a fairly automatic increase in the demand for other occupations.

A sudden sharp and prolonged reduction in demand, leading to a recession, might also be expected to alter this normal pattern of events. First, those industries in decline will almost certainly be the ones most susceptible to the recession and contract sharply. Large numbers of firms in these industries can be expected to close down altogether, causing large-scale, although possibly regionally concentrated, unemployment. The important point to note is that although declining, in the normal run of events they may not have been expected to disappear for many years. Thus their sharp contraction will have resulted in a large drop in employment which could normally have been expected to have been gradually absorbed by expanding industries over a prolonged period of time.

Secondly, mature industries may also stagnate, or even contract, with some firms also closing down and others cutting back on capacity. This appears to have been the case in the car industry, both in the USA and the UK. Capacity has dropped in both countries, most dramatically in the UK, in an industry which cannot be thought of as declining. Moreover, as we shall see in the next chapter, it will be difficult for the UK car industry, at least, to recover as much of the decline in capacity has been made good by increased imports. Finally, the growth sectors of the economy will also receive a setback, and they too might suffer bankruptcies and a reduction in capacity, particularly as such industries tend to be particularly highly geared. Generally speaking, the firms concerned can be expected to have borrowed considerable amounts in the expectation of a rapidly growing and secure market for their products. The failure of this expectation to be fulfilled may well cause them financial problems leading to collapse, as Schumpeter clearly envisaged. This again seems to have been the case with the computer industry, with the main UK micro manufacturers on the edge of collapse in 1985.

The net result of this will be that as the economy seeks to emerge from the recession, there will have been large-scale job losses in the declining industries, supplemented by redundancies in the established industries. In the normal run of things these would have been absorbed over a long period of time, by the gradual expansion of new industries. However, the contraction will have been so rapid that this would not be feasible, even had these new industries continued to grow at a normal rate. But of course, they will not have done so. At best they will probably have stagnated, and at worst they also will have contracted.

The problem viewed in this sense concentrates on a deficiency of supply in some industries, rather than too great a supply in other industries. It will simplify the remainder of the discussion if we refer to these industries as expanding and contracting respectively. The problem is not then one of excess capacity in declining industries; rather, one of insufficient capacity in expanding ones. Thus a policy aimed at closing down excess capacity, rationalisation or the removal of 'uneconomic' enterprises has little direct relevance for the problem of supply-deficient unemployment. Indeed because such industries provide the only available infrastructure to employ large numbers of workers such rationalisation policies are positively malevolent. Only if the capital, entrepreneurial or human resources thus freed were transferred to the expanding industries resulting in their more rapid growth might there be a reduction in unemployment. But it is difficult to see how capital from a steelworks can be transferred to promote the growth of the computer industry, or how skilled steelworkers can be immediately transformed into skilled programmers. Furthermore, if such a shutdown programme were to be achieved with the aid of government grants and redundancy payments, then it should be set against the impact equal expenditure would have if it were aimed more directly at the expanding industries.

To counter this type of unemployment, policies should be directed towards all industries. For the new industries this means the application of both demand and supply-side policies to promote their rapid growth. For mature industries, policies should ensure that the recession does not result in the needless scrapping of productive potential. But this is equally important for declining industries. Capital stock in these industries should not necessarily be scrapped, and workers made idle immediately their firms become unprofitable, or there is short-term overcapacity in the industry, as there are wider costs and benefits to consider. The first priority of a government should be to use Keynesian demand policies to prevent recessions developing, or at least limit them. Should they fail in this their second priority should be to prevent the destruction of supply-side capacity, even when that capacity is in declining and possibly unprofitable industries. These industries have to decline, but they should do so at a rate which allows their labour force to be absorbed into expanding industries.

Should the government fail in both these objectives and the economy slides from a recession into a depression where large-scale scrapping of capital has already occurred, then it will be much more difficult to restore full employment. There will need to be more emphasis on policies to expand new supply-side industries, although preserving the capacity of what remains of the existing ones must still rank as an important policy objective. The latter becomes particularly important if the structure of demand, and the optimal production processes, have not altered drastically from what they were prior to the depression, in other words, if the pattern of gradual industrial evolution noted above has continued through the recession. In this case the *desired* pattern of industrial production which emerges from the depression will be broadly similar to what it was prior to the recession. An alternative possibility is that the structure of demand and/or the optimal pattern of production processes and techniques will have changed substantially on re-emergence from the recession. This could be caused by a Schumpeterian-type cluster of innovations which Mensch (1975) argues can be expected to accompany a depression. In this case the previous industrial structure, the regional and industrial pattern of firms, their skill and capital structure will in substantial part no longer be appropriate to meet new needs. In this case greater emphasis may need to be placed on expanding new industries.

The first of these two scenarios would correspond to a state of the world where change was continual, gradual and exogenous. The second corresponds to a more discontinuous view of the world. This is what appeared to be the case in the 1930s, and is also arguably today. A whole cluster of innovations become marketed at the same time, possibly in response to the recession. In the 1930s the new industries were in cars, plastics, electricity and consumer durables. In the 1980s they appear under the collective heading of the new technology industries and include computers, wordprocessors, and biotechnology-based industries. In the next chapter I shall discuss whether innovation is stimulated by a depression as Mensch argued or not. I shall also discuss ways in which the growth of these new industries might be accelerated. But despite this emphasis on expanding new industries and capacity the bulk of the discussion will focus on ways to prevent the contraction of supply-side capacity.

EVIDENCE

The analysis has differed from the standard one in considering the impact of firm closure and the scrapping of capital on the productive capacity of the economy. It has also differed in one key assumption, *ex-post* there are no substitution possibilities between differing factors of production. Of course, this is an extreme position and it would be ridiculous to claim that there were no substitution possibilities at all. The key question is, to what extent is substitution possible? Casual observation—and the economist should not be too ready to dismiss this type of 'evidence'—would suggest that substitution possibilities are in a large number of cases small. Take transport. *Ex-ante* one can vary the capital : labour ratio to a considerable extent e.g. by buying a bigger truck. *Ex-post*, however, once the truck has been bought the capital:labour ratio is fixed. The same is true of capstan lathes, aeroplanes, typewriters, supermarket layouts, and so on.

Harder evidence comes in the form of the survey data shown in Table 2.3, which was obtained from the Confederation of British Industry (CBI, an employers' organisation). This is a quarterly survey of firms in manufacturing, and regularly includes a question on factors limiting output over the next four months. The figures show that in 1985, for example, 76 per cent of firms cited orders as a constraint. There are several points of interest in the table, such as the very sharp rise in this figure in the period 1980–83. Thus in 1983 93 per cent of firms were constrained by a lack of orders. The drop in this figure since then might reflect a slight recovery in the economy, or alternatively that firms have cut back on capacity so that it is more in line with demand, which would limit the economy's ability to respond to any increase in demand. This is what appears to have been the case in the 1971/72 recession. Then following the attempts of the Conservative government to reflate the economy, the number of firms reporting capital constraints on expanding output doubled from 14 to 28 per cent. Even more significant was the increase in those reporting skilled labour constraints, trebling from 12 to 37 per cent. Of these the constraint on skilled labour seems to have been more important, both because of the greater increase and because by 1974 it was still affecting 36 per cent of the firms, whereas only 16 per

Table 2.3: *Percentage of firms reporting that their output was likely to be limited by the following factors*

| | Orders | Factors limiting output | | |
		Skilled labour	Other labour	Plant capacity
1971	80	12	2	14
1972	78	12	3	14
1973	41	37	19	28
1974	40	36	16	16
1975	79	16	3	8
1976	79	13	3	11
1977	74	20	5	13
1978	76	22	4	11
1979	71	21	5	13
1980	88	8	1	6
1981	93	3	1	5
1982	92	3	1	5
1983	88	5	1	9
1984	80	8	1	13
1985	76	13	1	16

Source: CBI, *Industrial Trends Survey.*

cent of firms were then limited by capital constraints. Although whether this is still the case in the current recession is debatable given the depth of the recession and the indications that excess capital has been scrapped rather than mothballed.

However, the important point to note is that if there were perfect substitution possibilities between different types of labour and capital then at anything less than full employment there would be neither capital scarcities nor labour shortages. It is clear that throughout the period 1971–83 firms have been considerably more constrained by capital and skilled labour shortages than by unskilled labour shortages. If there is perfect substitution between factors of production, as so much of neoclassical analysis assumes, why did firms not substitute unskilled labour for either skilled labour or capital? The fact that they apparently did not is an indication that such substitution possibilities are limited in the short term at least. These facts are consistent with a putty-clay model rather than a putty-putty one. Further evidence comes from studies aimed at estimating the elasticity of substitution. These are almost always based on the assumption of a putty-putty capital model. If the short-run elasticity of substitution were in fact zero then the only changes in the capital:labour ratio over time would come from new investment. In this case estimates of the elasticity of substitution based on time-series analyses would be much lower than those obtained from cross-section studies of e.g. different industries or countries, where one is comparing different equilibrium situations, although neither would in fact be valid measures of the elasticity of substitution. These different industries might well have made different *ex-ante* decisions on the optimal capital:labour ratio, resulting in different *ex-post* ratios. But a measure of elasticity based on these different ratios would be of little value if capital was of the putty-clay variety. In fact time-series do tend to yield lower estimates (see Scarf and Shoven, 1985).

Helliwell *et al*. (1985) analyse a model with three factors of production (capital, labour and energy), and examine limited possibilities of a putty-semi-putty model. They estimate what they call a 'retrofitting parameter', which is a measure of the previous period's capital stock which can be retrofitted to embody the latest cost-minimising capital:energy ratio. The nearer this is to zero the closer is the model to a putty-clay one, whilst the closer it is to 1 - capital scrapping rate, the closer the model is to a putty-putty one. For the USA they find this parameter to be 0.45 and for the UK 0.05. The USA would therefore appear to have a much more malleable capital structure than the UK, although both countries exhibit substantial putty-clay characteristics. It should also be noted that this only relates to substitution possibilities between capital and energy, and it might be argued that these are greater than for labour and capital in any case for this they use a strict putty-clay model.

Finally, variations in the U–V curve (the relationship between unemployment and vacancies) and the Phillips curve, which have somewhat perplexed economists, can also be partially explained if we have limited factor substitution. At the beginning of a recession workers will be fired and new workers will not be trained. Once the economy moves out of the recession there will be skill mismatches resulting in a higher level of vacancies being associated with a given level of unemployment. Standard search theory would then suggest that a given level of unemployment will be associated with a higher rate of wage and hence also price inflation. Moreover, the deeper the recession, the more serious is the skill gap and the greater the shift in these relationships is likely to be.

However despite this evidence in support of a putty-clay regime, time-series data on capital stock do not show that the onset of a deep recession, such as occurred from 1979 onwards, results in large-scale scrapping of capital, thus causing a reduction in effective supply. This can be seen in Table 2.4 which seems to show that for the majority of European countries although there has been a substantial decline in the *growth* of potential output after 1973, a trend which accelerated after 1979, there has been no marked fall in either capital stock or potential output itself. At first sight this would appear to be fairly conclusive in disproving the hypothesis that as an economy enters a recession the number of firms, capital stock and effective supply all contract. The official figures simply do not show this happening. However, there are problems with these data, which can also be seen

Table 2.4: Changes in capacity output and capital stock in manufacturing

| | Annual average growth rates in: | | | | | |
| | Capacity | | | Capital stock | | |
	1960–73	1973–79	1979–84	1960–73	1973–79	1979–84
Austria	3.3	3.1	3.7	6.0	3.4	2.7
France	6.3	3.7	0.6	6.5	4.1	2.8
West Germany	4.6	2.4	0.9	6.0	2.3	1.8
UK	2.7	0.0	− 1.7	3.2	2.1	0.6
Canada	4.8	3.7	3.3	4.7	3.9	4.1
USA	3.6	3.1	2.5	2.7	3.8	4.1

Source: Economic Survey of Europe in 1984–1985, United Nations, New York, 1985.

from Table 2.4, which shows that the link between capital and potential output seems less than straightforward. For example, in the USA, there appears to be an inverse relationship between the two sets of figures. This is noted in the survey from which the above data are extracted and the authors conclude that time-series data on capital stock appear to have become less and less reliable in recent years. They are not quite sure why this should be so, but feel that the economic disturbances of the 1970s led to a reduction in the economic life of capital. The problem with this is that if firms had been scrapping and replacing existing stock more rapidly the UK would have experienced an investment boom, which has not been the case. A more plausible explanation is not that firms are replacing capital more rapidly, but that when firms go bankrupt, close plants or otherwise cut back on capacity much of their capital stock goes with them. The record numbers of bankruptcies and plant closures in recent years would then have resulted in a clear reduction in both capacity and capital stock, and rendered capital stock figures, which ignore this, useless. If this is so, then all the figures in the above table, certainly for the main European countries, would be much too optimistic. This view is supported by EUROSTAT figures which seem to imply that in the UK potential output in manufacturing *fell by 5 per cent in 1984 alone* (See Secretariat of the Economic Commission for Europe, 1985).

Finally, there is evidence of a more micro-nature concerning the closure of specific firms or plants. An early example of a declining activity being replaced by an expanding one is provided by Massey and Meegan (1979) who document the rundown of the General Electric Company (GEC) in the late 1960s and early 1970s. There were major closures in the heavy engineering side of its business with many jobs lost, plant closures and scrapping of capital equipment. However, in Schumpeterian terms this can be classified as one of those periods when gradual decline in one industry is made good by expansion in another. In fact it was GEC itself which provided these alternative opportunities. But it was not until 1973–74, as Lorenz (1975) has pointed out, that its fixed asset base was once more increasing with heavy investment in electronics, gas turbines, electronic motors, telecommunications and radio and television.

Another example of a company moving out of an area of declining profitability into one of expanding profitability is given in the Birmingham Community Project (1977) which documented the switch of Metro Cammell away from the production of general railway equipment to buses. Plant closures, bankruptcies and the scrapping of capital are a fact of economic life, yet official data sources, particularly in the UK but also in the USA, largely ignore them. Until figures do become available on capital losses it will remain difficult to get a full picture of what is happening to the supply side of the economy and capital stock figures will remain meaningless.

CONCLUSIONS

This chapter has primarily been concerned with going beyond 'Keynes' law', that demand creates its own supply, and examining what happens to the supply side of the economy during the business-cycle. It has been argued that during a recession effective supply is reduced as some firms go bankrupt and others close down plants and otherwise cut down on capacity. Many economists would like to view this as a process of 'creative destruction', in which the old and inefficient are swept away by the dynamic and the new. It will be shown in the following chapter that this view cannot be sustained and that all firms in all industries are at risk during a slump. Thus a recovery when it comes may be substantially impaired by the loss of supply-side capacity. A firm which has closed down, scrapped its capital and disbanded its workforce cannot suddenly start producing again once demand for its products revives. This will be the case, whether the firm is in the steel industry, the car industry or the computer industry.

Whether this leads to large-scale unemployment or not depends upon the nature of capital. The standard approach is to treat it as malleable jelly, and in this case full employment can be restored by either a fall in wages or a Keynesian-based policy of fiscal expansion. There will be costs in that the loss of this supply-side capacity will result in lower living standards, but unemployment should not be a problem. I have argued that this assumption is invalid and that a putty-clay model is more appropriate. In this case Keynesian policies to stimulate demand will not work. Equally, however, policies aimed at stimulating the supply side in the absence of an effective demand for firms' products are also doomed to failure. To emerge successfully from a depression both demand- and supply-side policies need to be followed. The demand policies need to be carefully targeted to stimulate demand in areas where employment is limited by a lack of demand. Supply-side policies need to promote the growth of new industries and prevent the collapse of existing ones. How this is to be achieved is something which will be pursued in the following chapter.

3 Retaining Supply-Side Capacity

We have attempted to show in the previous chapter that a crucial part of any successful strategy to prevent a recession from causing mass unemployment is to seek to retain the supply-side capacity of the economy, and where possible to expand it. There are several strands to this. First, the legal structure governing the liquidation of insolvent firms needs to provide for the survival of the production capacity of potentially profitable companies. There may be a role here for government intervention, if there is potential for market failure. There may also be a role for government intervention in saving firms which in commercial terms are not profitable. However, the protection of existing capacity is only half the story and policies should also be pursued which encourage the growth of new capacity in new areas. At the very least these must ensure that the environment which firms operate in is conducive to growth, entrepreneurship and the entry of new firms. But in order to pursue such policies a better understanding is needed of the processes by which some firms fail and other firms are born. Thus this discussion on appropriate policy strategies will be preceded by analysis of company failures and births in both the UK and the USA.

THE LEGAL STRUCTURE IN THE USA AND THE UK

The US Code of Insolvency
The American system places much more emphasis on the rescue of ailing firms than the British and most European

systems. A new code was introduced in 1978/79. The bankruptcy liquidation procedure in this is known as Chapter 7. Both voluntary (by the debtor) and involuntary (by creditors) petitions may be filed for liquidation. However, there is a separate procedure for firms in difficulties which want to reorganise. This is covered in Chapter 11 of the code. Under this, management often remains in charge of the firm, although a trustee can be appointed to oversee them. Once a Chapter 11 bankruptcy has been filed, secured creditors are prevented from foreclosing and removing their assets except with the Bankruptcy Court's approval. A further advantage to the firm is that new loans are more easily available, as well as new trade credit, since post-petition creditors take priority over all pre-petition creditors if the reorganisation plan fails. The essence of the reorganisation process is this plan which the code gives the debtor or its trustees the exclusive right for 120 days to file, and a further 180 days to gain acceptances for it. A committee of unsecured creditors is always appointed to oversee the firm, and further committees, for example, of secured creditors may be set up.

There are two procedures for adopting a reorganisation plan. The 'unanimous consent procedure' requires consent by all classes of creditors. Under this, secured creditors are treated individually rather than as a class, their claims may be cut back, but they then have a right to approve or disapprove the reorganisation plan. Unsecured creditors are treated as a group and also have the right to vote on the plan if their claims are impaired, where a two-thirds majority in amount and a majority in numbers of claims voting is required. In the reorganisation any parts of the firm may be sold. 'Cramdown' is resorted to if the reorganisation plan does not or seems unlikely to secure the required majorities. The plan can then be confirmed by the Bankruptcy Court as long as a 'fair and equitable' standard is applied to each dissenting class of creditor. For secured creditors this requires that they retain their pre-bankruptcy liens and that they receive periodic cash payments equal to the amount of depreciation on the property. A key aspect of the reorganisation plan is the evaluation of the firm's net future earnings. If this value is greater than the liquidation value of the firm the reorganisation is justified. If it is less than the firm's debts then old equity holders get nothing and frequently existing creditors become the new shareholders as part of the settlement. Thus this evaluation is often a source of contention between debtor and creditors.

In practice the use of cramdown involves heavy transaction costs as the Court usually requires valuations by outside appraisers, expert testimony, and so on. Thus, in this sense it is only likely to be used by the largest firms. However, there is some evidence that this has been used by firms to sell off their operations as a going concern, and the proceeds distributed to creditors. In practice this is therefore not a reorganisation, but a liquidation without the costs and delays normally associated with a formal bankruptcy liquidation. There are also claims that this procedure has been used by large corporations to renege on contracts. For example, in 1983 when Continental Airlines and Wilson Foods sought protection from creditors under Chapter 11, the unions claimed that the main purpose was to abandon expensive labour contracts, which duly happened. Similarly Manville Corporation filed for Chapter 11 bankruptcy despite assets of $1.2 billion because product-liability suits by victims of asbestos-related diseases would inevitably lead to bankruptcy (see *The Economist*, 3 March 1984). However, these seem to be more teething problems than long-term ones. In 1983 the Supreme Court ruled that companies would need to prove that labour contracts were 'burdensome' before protection was granted; whilst the Bankruptcy Amendment Act 1984 further limited the ability of businesses to terminate labour contracts unilaterally as part of the bankruptcy proceedings.

The UK Insolvency System
In England and Wales there are three classes of company liquidation, two of which involve insolvency. Compulsory liquidations stem from winding-up orders following petitions to the Court from creditors. There were 9619 such petitions disposed of in 1984 and just over a half resulted in a winding-up order. Creditors' voluntary liquidations occur when the company and its creditors agree on the liquidation procedure without recourse to court proceedings. In the final class of

liquidations—members' voluntary liquidations—the company winds up for reasons other than insolvency, e.g. the retirement of the owner or the merger of the company with another. However, it should be noted that many companies simply cease trading without going through the formality of insolvency proceedings, which of course cost money. These are nearly always small companies with no assets to dispose of, and they will eventually be struck off the Register of Companies.

Upon a company going into creditors' voluntary liquidation it must agree with its creditors on the appointment of a liquidator. It is his task to wind down the company and in so doing to realise the maximum amount from the company's assets to distribute to its creditors. *There is no obligation upon him to take account of the 'public interest' nor the interests of the workforce in doing this.* As in the USA not all creditors share equally in the distribution of assets, some being secured creditors and others having preferential status whose claims are realised first. Preferential debts consist of money owed to the community in the form of taxes, rates and social security contributions, together with wages and salaries of employees and their holiday remuneration. Any remaining assets, once realised, are then shared in equal proportion between the remaining creditors, each of these remaining creditors will therefore suffer the same proportionate loss.

A similar procedure follows a successful petition to the Court to wind up a company. In this case an Official Receiver is appointed by the Court to investigate the reasons for the company's insolvency. In the event that there are sufficient assets to warrant it he is then frequently appointed liquidator to the company. The same rules of distribution of the realisable assets apply in both categories of liquidation, although compulsory liquidations tend to involve smaller companies with smaller debts than creditors' voluntary liquidations.

A receiver—not to be confused with the Official Receiver, although the media frequently do—can be appointed prior to a firm going into insolvency by the holder of a debenture. A debenture is a document given by the company as evidence of a debt to the holder, often a bank, and usually arising out of a loan. It is generally secured by a charge, frequently a floating charge. This is a device virtually unique to English law. Its chief characteristic is that it is not a charge on a specific set of assets, but floats across the company's assets as they change over time. This therefore allows the company to carry on trading in a normal manner, disposing of and acquiring assets as normal, but also allows the bank to freeze those assets at any instant of time should money become payable under a certain condition laid out in the debenture with the bank having to take steps to recover its security. A receiver can then be appointed by the bank to sell off as many assets covered by the floating charge as are necessary to repay the bank's loan and any preferential creditors. On the appointment of a receiver the assets become specifically charged in favour of the debenture holder, and the company's powers over them cease, although the company remains in business until wound up. If it is necessary to carry on the business the Court usually appoints the receiver to be receiver and manager. This is generally done only if it is hoped to sell the company as a going concern. *The receiver has no other significant obligations, neither to the remaining creditors, the workforce, nor the public interest, and it frequently is the case that by the time the receiver has completed his task only the empty shell of a company is left.*

Thus the prime object of a liquidation is to realise assets in an attempt to repay creditors, and often a specific group of creditors, as much as possible. There is no obligation on the liquidator to keep the firm operating as a going concern and preserve jobs. Parts of it might be sold to separate bidders, but it is unlikely to survive as a going concern in its entirety. Jobs are frequently lost and effective supply reduced. Effective demand is also reduced due to the reduction in redundant workers' income whilst unemployed. There may also be knock-on effects to supplier firms. This situation is most common in a recession and, as Figure 3.1 shows, the UK in the years 1980–84 has seen record levels of insolvencies as whole regions and industries have been decimated. Compare this with the main purpose of the Chapter 11 provisions of the US bankruptcy code which are to enable more companies to survive a bankruptcy, and we have a major reason why the US economy has been so much more resilient in recovering from recession. It also frequently happens that after a Chapter 11 bankruptcy a more cost-competitive and successful firm emerges and, of course, jobs are preserved. This is very important at a time of recession and has led the British government into an attempt at reforming the British system along the lines of the American one. The Cork Committee was set up in January 1977 to look at the whole question of insolvency and personal bankruptcy. Their report, which was presented to Parliament in June 1982, covered many areas. But with respect to the approach to be adopted to companies in serious difficulties their main proposal was for the creation of a new post of 'administrator'. They recommended that he be appointed by the Court primarily in cases where the company has not granted a debenture secured by a floating charge, and hence a receiver cannot be appointed. If a floating charge exists then the holder of it must be given prior notice of the appointment. The administrators task would be to consider the reorganisation of the company and its management with a view to restoring profitability, to make proposals for the most profitable realisation of assets for the benefit of creditors and shareholders, and possibly to carry on the business where this is in the public interest, but it is unlikely that this can be done under the existing management. In some respects the administrator's powers would go beyond those of a receiver. In the hope of successfully reorganising the company he would be allowed to suspend the rights and proceedings of all creditors, including a twelve-month prohibition on certain secured creditors realising their security except by agreement or with the permission of the Court.

The government's response to the Cork Report has in this respect been to water down the original proposals. They accepted the concept of an administrator to be appointed by the Court to facilitate the rehabilitation and reorganisation of companies faced by insolvency. No administrator was to be appointed where the holder of a floating charge wished to exercise his right to appoint a receiver and manager. Upon appointment the administrator is to assume management of the company and undertake rehabilitation measures. He would also be required to submit his proposed policy to the company's unsecured and secured creditors, who both have a veto over them. Whilst he is operating no petition for winding up may be made without leave of the Court and a stay of six months was to be imposed on all proceedings on behalf of creditors. Thus the creditors would appear to have a fairly effective veto on the actions and appointment of an administrator. Indeed he will only be appointed in the first place if the secured creditors agree. These are generally banks who have lent to the firm on a secured basis. In the case of an insolvent company they have the right to appoint a receiver. He can if he wishes sell the firm as a going concern, thus ensuring continuity of employment. But where the receiver differs from an administrator is that his first responsibility is clearly to those appointing him, i.e. the bank. Thus if the appointment of an administrator is likely to be against their interest they are unlikely to agree to it, whereas if they do, then it is likely that he would in any case act no differently from a receiver. It therefore seems unlikely that this new legislation will have any significant impact on the number of insolvent or distressed firms surviving to make a future contribution to employment and output.

COMPANY DEATHS IN THE US AND THE UK

In keeping with the general lack of interest in the supply side of the economy, economists have done little work on either the causes of company deaths or births. There is a small volume of literature, mostly American and mostly on the theoretical aspects of bankruptcy. Bulow and Shoven (1978) claim that according to traditional economic theory a firm in financial difficulties will be forced into insolvency by its creditors, if its going concern value is less than its liquidation value. They also argue that in some circumstances the bank might be led to help the firm continue even when this condition does not hold. This conclusion is based upon a model with just three groups of claimants. Bankruptcy occurs in this framework when the two negotiating claimants, the bank and equity holders, have a more valuable joint claim under bankruptcy than under continuation. They show that the optimal decision rule for the bank appears to be that if the value of the firm's equity holdings under continuance is greater than the difference between the bank's claim under continuance and bankruptcy, the firm should be kept going. Van Horne (1976) used a state preference framework to analyse the creditors' optimal decision. In the two-period case debtholders should initiate bankruptcy proceedings if the present value of debt at time 0, assuming bankruptcy proceedings are forgone, is less than if bankruptcy is initiated. The former equals the value of any distribution in period 0 plus the cumulative value of receipts at time 1 in states in which bankruptcy occurs plus the cumulative value in those states in which bankruptcy does not occur. The remainder of the paper generalises this decision rule to *n* periods.

However, these papers are rather abstract and suffer from the curious omission of trade creditors. This is particularly serious as research done by the Wilson Committee (1979) found that in the UK the two most important forms of credit for small firms in 1975 were trade credit and bank overdrafts and loans, which amounted to 64 per cent and 25 per cent of current liabilities respectively. I have elsewhere (Hudson, 1986a) included trade creditors in the analysis and concluded that the optimal decision for creditors as a whole is to liquidate an insolvent firm if the liquidation value exceeds expected net discounted revenue, adjusted to exclude any revenue in excess of current debts. Such revenue would go to the equity-holders, rather than the creditors, and as such is irrelevant to the latter's decision on whether to press for closure. The decision for the bank is somewhat different. It will extend a loan to a troubled firm if it expects there to be some time in the future when, in discounted terms, the liquidation value of the firm is expected to exceed the total debt owed to the bank at that time. It should be noted that the possibility that the firm will ever get out of its financial crisis is irrelevant to the bank's decision. It may be taking risks in lending to financially troubled firms, but these risks will be borne by the ordinary unsecured creditor. In both the

USA and the UK this is surely something which should be of concern to policy-makers, not just on equity grounds, which are not the direct concern of this book, but because if a firm fails with large debts, this might have important knock-on effects on the viability of other firms.

For an individual firm, the probability of its going into liquidation is determined primarily by past and current profits. I shall assume that this will be a function of aggregate profitability, its age and a vector of firm-specific factors such as innate entrepreneurial skill and location. Age will be important as a new firm is unlikely to reach an equilibrium level of profits immediately. The owners will be on a learning curve, where they find not only potential customers, but gain the knowledge necessary to run the business. Secondly, the fact that a company has been in existence a number of years is an indication that the owners are capable entrepreneurs and the industry is a viable one. Thus, age also acts as a proxy for other firm-specific factors. However, it takes time for a firm to build up debts, for creditors to perceive that the company cannot pay and for liquidation proceedings to begin. We might therefore also expect to see an initial 'honeymoon period' between a company being established and its getting into difficulties. Support for the first of these hypotheses can be found in Marcus (1967), who found that the proportion of firms who earned zero or negative income is highest for newly-formed firms and declines sharply to age five. Thereafter no systematic relationship was found. Similarly in a study of the Lancashire cotton industry in the nineteenth century, Lloyd-Jones and Le Roux (1982) found that of the 57 firms under six years old in the 1815 population structure, 86 per cent were destined quickly to become exit firms. Lomax (1954), in a study of failures in New York between 1844 and 1926, showed that mortality was highest amongst new firms. Finally Altman (1983) in a study using quarterly data on American business failures found evidence for both a 'honeymoon period' and a subsequent period of high risk.

An increase in the rate of interest will directly increase a firm's costs and therefore reduce profits, thus increasing the probability of its going into liquidation. In addition it also affects the bank's decision on whether to give a loan to a financially troubled firm. An increase in the rate of interest can be regarded as either increasing the payments due to the bank in future periods, or further reducing the present value of any future profits. In this case the previous analysis would suggest that this will reduce the likelihood that the bank will give credit to the firm. However, this is based on the assumption that the market for credit clears. This may not be so for two reasons. First, Goodhart (1984) has noted that for many periods in recent years the banks in the UK have been restricted in their lending by government or Bank of England directives. Only with the introduction of the competition and credit control policy in 1972 has this been a specific aim of government policy, and even then the imposition of the 'corset' has still on occasion imposed restrictions. Arguably this has not been the case in the USA; however Jaffee and Modigliani (1969), Jaffee and Russell (1976) and Keeton (1979), amongst others, argue that in any case interest rates are not used to clear the market for credit. Some explain this by 'social conventions' forcing banks to charge a uniform rate to non-identical borrowers. But Stiglitz and Weiss (1981) suggest that the market-clearing role of interest rates is diluted by its effect on the risk distribution of borrowers and upon existing borrowers' attitudes to risk. On both counts an increase in the rate of interest can be expected to increase the risk content of the bank's lending and this will prevent its using interest rates fully to equate demand and supply. They also argue that an increase in interest rates may coincide with only risky projects being financed. Therefore, in a situation where the bank rations credit between a number of would-be borrowers, a rise in interest rates will lead to a switch in credit towards borrowers with a low-interest elasticity of demand. Firms facing insolvency clearly fall into this category. Thus, with rationing, a rise in interest rates is likely, other things being equal, to lead to an increase in the number of distressed firms receiving credit facilities. Hence *a priori* it is not possible to state with certainty the impact of a change in interest rates on the probability of a troubled firm being saved by the bank. This will depend upon whether credit markets are rationed or not.

When we come to analyse company births I shall argue that an unemployed worker will be more likely to start a new firm than an employed worker. However, many of these firms will be more marginal in two senses. First, their prospects for success may be less than for other firms. They may be setting up in industries or areas which will make it difficult for the firm to grow and survive. In many cases the expected profits will be such that had the owner been in employment he would not have considered setting the firm up. Secondly, such people are being forced into entrepreneurship, a role for which they may be ill-suited. They may well, for example, be more risk-averse than entrepreneurs who give up paid employment to start a new firm. They may also have had less relevant experience. For all these reasons we might expect a particularly high failure rate amongst such firms. To allow for this we shall be including the average of unemployment in years $t-1$ to $t-3$ when analysing company failures in period t. The final variable we shall include will be inflation as it has been argued that firms find it easier to increase real prices when prices in general are going up, and thus loss-making firms might find it easier to cover their costs and therefore survive.

Company Deaths in the UK

The above theories receive some support if we analyse liquidations in England and Wales. The results of regressing insolvencies on profits, real interest rates, inflation, average unemployment and lagged births are shown below:

$$CVL_t = 1.023 + 0.0716 AU_t - 0.0242\pi_t - 0.00924 r_t -$$
$$(5.38) \quad (6.02) \quad\quad (4.45) \quad\quad (3.08)$$

$$0.0207 P_t - 0.425 B_{t-1} + 0.325 B_{t-2} - 0.377 B_{t-3}$$
$$(4.92) \quad\quad (4.51) \quad\quad (2.69) \quad\quad (2.60)$$

$$+ 0.0483 B_{t-4} - 0.0311 B_{t-5}$$
$$(3.91) \quad\quad (2.95)$$

$$R^2 = 0.914, \; DW + 1.72, \; \text{Period} = 1953{-}83 \qquad (3.1)$$

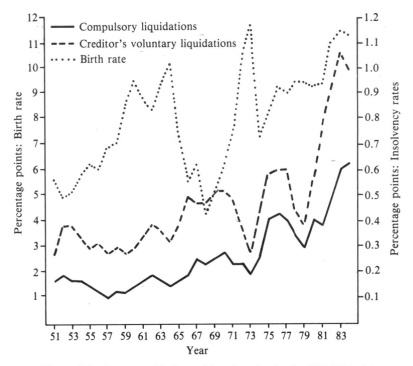

Figure 3.1: Company births and insolvencies in the UK 1951–84

$$\text{COMP}_t = 0.201 + 0.0454 A U_t - 0.00642 \pi_t - 0.00542 r_t$$
$$\quad (2.29) \quad (11.46) \qquad (3.19) \qquad (5.31)$$

$$\quad - 0.000151 P_t - 0.102 D81 - 0.0101 B_{t-1}$$
$$\qquad (0.10) \qquad (4.66) \qquad (3.31)$$

$$\quad + 0.00108 B_{t-2} + 0.00296 B_{t-3} + 0.0117 B_{t-4}$$
$$\qquad (0.27) \qquad (0.61) \qquad (2.93)$$

$$\quad - 0.000851 B_{t-5}$$
$$\qquad (0.25)$$

$$R^2 = 0.977, \ DW = 1.83, \ \text{Period} = 1953-83 \qquad (3.2)$$

where CVL are creditors' voluntary liquidations and COMP are compulsory liquidations, both as proportions of the number of firms in existence at the beginning of the period.

This is the appropriate form for the dependent variable as it represents the failure rate, rather than the number of firms *per se* which will obviously vary with the size of the population. AU is average unemployment in period $t - 1$ to $t - 3$; π is the ratio of profits to corporate GDP; r is the real interest rate, defined as the difference between the nominal interest rate and lagged inflation; P is inflation; and B_{t-i} is the number of companies registered in period $t - i$ as a proportion of the total number of companies trading in period t. These regressions were estimated jointly along with a third equation relating to corporate births using the seemingly unrelated regressions technique. This is discussed, and more exact definitions of the data given, in Hudson (1986a). The profits variable is correctly signed and significant at the one per cent level. This is current profits; lagged functions were tried, but failed to be significant. This should not be taken as indicating that such a lag does not exist as there are obvious multi-collinearity problems in its identification. The coefficient on interest is also significant in both equations. Its negative sign suggests the existence of credit rationing. However, it is important to realise that an increase in interest rates will reduce profits and this in the long run is likely to cause a net increase in insolvencies. The unemployment variable is also significant in both equations. This is important and tends to confirm the hypothesis that companies formed by the unemployed are more likely to fail than other firms. However, the inflation variable is only significant for creditors' voluntary liquidations. The dummy variable D81 is included to capture the effects of the civil service strike in 1981 on compulsory liquidations. Its significance indicates that the number of winding-up petitions presented by government bodies was adversely affected by the strike.

The lag structure on incorporations provides strong support for the honeymoon hypothesis, with the coefficient on births lagged one period being significantly negative. There is also some indication of the following period of high risk. In interpreting these coefficients it should be borne in mind that many of the firms formed in period $t - 5$ will no longer be trading in period $t - 1$, thus an equal coefficient on B_{t-5} and B_{t-1} will indicate a much stronger effect on those firms which

Table 3.1: The age structure of insolvent firms in the UK

	1	2a	2b	2c	2d	2e	2f	2g	2h	2i
	%	%	%	%	%	%	%	%	%	%
1 year or less	1.7	3.7	1.2	4.8	10.0	0.0	3.0	2.7	6.0	1.0
1–2 years	10.7	12.4	11.8	13.3	16.7	3.4	13.6	12.4	7.0	16.0
2–3 years	15.4	12.8	15.3	15.2	8.3	10.3	16.7	7.1	13.0	16.0
3–4 years	10.6	9.4	8.2	8.6	5.0	3.4	12.1	11.5	12.0	10.0
4–5 years	11.9	8.1	7.1	4.8	6.7	6.9	7.6	12.4	13.0	4.0
5–6 years	11.1	5.9	8.2	8.6	8.3	10.3	3.0	5.3	3.0	1.0
6–7 years	6.4	4.4	7.1	6.7	1.7	3.4	7.6	2.7	1.0	3.0
7–8 years	4.9	6.7	10.6	3.8	6.7	17.7	4.5	5.3	6.0	7.0
8–9 years	5.9	4.7	3.5	1.9	1.7	10.3	10.6	2.7	3.0	10.0
9–10 years	3.0	3.4	4.7	1.0	3.3	6.9	4.5	2.7	6.0	1.0
over 10 years	19.4	29.5	22.3	31.3	31.6	27.4	16.8	35.2	30.0	31.0
Number of firms	596	595	85	105	60	29	66	113	65	68

Key: 1, all compulsory liquidations; 2, creditors' voluntary liquidations: 2a, all creditors' voluntary liquidations, 2b, construction, 2c, retail/wholesale, 2d, textile manufacturers, 2e, property companies, 2f, business services, 2g, manufacturing, 2h, general consumer services, 2i, transport and miscellaneous.

Source: Sample survey carried out by the author and financed by the ESRC.

are left from period $t - 5$. Stronger evidence for both the honeymoon and high-risk periods comes from Table 3.1, which shows the results of a sample survey of firms going into insolvency between 1978–81. It is immediately clear that the majority of companies which go into liquidation are young ones, although not many companies go into liquidation in their first year. The pattern of the lagged relationship was as anticipated, with the peak in the lagged distribution for both types of liquidation being reached after four years and compulsory liquidations after six years. However, the lag structure for compulsory liquidations may be somewhat misleading in that this type of insolvency procedure frequently involves the prior restoration to the Register of Companies of firms which have been struck off in the past. The actual 'death' of such a company would have occurred earlier than the time indicated by the winding-up order. The table also shows how this age structure has varied across industries for creditors' voluntary liquidations. It is not possible to identify the industry of a company in compulsory liquidation from published data.

Company Deaths in the USA

Figure 3.2 also shows the failure rate of US firms per 10,000 listed industrial and commercial enterprises. A failure is defined as a concern that is involved in a court proceeding or a voluntary action that is likely to end in loss to creditors. All industrial and commercial enterprises that are petitioned into the Federal Bankruptcy Courts are included in the failure records, as well as certain other closures, for example, voluntary discontinuances with known loss to creditors. The series follows a somewhat unusual pattern. It rises almost continuously until 1961, following which there is an equally marked downward trend until 1978–79, following which

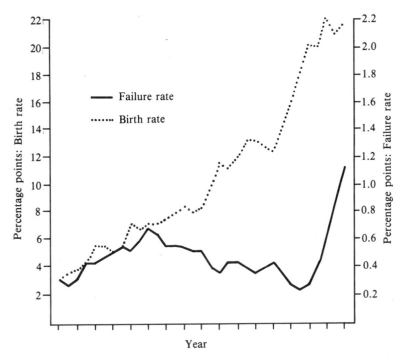

Figure 3.2: Company births and failures in the USA, 1951–83

there is a dramatic increase. It is interesting to note that this most recent upturn coincides with the introduction of the new bankruptcy code, and it may be that changes in the structure of the law have made bankruptcy a more attractive proposition to companies. However, it is also possible that the banks may have become more hesitant to lend to firms on a secured basis due to the possibility of a Chapter 11 bankruptcy preventing the bank from realising its security in the event of failure. To test this we have constructed a dummy variable, LAWD, operative for the period since 1979 when the bankruptcy code was introduced. However, it should also be borne in mind that this period also coincides with a sharp drop in profits, which by itself would be expected to result in a higher incidence of failure.

LAWD was the only dummy variable constructed for this regression. The remaining variables were as defined for the UK. Once more the technique of seemingly unrelated regressions was used to estimate this equation, this time in conjunction with a company births equation. The results are shown below:

$$FAIL_t = 99.42 + 4.75\,AU_t - 3.51\,\pi_t + 2.51\,r_t - 4.36\,P_t$$
$$\qquad (6.91) \quad (3.40) \qquad (4.37) \quad (4.12) \quad (7.70)$$

$$\qquad + 28.33\,LAWD - 7.69\,B_{t-1} + 5.25\,B_{t-2}$$
$$\qquad\quad (5.37) \qquad\quad (4.86) \qquad (2.40)$$

$$\qquad - 0.336\,B_{t-3} - 0.842\,B_{t-4} - 2.32\,B_{t-5}$$
$$\qquad\quad (0.14) \qquad (0.32) \qquad (1.17)$$

$$R^2 = 0.874, \; DW = 1.68, \; \text{Period: } 1951-83 \qquad (3.3)$$

FAIL is the failure rate shown in Figure 3.2. This equation is very similar to those for the UK, unemployment, profits and inflation are all correctly signed and significant at the 1 per cent level. The coefficient on real interest is also significant at the 1 per cent level, but this time it is positively signed. Thus, unlike the UK it would appear that credit markets are not rationed. The conclusion that the money markets in the UK are more imperfect than in the US is perhaps not altogether surprising. The positive coefficient on LAWD is also significant at the 1 per cent level, and would suggest that the recent changes in the bankruptcy legislation have increased the number of firms becoming bankrupt. The average number of firms going into reorganisation increased from an average of 3263 in the period 1975–78 to 13912 in the period 1980–83 immediately following the introduction of the new code. Whereas the size of the coefficient indicates that the annual increase in the number of companies going into bankruptcy as a result of the introduction of the new code is about 8000. Thus this is not inconsistent with the hypothesis that this increase is primarily due to more firms going into reorganisation, and there is no evidence to suggest that, as yet, the banks have changed their behaviour to lenders.

The hypothesis of a honeymoon period followed by one of high risk in the life cycle of a company again receives support from the coefficients on lagged births, and is further confirmed by Table 3.2, which shows the age structure of failed firms. This is very similar to those in Table 3.1, particularly for creditors' voluntary liquidations. There are also similarities between the two countries in how this age structure varies across industries.

Table 3.2: The age structure of insolvent firms in the US in 1983

	1	2	3	4	5	6
The US:	%	%	%	%	%	%
1 year or less	2.7	2.2	1.5	3.0	1.7	4.6
1–2 years	8.7	7.4	8.1	10.9	4.1	9.4
2–3	13.3	13.8	12.5	16.3	8.3	12.0
3–4	12.3	12.3	12.3	13.2	8.7	13.8
4–5	10.0	9.8	9.6	10.7	9.6	9.7
5–6	8.8	8.4	9.4	8.8	9.5	8.1
6–7	7.0	7.2	6.8	6.8	8.0	6.6
7–8	6.2	5.7	6.3	5.6	7.9	6.3
8–9	4.6	4.5	4.6	4.2	5.7	4.5
9–10	3.6	3.5	3.9	3.3	4.8	3.0
over 10 years	22.8	25.2	25.0	17.2	31.7	22.0

Note: Column 1, all businesses; 2, manufacturing; 3, wholesale; 4, retail; 5, construction; 6, services.
Source: Dun & Bradstreet, *Failure Record*, 1982–1983

COMPANY BIRTHS IN THE USA AND THE UK

It will be assumed that an individual will set up in business if he expects to be financially better off than if he does not. This is, of course, the standard economic approach to any question, and ignores such possibilities that entrepreneurs may be motivated by factors others than monetary reward. One could replace the above assumption with one based on a utility function approach. But in any utility function income is bound to play an important role. Hence, I shall assume that for an individual the probability that he will wish to start a firm will be determined by the ratio of expected profits to current income. In addition, because the former is likely to be riskier than the latter, the individual's degree of risk-aversion is also important.

In general we would expect those individuals with low degrees of risk-aversion to be the ones who set up new firms. The profits expected from setting up a new firm may be linked to the average profitability of existing firms together with some variable proxying the number of potential opportunities for new businesses. In the empirical work which follows, real consumers' expenditure will be used for this. If the individual is unemployed current income will equal any benefits received whilst unemployed. Future income will depend upon how soon he can expect to get a job and at what wage. Standard search theory would suggest that both of these will depend upon the number of relevant vacancies and the number of job searchers competing with him for those vacancies. If we ignore on the job search, the latter can be proxied by the number of unemployed. The more vacancies and the fewer unemployed, the quicker he can expect to find a job and the higher also will be the expected wage at which it will be offered. Thus, the probability of an individual setting up in business should increase if he becomes unemployed, and the more slack in the labour market the greater will be this increase.

In many cases whether the individual sets up in business or not may depend upon whether he can get the appropriate credit from the bank or some other agency. Some, of course, will not need such facilities, either the company does not need substantial sums of money to establish, or alternatively the individual has the necessary finance himself. But many businesses will need such facilities and the banks are unlikely to give money to all who ask. The decision is once more likely to depend upon the rate of interest, although as with closures the exact nature of this relationship is not clear, as it will once more depend upon whether the market for credit is rationed.

Company Births in Great Britain

As can be seen from Figure 3.1 the number of company births has been increasing steadily since the early 1950s with one exception. This was during the period 1965–71 when company births suffered a sharp decline. Recent years have seen this increase accelerate and the number of new companies registered with Companies House in 1983—96,068— was a record. At first sight it might appear that this was indicative of a healthy economy where new enterprise was flourishing and that these new firms could be expected to make a significant contribution both to reducing unemployment and promoting new ideas and industries. However, the previous analysis on company failures has indicated that new firms are particularly susceptible to failure.

In addition to the set of explanatory variables discussed in the previous section, there have also been a number of institutional factors which may have had an impact upon the number of new incorporations. The limited company is not the only legal form open to new firms, they may alternatively choose some unincorporated form of business enterprise such as a partnership. Equally every company registration does not necessarily signal the birth of a new firm, as an unincorporated business may choose to 'move up' and become incorporated. Each option has advantages and disadvantages. The owners of a limited company have, of course, the protection of limited liability should the company fail. But they also have to reveal more information concerning their activities. Changes in these relative advantages and disadvantages might therefore be expected to have an impact upon the number of companies choosing to become incorporated.

There are several such changes which occurred during the period with which we are concerned, with perhaps the most important relating to changes in the tax structure such as the introduction of selective employment tax in 1966 at a rate of £1.20. This was increased to £1.80 in 1968 and abolished in the 1972/73 tax year. This was an employment tax which was applied to specific industries, particularly in the service sector, with self-employed workers being exempt. Thus, as the two reports of the Reddaway Committee (1970, 1975) noted, this almost certainly stimulated purely nominal changes in status by some small firms as well as representing an added cost to others. It also probably reduced the number of new firms in these sectors choosing to incorporate. Corporation tax was also introduced in 1966. This replaced profits tax and led to the great majority of small unincorporated businesses paying tax on their profits at rates substantially below the fixed rate of corporation tax to which incorporated businesses were subject. This bias in favour of unincorporated businesses lasted until the 1972 budget when the Chancellor announced further reforms to take effect from April of the following year. These changes in the institutional environment will be proxied by the use of dummy variables.

The result of regressing the number of new companies registered (BIR_t) in period t on the set of independent variables discussed above is shown in equation (3.4), which was estimated using the seemingly unrelated regression technique along with the insolvency equations:

$$BIR_t = - 48910 - 21685\,V_t + 2426\,U_t + 1228\pi_t + 104r_t$$
$$\quad\quad (3.22)\quad (3.28)\quad\quad (4.93)\quad\quad (3.73)\quad\quad (0.55)$$

$$\quad + 560.4\,C_t + 0.364 BIR_{t-1} + 15069 D73$$
$$\quad\quad (4.62)\quad\quad (2.89)\quad\quad\quad (3.31)$$

$$\quad - 9328 D66 - 71$$
$$\quad\quad (3.64)$$

$R^2 = 0.971$, Durbin's h statistic $= 0.773$, Period $= 1953-83$.

$$(3.4)$$

Both current unemployment (U_t) and vacancies (V_t) are

significant at the one per cent level. Profits (π_t) and consumers' expenditure (C_t) are also significant, as are the two dummy variables included in the equation. The first of these, D66-71 was operative throughout 1966–71, the period when there was both a major anomaly in company taxation and selective employment tax was in operation. The second dummy variable, D73, was included to capture any reaction to the removal of both the tax and the anomaly. The signs on these two variables suggest that the net effect of the unfavourable legislation during the period 1966–71 was to reduce the number of new limited companies being registered. Many of these would probably have set up in unincorporated forms, e.g. partnerships, and switched once the legislation was changed by 1973. The positive sign on interest rates again suggests credit rationing, although this time the coefficient is not significant.

Company Births in the USA

The trend in new incorporations can be seen in Figure 3.2. The data represent the total number of stock corporations which issued charters under the general business laws of the various states. These include completely new businesses that are incorporated, existing businesses that are changed from the non-corporate to the corporate form of organisation, existing corporations that have been given certificates of authority to operate in another state and existing corporations transferred to a new state. Thus it can be seen that the massive number of 600,000 incorporations in 1983 would not all be totally new enterprises. None the less this is a valuable indicator of new corporate development and the rapid rise in this series since 1970 is impressive. The regression results are shown in equation (3.5):

$$\text{BIR}_t = -157411 + 4883\,U_t + 4990\pi_t + 179.1\,C_t$$
$$\qquad\quad (3.66)\quad (1.98)\quad (2.99)\quad (3.52)$$

$$+\ 0.848\text{BIR}_{t-1}$$
$$(10.88)$$

$R^2 = 0.990$, Durbin's h statistic $= 0.61$, Period $= 1951–83$

$$(3.5)$$

These were estimated jointly with the failure rate equation using the seemingly unrelated regression technique. All coefficients are significant at the 10 per cent level. The unemployment variable, in particular, is correctly signed and together with the results from the UK clearly suggest that the unemployed are more likely to set up their own business than employed individuals. Vacancies were omitted from this regression as US data are only available back to 1961. The explanatory power of the equation is very high, but this is only to be expected in time-series data with a clear upward trend. A dummy variable was put in for the period 1982–83 to capture any incentive effects from Reagan's tax cuts, but the coefficient was incorrectly signed, and the variable has subsequently been dropped from the equation. Also omitted was the interest rate variable which was insignificant. The insignificance of this for both countries does seem to suggest that new corporate registrations are not directly affected by credit conditions.

POLICIES TO RETAIN SUPPLY-SIDE CAPACITY

The empirical work has confirmed the importance of the age structure of firms in determining the number of insolvencies, with the hypothesis of honeymoon, high-risk and establishment phases in a typical firm's life-cycle receiving considerable support. Thus a large increase in company registrations is likely to lead to an increase in insolvencies two to three years later, and this should be borne in mind both when using data on new company registrations as an indicator of the strength of new entrepreneurial vigour, or alternatively using data on company failures as an indicator of the vitality of the corporate sector. This is particularly the case when such increases are caused by high levels of unemployment coupled with few employment opportunities. Such a development can be viewed somewhat ambiguously from a policy standpoint. On the one hand, the unemployed can be seen to be seeking their own solution to the unemployment problem, which if successful will also help increase the number of employment opportunities for others. But the empirical evidence is that people 'forced' into an entrepreneurial mould are not making successful businessmen, and we can expect an even higher incidence of failure amongst such firms than in general. There are no UK data on the reasons why companies fail, but for the USA the main cause appears to be managerial incompetence. Dun and Bradstreet's statistics show that in 1980 over 94 per cent of all failures were identified with lack of experience, 50 per cent with unbalanced experience, and 46 per cent with incompetence. This suggests the need to look at policies both to reduce the failure rate due to inexperience and incompetence and also to reduce the supply-side multiplier effects on trade creditors of an insolvency.

Directors of limited companies in both countries are able to trade in the knowledge that however great their company's debts, they themselves will be subject to only limited liability. This is often quite low, for example in the UK in 1984 out of the 96,155 new firms incorporated, 56,415 had a share capital of £100 or less. Moreover, due partly to inflation the real value of the share capital of an average newly incorporated firm has been falling sharply over time. Thus in effect the concept of limited liability has been replaced by one of virtually no liability, and regardless of how great a company's debts the personal costs to the directors can be minimal. This hardly seems fair or efficient, and one doubts whether this is what was intended when the concept of the limited liability company was first introduced. There should be a statutory minimum liability which anyone setting up a limited company should be subject to. This should be sufficient to provide an effective penalty should the firm be liquidated, but not so great as to deter serious attempts at starting a new company. The purpose of this would be both to allow a greater distribution of assets to creditors in the event of failure, but more importantly to make entrepreneurs consider seriously the probability that their business will succeed and whether they have taken sufficient steps to maximise this probability.

At present directors require no formal qualifications or training in either the USA or the UK. This is not the case everywhere and several European countries have recognised the need for such training and a broad range of schemes are available, some of which are compulsory. In Italy, for example, Law No. 426 of 11 June 1971 restricted entry into a business to those who have passed a proficiency test, have worked in the business for at least two years, or have attended a professional course run by the state. Such an innovation should lead to fewer unviable firms being established, and fewer subsequent failures, with reduced knock-on effects to other trade creditors. There should also be an improvement in the average abilities of all entrepreneurs, which should both increase their chances of survival and their subsequent efficiency if they do survive. This would appear to be particularly important with respect to entrepreneurs who were previously unemployed, and whose firms seem particularly susceptible to failure. Against this there is the possibility that it will prove a deterrent to enterprise. Probably, it will and almost certainly there will be a reduction in the number of new companies, either because the would-be entrepreneurs were deterred by the prospect of the course, or learnt that either they or their prospective companies were unlikely to succeed. This should be viewed as an advantage not a disadvantage, as such individuals would be almost certain to fail.

Government Rescue of Ailing Firms
Is there a direct role for the government to play in the rescue of failing companies? To pose the question another way, does the market by itself ensure that all companies which should be rescued are rescued? Clearly, in the UK, given the emphasis on realising assets in a liquidation rather than saving the company, it probably does not and certainly this appeared to be the view of the Cork Committee. But even in the USA, where much greater emphasis is placed on the rescue of firms, there is still a case for government intervention to rescue firms which the market will not save. For simplicity we might assume that such firms are in the long-run unprofitable, i.e. ignoring any current debts the net present value of any discounted future profits is less than sufficient to warrant their being kept open on commercial criteria. This does not necessarily mean that they would make a loss, merely that profits are less than Marshall's 'normal' level required to keep the firm operating in the long-run.

The case for government intervention rests upon any social costs and benefits attached to the potential closure of the firm, and these can be expected to vary with the business-cycle and in different regions of the country. When employment opportunities are plentiful, a redundant workforce will quickly find alternative employment, although even here there may be a need for government retraining programmes for those with very industry-specific skills. But when this is not the case, then within the region affected by the job closures there is likely to be substantially more unemployment possibly for several years. The costs of this are twofold. First there are the financial costs to the government, the costs in unemployment insurance, which will generally be borne by either local or central government need to be added to lost tax revenue, both direct and indirect, as a result of the firm's employees becoming unemployed. Secondly, there are the personal costs to the individuals concerned of a long period of unemployment, which may well result in a deterioration in mental and physical health leading to a permanent loss in productive skills. Both of these costs will be reinforced by possible multiplier effects on both the demand and supply sides of the economy. These may well justify the government either subsidising or taking into public ownership firms which the market would let close. The commitment need not be an indefinite one. In some cases circumstances might change to make the firm a viable and profitable enterprise so that it can be returned to private ownership. In others, as economic conditions improve and alternative employment opportunities increase, the unprofitable firm can be gradually run down.

Such a course of action would not be entirely new to governments. In the UK there is a long record of government intervention to rescue failing firms. These include the car manufacturer Austin Rover, the engine manufacturer Rolls Royce and large sections of the shipbuilding industry. Amongst state-owned industries many coalmines and steelworks have been kept open beyond the period which private commercial criteria would indicate as being optimal. The United States government has, somewhat surprisingly perhaps, possibly been even more ready to intervene to rescue failing companies. A prime example of this is the railroad industry. In 1971 almost all intercity passenger operations were taken over by a federal government-controlled and subsidised corporation (Amtrak). Local government had already become involved in commuter operations in metropolitan areas. Then, after several bankruptcies involving Penn-Central and other eastern systems during the period 1970–72, the federal government had to take over their total operations, including freight. These operations were consolidated under two federal public authorities, the US Railroad Association and the Consolidated Railroad Corporation. More recently the administration has intervened to save both Chrysler, whose demise would have cost the Treasury $280 million in annual taxes and the Continental Illinois Bank, whose failure would have brought down more than 2000 smaller banks. Whilst in both countries, agriculture has been continuously subsidised for many years. However, in both the UK and the USA each rescue tends to be a one-off decision, made on *ad hoc* criteria, and often vehemently criticised by those who argue that market forces should prevail. There is no general recongition and acceptance of the need to retain supply-side capacity by government intervention, nor that such rescue packages should be standard procedure.

By and large, this concern to save troubled companies is limited to the largest corporations such as Rolls Royce and Chrysler. There is seldom a similar concern shown for small to medium-sized companies. Yet the same arguments which make it valid to rescue large companies also make it valid to rescue smaller ones. One possible policy option for governments would be to fund an agency to which insolvency practitioners could turn in an attempt to secure the continued existence of companies which the market will not save. This agency could buy the firm with a view to restoring it, via a capital injection, into a profitable enterprise which could then be returned to the private sector. In the situation where it cannot be made profitable and the firm is to be kept going in private hands, a continuing subsidy would have to be paid to the owners, or the company taken into public ownership. The agency would not, taken alone, be expected to make a profit out of these operations. But for the government as a whole, taking into account the extra tax revenue and the lower welfare payments, which are the direct result of its operations there may well be a net overall surplus. In deciding which firms to support the prospective agency should take into account local factors, such as the state of the local labour market which determine the speed with which resources will be transferred from an insolvent firm into other employment. *A priori*, firms in areas of high unemployment are likely to have a strong case for saving, at least on a temporary basis. The agency's funds should vary in a cyclical manner. During a recession there will be an increase in all regions in the number of firms warranting support and it should have sufficiently elastic financing to meet such changing needs.

This conclusion that declining industries should be supported by government policies runs counter to both traditional analyses of structural unemployment and Schumpeter's analysis of the business-cycle. The problem as we have viewed it concentrates on a deficiency of supply in some industries, rather than too great a supply in other industries. Thus a policy aimed at closing down excess capacity, rationalisation or the removal of 'uneconomic' enterprises has little direct relevance for the problem. Only if the capital, entrepreneurial or human resources thus freed were transferred to the expanding industries resulting in their more rapid growth might there be a reduction in structural unemployment. In the midst of a recession this is not generally the case. Indeed the reduction in demand following large-scale closures is more likely to reduce the effective demand for these expanding industries, hindering their expansion.

The difference with Schumpeter arises because of a differing view as to what causes the downswing of a cycle. In Schumpeter's analysis it is caused by over-expansion of new, initially highly profitable industries. Firms attracted into these industries expand capacity and profits are eroded. Faced with this over-capacity contraction would be set in with the possibility that the economy would overshoot equilibrium and a slump develop. Thus the slump is the final stage of the cycle, and has nothing to do with the decline of long-established industries. The decline of employment in these older industries is inevitable and natural, and should not be opposed as that would be to hinder advance. New opportunities to take up any slack will always appear. Our analysis begins not with a boom, but with a recession caused by a drop in demand. Firms in all industries will be affected by this, but declining ones will be particularly at risk. They may then decline, not at Schumpeter's optimal rate but too rapidly, that is before new and growing industries are of sufficient size to absorb the slack. This demand-side stimulus to a slump is something Schumpeter never considered. His arguments against subsidies were based on an entirely different scenario. I would tend to agree with him that in the normal run of events firms in declining industries should not be subsidised nor rescued. But recessions of the depth currently gripping the UK lie outside the normal run of events when Schumpeterian analyses can be considered valid.

Government Intervention to Save Plants and Subsidiaries of Companies

Even more contentious than the idea that governments should save failing firms, is the idea that they should interfere with the internal decision-making of companies to prevent them from closing down part of their operations. Many would argue that such interference is unwarranted and in the end bound to be inefficient. On what grounds can the government interfere with a company which wishes to close down part of its operations in order to enable it to expand in other, more profitable areas? If such action is to the benefit of the company will it not also benefit society as a whole? The argument against this hypothesis can be taken in several stages. First, many firms close plants not to finance new investment, but to acquire existing concerns. This may be profitable for the company, but for the economy it is a net loss. Secondly, present government policies are not neutral to the firm's decision, they actually encourage closure decisions. Companies which close down plants in the USA, for example, receive a number of direct economic subsidies. According to Lustig (1985) these come in the form of tax write-offs for plant and equipment losses, liberalised depreciation rules, investment tax credits and preferential treatment for capital gains. Thus General Electric had tax liabilities of $22 million entirely cancelled at the time it made 22,000 workers redundant, whilst US Steel benefited by $200 million when it closed its Youngstown plants.

This incentive to scrap capital should be removed, unless it is seen to be in the national interest. However, arguably one can go further and argue that the decision to close plants should to some extent take explicit account of any social costs which the community has to incur. If the proposed closure is meant to finance the development of another enterprise, perhaps in another part of the country, then any social benefits from this should also figure in the calculation. Considerable private and social capital supports any large concern such as steelworks in Youngstown or Consett in North-East England. Roads, schools and houses are built around such a plant, and individual workers make their own, often life-time, investment in training. Severance, or redundancy, payments are one way in which such costs are already taken into account in closure decisions, but these are variable and cover only the workers. Nowhere are severance costs paid to communities as a whole, although some large firms do pay them on a voluntary basis. This argument receives some support form the comments of Judge Thomas Lambros of the US District Court for Northern Ohio in the case of Lyle Williams, Congressman *et al. v.* United States Steel Corporation. He argued that property rights had been established by the lengthy relationship between United States Steel and the Youngstown community. Thus the steel industry should remain in the community or, arguably, the industry should be required to contribute to the costs of rehabilitating both the community and workers.

I am not here arguing that companies should never close down plants or activities to move towards more profitable ones. The social costs associated with such closures will vary with the business-cycle, and at normal times alternative employment opportunities will present themselves to both individual workers and communities. To attempt in such circumstances to stop the natural process of change and development would be fundamentally to damage

Schumpeter's process of creative destruction, upon which progress, prosperity and international competitiveness ultimately depends. However, when unemployment is high the costs to communities and workers of closures will also be high. A policy linking, by statute, individual and community separation/redundancy payments to local prevailing levels of unemployment would not only be fair and equitable it would also be efficient. Firms would be encouraged to change, to adapt in times of prosperity, rather than as happens at the moment in times of recession through so-called rationalisation programmes. Individuals and communities would also receive compensation in line with the harm they are likely to suffer. It is clearly irrational for workers in the prosperous south-east of England, were job opportunities are relatively plentiful, to receive the same redundancy payments as workers in the north-east where they are not.

ALTERNATIVES TO DIRECT GOVERNMENT INTERVENTION

In such cases where only part of a company is being closed there has been an increasing number of examples of a rescue being mounted internally, i.e. either a worker or management 'buy-out'. In the UK in the three-year period 1982–84 these ran at about £200 million a year. However, as 1985 saw large corporations increasingly attempting to divest themselves of unwanted subsidiaries, management buy-outs were likely to exceed £1 billion, although by no means all of this was to save ailing companies. The capital for these ventures comes from either specialist institutions or foreign, particularly US, banks. Prudential Assurance, for example, has recently set up two funds to provide £98 million of venture capital providing finance for management buyouts as well as start-up capital for high-technology companies in both the USA and the UK. This is a development which should be encouraged by government policies.

An alternative source of finance available for both the rescue of troubled firms, and the creation of new supply side

Table 3.3: Foreign investment decisions[1] in the UK, 1984

Country of Origin	Number of projects	Jobs created[2]	Jobs safeguarded
US	134	16 376	6 651
West Germany	38	1 138	883
Canada	18	300	344
Japan	16	6 192	—
Irish Republic	12	433	398
Rest of world	67	3 686	9 715
Total	285	28 125	17 991

Source: Financial Times, 8 January 1986.
Notes: 1. Investment decisions include first-time investment, expansion, takeover and joint ventures.
2. Jobs created are an estimate of long-term employment associated with the project; not every decision is accompanied by an employment estimate.

capacity comes from foreign based or multinational companies. This, for the UK, is already an important source of finance as Table 3.3 shows, with the USA, Japan and West Germany being the leading providers of new employment. Such finance is particularly attractive in that it may bring with management expertise, new ideas and possibly new products and markets also. However, recent history also suggests that, especially when it is a case of rescuing an existing company, the end result may be detrimental to the home economy. The best example is, perhaps, provided by the car industry. At the beginning of 1986 there was just one major endogenous car manufacturer in the UK, Austin Rover, with Jaguar and Rolls Royce important specialist producers of luxury cars. Ford has long been a subsidiary part of a large multinational organisation based in the US. But, until relatively recently, Vauxhall and Talbot were also British-owned institutions. Vauxhall, however, is now part of the General Motors group and Talbot is a subsidiary of the French-based Peugeot company, which acquired it from Chrysler for a nominal US $1 in 1979. The effect of this on hidden imports of cars has been documented by Jones (1985). In 1973 these accounted for 0.3 per cent of UK sales, by 1978 13 per cent, and by 1983 had reached 23.5 per cent. Over this same period open imports of (mainly) European and Japanese cars, with the help of voluntary restraint by the Japanese, had risen by just 7.6 per cent to 34 per cent of total sales. The bulk of this increase in hidden imports is accounted for by Ford. Vauxhall and Talbot together imported some 10 per cent of total UK sales in 1983, compared with 1 per cent which they produced in the UK and about 8 per cent which was 'assembled' in the UK.

This increase in hidden imports has partly been at the expense of BL's market share, which fell from almost 32 per cent in 1973 to under 18 per cent some ten years later. However, the multinationals also cut back on UK production capacity either by closing down plants altogether, as happened at the Talbot plant at Linwood in Scotland, or by failing to invest as General Motors did during the period 1979–82. Thus at the beginning of 1986 Talbot employed just 5000 workers, whereas a decade earlier its predecessor employed some 30,000. The implication would appear to be that, in the car industry at least, foreign buyers use their UK subsidiaries to increase their imports to the UK, and have to an extent been content to run down domestic productive capacity, although it is less clear whether this was initially their intention. However, that is of little moment and the important point would appear to be that they have been able to undermine the British car industry. More generally governments need to be aware of the dangers of letting foreign companies gain control of domestic firms.

This is, of course, more a problem for European countries than for the USA. In 1982 foreign-owned companies in the United States owned just 1744 firms, employing 2.377 million workers. However, as Table 3.4 shows, these figures have been increasing extremely rapidly in the last decade. In addition overseas investors provided 27 per cent of new US venture capital in 1985. Clearly, a major reason for these trends is a desire to gain a foothold in the most important market in the world at a time when protectionist tendencies are increasing. Clear examples of this are once more provided by the car industry. Honda decided in 1979 to build a US factory in Ohio. By 1985 it was producing 150,000 cars, and planning to double this. Because the Japanese government

Table 3.4: Foreign-owned US firms

Year	Firms	Establishments	Employment (000s)
1982	1,744	48,287	2,377.4
1979	1,365	30,962	1,655.8
1976	657	15,122	823.1

Source: Various editions of the *Statistical Abstract of the United States.*

allowed Honda to export only 400,000 cars to the USA in 1985, this extra production allows Honda to lay claim to being the major Japanese car manufacturer in the USA. However, approximately 50 per cent, in value, of the parts used in its US manufacturing plant are imported from Japan. At the same time American manufacturers have been contracting. For example, Ford has cut its US hourly workforce from 190,000 in the late 1970s to 110,000 in 1985, closed eight US plants and cut its white-collar staff by 30 per cent. Access to American technology is also an important reason for this increasing overseas presence in US business, and if it were to continue this might emerge as an important political issue in the future, putting pressure on US administrations to consider the consequences of letting the control of major companies pass outside their borders.

TRADE RESTRICTIONS

Both the UK and the USA's problems in trade have been caused by unrealistically high exchange rates. For the UK this seems to have been caused partly by the effects of North Sea oil and high interest rates, and partly by the government since 1979 seeking to control inflation by keeping import prices low. In the USA, a similar concern with inflation and a corresponding tight money regime with high interest rates have also served to keep the dollar overvalued on the international money markets. Another factor has been the emergence of the dollar as a symbol of American economic virility. If in both countries the exchange rates had been more in line with the competitive position of the relative economies as a whole, then the problems of the recent years with increasing import-penetration would not have been so severe and the calls for trade restrictions less vociferous. In future this should be of prime importance for governments concerned with macroeconomic stability and the need to avoid recessions.

Traditional calls for protectionism have been growing in recent years both in Western Europe and North America. On economic grounds the case against import restrictions has always been that they distort the natural flow of trade and the operation of the principal of comparative advantage by which economies concentrate on producing what they are relatively most efficient at. This, it can be shown, will produce the most efficient pattern of production and all countries will benefit. Thus, as usual, the economist's traditional response to import tariffs is primarily based on consideration of two equilibrium positions, where welfare is reduced when trade restrictions are imposed. Unfortunately, the UK and other European economies are most definitely not in equilibrium, and such arguments lose much of their force.

These increased calls for protectionism are perhaps slightly misplaced when the major reason for the trade imbalance is an overvalued currency. However, there are structural problems affecting dynamic economies which illustrate the need for some form of tariffs. In the computer industry, for example, it is becoming increasingly difficult for manufacturers to compete with the world-wide dominance of IBM, whether in mainframes or micros. In 1980 IBM's share of the UK market was 33 per cent bigger than ICL, the only UK mainframe producer. By 1984 IBM UK's turnover at £2340 million was 156 per cent bigger than ICL's £917 million. This is reflected in the information technology sector trade balance. In 1980 this was just £80 million, four years later it had reached £928 million. In microcomputers the beginning of the 1980s saw the UK with many small manufacturers, but with three firms particularly successful and innovative, Acorn, Sinclair and ACT. By the middle of the decade Acorn and Sinclair had been taken over by Olivetti and Amstrad respectively, and ACT had effectively dropped out of the personal computer market. It is still not clear whether, on current trends the UK, or for that matter Europe, will have a computer hardware industry at all by the end of the decade. This is not a direct concern of this book, but the implications of such a development for Europe's ability to move out of a recession are. The main problem for both ICL and ACT has been the difficulty of competing with IBM, a difficulty which other American firms are also experiencing. For Europe this is particularly worrying as the continued expansion of new industries is seen as essential if full employment is to be restored. The Schumpeterian process of over-capacity and bankruptcies in the wake of a new product can be seen to be at work here. But what Schumpeter did not foresee is that world domination of the industry would be achieved by just one or two firms. Neither the UK, nor Europe as a whole, can afford to see its investment in these new industries being wiped out in this way.

Thus there is a case for import controls to protect specific industries. As with the microcomputer industry, these will generally be new industries, the infant industry case, or alternatively industries which are in severe disequilibrium. An example of the latter would be the US car industry following the OPEC oil price rises. These switched demand towards smaller, more fuel-efficient cars which the US industry was unsuited to meet. The result was a permanent increase in foreign penetration. There is also a case for import controls when there are supply-side constraints on the expansion of output and employment, and an increase in demand might lead to a more rapid expansion of effective supply, but would simultaneously result in increased imports. These should, in general, be aimed at protecting the balance of payments rather than individual industries. But to prevent a trade war, which would have severe potential dangers, all forms of controls should be internationally agreed. There must be a mechanism by which restrictions are enforced during such an expansion, and then gradually abandoned. For example, such restrictions might only be imposed whilst the country is engaged in an expansionary policy to reduce severe unemployment. In addition unemployment would need to be in excess of some given level before such policies could be applied, and the country would also have to show that it is encouraging expansion by easy monetary policy or a large government deficit. Once unemployment fell below a given level, then the restrictions would automatically end. Should the balance of payments move into surplus whilst the policies are in operation then some of the restrictions would have to be renegotiated in succeeding years, or the process of expansion accelerated.

To someone brought up in the international community this must seem close to heresy. However, such restrictions are an important part of any expansionary policy to restore full employment, and to preserve supply-side potential during periods of structural disequilibrium. Without them, the task of macroeconomic management will be more difficult, time-consuming, even perhaps impossible. Moreover, if there is no orderly way in which such restrictions can be negotiated, then the possibility must exist that governments will resort to them in an *ad hoc* and disorderly way, risking the disintegration of the system GATT has painstakingly constructed over a period of nearly 40 years.

WAGE FLEXIBILITY

As we have seen, it was Keynes' contention that the effects of a cut in wage rates would be problematical due to the fact the the demand curve for labour would simultaneously shift downwards. In general, this is a position I am in some measure of agreement with. There is the possibility that a fall in real wages would encourage the entry of new firms, particularly in labour-intensive industries. These firms would be attracted by the low wages, but again there is the presumption that there would at the same time be an increase in demand. Perhaps this would come about through these firms being more competitive than foreign competitors and gaining new markets domestically and abroad. But it should be recognised that this development would involve an economy in moving 'backwards' towards a less developed, less capital-intensive industrial structure, with lower real wages and living standards in the long term. Full employment in the UK could probably be restored if all the unemployed were prepared to work for subsistence wages. But this is hardly a satisfactory solution to the problem.

There is one case, however, where wage flexibility leads unambiguously to both an increase in effective supply *and effective demand* over what would otherwise be the case. This is where a firm would close down in the absence of such a reduction. The firm may have become, either temporarily or permanently, unprofitable given its current cost structure. A cut in wages might shift the firm back into profitability, thus saving it. In this case effective supply is maintained at its existing level, whereas otherwise it would fall due to the loss of the firm's productive capacity. Similarly effective demand is maintained at its existing level, although there is a redistribution away from workers towards shareholders, which is again higher than what it would otherwise be if the firm were to close down and the workers to become unemployed. Such renegotiation of labour contracts is both more common and more easy in the USA. There are two reasons for this. First, unions are less influential and less widespread in the USA than in the UK. Secondly, as we have seen, Chapter 11 of the US bankruptcy code explicitly allows for the renegotiation of contracts by troubled firms.

In general the greater flexibility of labour contracts in the US compared with most European countries gives much more flexibility to firms in altering their costs in line with demand for their products. Layoff unemployment is a widespread phenomenon in the USA. During a recession workers are temporarily laid off, to be rehired again at a later date. This allows the firm to cut its costs very rapidly in line with changing conditions. In the UK this option is not available. Placing the workforce on a reduced working week is sometimes resorted to, but in many cases the only strategy open to firms seeking to cut costs is a permanent contraction. The result of this is a permanent loss of jobs. This is not to deny that the system of layoffs does impose uncertainty costs on individual workers. The US system involves a higher probability of short-term job loss, but the UK system appears to carry with it the higher probability of long-term job loss.

FISCAL MONETARY AND INDUSTRIAL POLICIES

The empirical work showed that by and large small businesses prosper more readily in periods of boom than slump. Company closures are closely linked to profitability, and have tended to increase as an economy enters a recession. Company births too are directly related to profitability and the level of activity in the economy. Their link with unemployment provides some promise that supply-side potential is likely to regenerate itself out of the waste of the recession. But the empirical work also showed that it was probable that firms started by unemployed workers have a higher failure rate than other firms. More generally the high incidence of young firms amongst company failures is testimony to the difficulty all firms have in getting started. In general, then, the hope that the supply side of the UK economy can move out of the depression through the unaided efforts of small entrepreneurs seems optimistic. However, their task will be made easier given an appropriate climate of steadily increasing demand within which to operate. Fiscal, monetary and exchange rate policies can play an important role here. Interest rates also have a more direct role however than merely stimulating aggregate demand. They are an important part of a firm's costs, particularly a new firm attempting to grow rapidly.

Of course small firms cannot be the whole story; existing large firms arguably have an even more important role to play not just in maintaining current output and supply potential but in expanding into new areas. it will be recalled that in Schumpeter's second development model the R & D efforts of large firms were the principal way in which new innovations were developed. Yet R & D tends to be one of the first areas of expenditure which are cut when a firm needs to cut costs. Thus again it would seem reasonable to argue that an expanding economy is more conducive to the development of new innovations.

In addition to the macro-orientation of fiscal and monetary policy, they can be used at the micro-level. An important determinant of new investment and growth is likely to be the level of corporate taxation. This reduces both the amount of money available for investment and the incentive to invest. As indicated earlier there is no clear consensus on the effectiveness of corporate tax cuts. None the less as we saw in Chapter 1, the Reagan tax cuts, contained in the Economic Recovery Tax Act 1981, did coincide with a very rapid increase in investment at a time when interest rates were exceptionally high. Thus despite Bosworth's (1984) reservations, the resulting investment boom does not seem inconsistent with the reasonable *a priori* theoretical view that corporate tax cuts should encourage investment. Such cuts would therefore seem to offer a policy strategy capable of simultaneously stimulating effective demand and effective supply. Such taxes are placed on entrepreneurship and hit hardest at the most efficient firms. The least efficient firms, those which make no profits, pay no taxes. A gradual switch away from company taxation to other forms of revenue-raising, such as a wealth tax, would seem to be an important part of any supply-side policy. If such a policy did result in an increased rate of expansion of the supply side of the economy, and there were no undue adverse effects, then it might be hoped that eventually such taxes could be removed altogether.

Perhaps the most successful example of a capitalist government directing credit at particular industries is the Japanese one. This involves subsidised lending by the Japanese Development Bank and subsidies for applied research. The Ministry of International Trade and Industry (MITI), Japan's most important industrial policy agency, controlled about 12 per cent of public research and development funds in 1983, or about $708 million. Japanese industrial policy has been very successful in encouraging the growth of the machine tool industry, although it is not always easy to pick the winners, and the recently favoured aluminium smelting and petrochemical industries are now in decline. It must also be said that the UK government has been particularly unsuccessful in choosing the limited number of companies it has chosen to subsidise. However, a major reason for this must be the intrusion of political factors in many of these decisions.

More generally UK government's can be criticised for not

having a consistent and continuing set of policies to promote industrial growth, particularly in newly developing industries. In part this is the consequence of differing policies being followed by governments of differing parties. Certainly this does not happen to the same extent in France or Japan. In the computer industry, for example, there have been sporadic government initiatives such as the formation of ICL in 1968 which then received £40 million of aid in the 1970s. Other companies also received aid of various kinds from the National Economic Development Council and the National Enterprise Board (which has since been abolished), while the software industry was encouraged by the Software Products Scheme. But these have tended to be reactions to one-off problems rather than elements of a unified strategy. In contrast the Japanese have been much more deliberate. For example, at the end of the 1970s they realised the key importance information technology would play in the 1990s and developed the 'fifth-generation project'. This covers a ten-year period, setting specific targets and providing financial resources.

Governments in the USA have consistently shunned the need for developing an industrial strategy, preferring to let market forces determine which firms survive and in which direction industries should develop. However, the USA would appear to be in a different position from the UK. It has the largest market in the world, the largest companies and more of them. These companies have the resources to develop and finance their own strategies. Should some of them fail, then other US companies will be ready to fill the gap. The UK generally has at the most only one major company in any one industry, and if it fails the gap will be filled by imports. The US has also been fortunate in the close ties which have developed between their universities and corporate business, one of the fruits of this being 'Silicon Valley'. However, US firms are protected from competition in one very important area—defence. In general defence contracts are limited to US firms who also benefit from R & D spin-offs. Whether these factors will be sufficient to allow the US to continue competing with the Japanese as the benefits of their more co-ordinated approach begin to be reaped in the next decade we shall have to wait and see.

CONCLUSIONS

The purpose of this chapter has been twofold. First, to gain some insights into the processes by which new firms are born and existing firms close. The theoretical and empirical work on insolvencies and new company registrations has highlighted the susceptibility of young firms to closure. It is therefore important for policy-makers to attempt to provide an environment in which as many new firms as possible survive these early years to become successful companies providing new employment opportunities. Equally it is important to ensure that as few incompetent and inexperienced entrepreneurs set up in business as possible. Compulsory training schemes for new firms may well be one way of achieving both objectives. This is particular important for firms set up by the unemployed, which would appear to be more suceptible to failure than other firms. One implication of this research is that it seems unlikely that the supply side of the economy will rapidly and automatically expand towards a new equilibrium once recession forces a reduction in effective supply. In particular any hope that this might be achieved by the development of new enterprises must be treated with caution. Just as Keynes argued that the demand side of the economy can remain below the full-employment equilibrium level, so it would appear that the supply side of the economy may do the same. This potential double impediment to the restoration of equilibrium in the economy is a serious problem for policy-maker.

With respect to insolvencies it should be the aim of government policy to provide a framework which prevents the needless scrapping of capital and the disappearance of firms as going concerns, whilst enforcing the discipline of the market-place on individuals. Inefficient and unsuccessful management should not be shielded from the consequences of their actions by the need to keep their firms as going concerns. Nor should they be shielded from misfortunes arising outside their control. Effective management must continually search for new processes, new products and new markets. They must anticipate misfortune, and be ready with contingency plans. Entrepreneurial activity can be the source of great rewards, but the profit mechanism can only be effective if it is accompanied by the fear of failure. The US system seems to have been particularly successful in managing to reconcile these conflicting objectives, via the Chapter 11 provisions of the bankruptcy code. This, together with greater flexibility in the labour market, is surely one of the reasons why America appears much better equipped to survive a recession without a significant reduction in its supply-side capacity. Thus once demand increases, there is sufficient supply-side capacity to meet this increase and increase employment. The UK, on the other hand, appears to have been particularly unsuccessful in managing the rescue of troubled firms, and despite recent attempts at reform, the future promises little better.

Even when there is an efficient free-market mechanism to provide for the rescue of failing, but potentially profitable, firms, there might still be a need for direct government intervention in cases where there are significant social costs accompanying the closure of apparently unprofitable firms. This is particularly important in a recession, when declining industries might be forced into closure, before new and expanding industries have had time to build up alternative employment prospects. This is of course likely to be very controversial, and in particular totally opposite to Schumpeter's conclusions. But it makes little sense in seeing old industries decline, until new industries are available to take up the slack.

Apart from concerning themselves with failing firms and industries, governments need to be much more aware of the supply side of the economy. They should be concerned about the structure of ownership of industry, and take all possible steps to encourage the growth of new and expanding industries. In an age of multinational giants, it may be that governments can no longer take a *laissez-faire* attitude to foreign competition. Active government encouragement, by e.g. a policy of government preferment in procurement programmes, in certain industries may become essential. If the UK is to move out of recession the government also needs to develop a consistent strategy towards industry and channel research funds in accordance with that strategy. The US is currently not in recession, although this may change, and in any case is arguably so large that it does not need active government involvement in directing the course of development in the economy. However, it is my belief that this *laissez-faire* attitude will become increasingly difficult to maintain in the face of other countries' more co-ordinated approach. By the 1990s the US may well feel compelled to develop an industrial strategy, but by then it may be too late. Finally, there may also be a case for negotiating a system by which governments can impose trade restrictions automatically once unemployment rises above a certain level, or following major supply-side shocks which throw the economy into disequilibrium.

4 A New Empirical Approach

In previous chapters it was argued that the approach of disequilibrium theorists was superior to those who ground out their analysis within a market clearing framework. I have also attempted to expand upon this analysis to analyse the impact capital scrapping and bankruptcies have on unemployment and output. In this chapter we shall argue that a new empirical approach is also needed to model more closely the complexities of the real world. To attempt to do this using a handful of equations may yield valuable insights into the way the real world might behave. But I believe that it seriously limits the degree of rigour the economist can bring to his model. Too often the choice is between mathematical tractability and realism of assumption, and too often it is the former which prevails. To base policy conclusions on such models without realising the extreme simplifications involved is naive in the extreme. Yet this is common, even standard, practice in macroeconomic analysis. Lucas's classic 1975 paper, for example, consisted of just nine basic equations. These represented an economy with a single homogeneous output, two homogeneous factors of production, constant returns to scale in production, perfectly competitive markets, and later rational expectations. Using this model he was able to provide important and valuable insights into the way in which economies might behave in certain circumstances. But that this should have led to the policy neutrality hypothesis gaining ground in policy-making circles, as it did in many Western European countries, is difficult to understand.

Keynesians too adopt the same general approach. Layard and Nickell (1985) in analysing unemployment in Britian have two basic behavioural equations, These are:

$$N_i = f(Y_i/K_i)K_i \qquad (4.1)$$

$$Y_i = D(P_i/P, \sigma) \qquad (4.2)$$

where N_i is the labour demanded by the ith firm, Y_i its output, K_i its capital stock, P_i/P its relative price and σ aggregate economic demand. The assumptions they make include a given number of perfectly competitive firms, constant returns to scale in production with a single homogeneous type of labour and also capital, and that expectational errors in prices and wages are proxied by second differences ($\Delta^2 \log P$ and $\Delta^2 \log W$). On the basis of this model and the resulting econometric work they are able to reach fourteen conclusions of which the following are a sample:

1. The contribution of the rise in the unemployment benefit ratio has been of the order of 0.4 percentage points.
2. The impact of unions on unemployment in the post-war period is to have increased it by about 2 percentage points.
3. Increased income and indirect tax rates have had no effect on unemployment.
4. Increases in non-wage labour costs (primarily national insurance contributions) have increased unemployment by about 2 per cent.

However, the world is not made up of perfectly competitive firms, constant returns to scale are by no means the norm and the above error learning mechanism is most unlikely to be anywhere near accurate. Thus the validity of their results must be at least questioned. Yet this is the standard mode of analysis in economics and is one reason why so much econometric work today carries so little conviction. Of course this type of approach is useful, in, for example, concentrating attention on a few key aspects of a problem in a form which can readily be digested by a single person. In addition, in having to put down one's ideas in the form of a mathematical model one is forced to consider in detail areas which could otherwise be glossed over. Exactly how useful the approach is will vary inversely with the degree of heroic simplification used. This should be borne in mind when interpreting econometric results, and such results need to be put forward in policy circles with a great deal less temerity than is often the case. To cut unemployment benefit because some equation indicates that this will reduce unemployment may prove embarassing to the economist when no such effect materialises. But the lesson will have been paid for by those in receipt of the benefit.

MACROECONOMIC MODELS

There have been two main attempts to break away from the above oversimplification of economic problems. The first centres on attempts to build macroeconomic models of the whole economy. This began with the work of Tinbergen in the 1930s. The early postwar models were generally small, the important Klein–Goldberger (1955) model of the US contained 15 stochastic and 5 non-stochastic equations with 20 endogenous and 14 exogenous variables. Both the Brookings and the Wharton model are direct descendants of this. The Brookings model was much more disaggregated than its predecessors, and included sectors not previously modelled. At the time of its development in the 1960s it contained 265 variables. Development on the Wharton group of models, which are mainly used in forecasting work, began in 1967, the original version consisting of 118 variables.

There are now many such models in both the US and the UK. These are often very large, for example, the UK Treasury model now contains well over 700 equations and 1000 variables, whilst the Data Resources Incorporated (DRI) model of the US contained 718 endogenous and 170 exogenous variables in its original version. These models have mainly been used for short-term forecasting, to give information about the likely state of the economy in the next year or so. They can also be used for *ex-post* policy/structural simulation, to provide information about what the likely effects of different policy scenarios would have been under different states of the world. They have also been used to examine the dynamic properties of models. Finally, there have been some attempts at using them for *ex-ante* policy optimisation.

There are several points to note in the way they have developed. Firstly, the emphasis is on the short term. The UK Treasury model, for example, can only safely be simulated for five years. Beyond that, as the Treasury recognises, it gives increasingly unreliable results, and to-date, macro-economic models have been used almost solely for short-term policy analysis. This serves an important function, governments need to know the effects of policies on their likely revenue and expenditure in the short period. In addition such a model can be used in fine tuning the economy. *However, it also implies that there has been no serious attempt at medium or long-term planning, with the result that long-term decisions have been either the cumulation of short-term ones or arrived at in more ad hoc ways.* Realisation of this has led to considerable recent interest in long-term models, such as the CUBS model in the UK. Work on these is still in their infancy and at the moment they tend to be supply-side models only. But the long-term goal must be a full macroeconomic model with both supply and demand side constraints.

One of the main problems in the way of making these models more long term lies in their treatment of capital stock. The role of investment tends to be limited to its contribution to output in the current period, and ignores any effect on capital stock in future periods. In most models it would not matter if it did, for capital stock plays no role in determining the potential of the supply side, nor in affecting productivity growth. In fact the latter, in the UK Treasury model, is an exogeneous constant. One can understand why, apart from traditional Keynesian emphasis on the short term, this should have been the case. Capital stock is notoriously difficult to measure, but to ignore it altogether on these grounds seems a less than satisfactory solution.

The second point to note concerns the aggregative nature of these models. They are not, for instance, trying to model some individual consumer maximising his utility function subject to an income or wealth constraint. Instead they are concerned with how the mass of consumers behave in aggregate. This argument relates to Lucas's (1975) criticism that macroeconomic models are not truly structural. By this he means a model which is invarient under specified different states of the world, and hence can be used in predicting the impact of policy intervention. This definition, which is expanded upon in Sims (1977), differs from the standard econometric one of structural, which is used with reference to the structural form of a simultaneous equation model. Lucas's argument was that current models estimate behavioural equations on time-series data relating to specific states of the world. Change that state by some new policy initiative and the previously estimated equations will no longer offer a satisfactory guide as to how economic agents will act. This difficulty arises because of the difficulty of modelling aggregate behaviour by equations which are necessarily proxies for the way people in the aggregate behave. In general such proxies tend to explain past behaviour well, but predict future behaviour badly. Only when we can move away from such proxies will we be free of the Lucas critique. But this will not happen until we begin to model aggregate behaviour as the sum of the actions of individual agents engaged in some type of maximising behaviour.

APPLIED GENERAL EQUILIBRIUM MODELS

As we have seen, the general equilibrium approach lies at the heart of economics. It brings together all the agents of the economic system, and examines them as a whole rather than in isolation. Parts of it therefore date back to Adam Smith who ascribed the profit motive as being the guiding principal of producers, and on the demand side, to John Stuart Mill's analysis of the response to changes in taxes and import duties. But the first economist to put this together within a general equilibrium framework was Walras in the late nineteenth century. A central feature of Walras's contribution was the realisation of the importance of an equilibrium set of prices. His first argument that such a set of prices existed rested on the equality between the number of prices and equations in the system. His second line of approach centred on the now famous tatonnement process by which the auctioneer revises prices in accordance with the difference between supply and demand. However, although important by themselves neither of these arguments are adequate to meet their objective. The first is not sufficient to prove existence and the second process need not converge to an equilibrium even if it exists. In fact an existence proof was not provided until the 1950s, when Arrow and Debreu (1954) used the notion of a Nash equilibrium in an *N*-person game. Debreu (1959) provided an alternative proof based on fixed point theorems, which were first introduced into economics by Von Neumann. Further developments were made by Gale (1955) and McKenzie (1959). However, progress on the second of the above problems, that of actually computing the equilibrium price set, was not made for two further decades.

Applied general equilibrium models have mainly been used in trade and tax applications. To analyse the effects of a change in tax rates, the model is solved with the initial tax rate and then re-solved with the new tax rate. Thus the long run equilibrium effect of the change can be calculated. Most of the applied work has been based on the fixed coefficient type model of Leontief (1941, 1953). Harberger's work (1959, 1962, 1966, 1974) has been of particular significance. The Harberger model was represented by just three reduced form equations. It assumed perfect factor mobility between industries, two factors and two products, fixed aggregate supplies, perfect competition in all markets, a closed economy, and linear homogeneous production functions. It was able to generate estimates of the efficiency and incidence of various taxes. Harberger's approach was a considerable advance over partial equilibrium models. But it quickly becomes intractable in dealing with more than two sectors or factors. In addition the model is only valid for small tax changes.

An alternative approach has been developed by Shoven and Whalley (1972, 1973 and 1974) based on the Scarf (1967 and 1973) algorithm used to compute equilibrium prices using fixed-point methods. This involves the subdivision of a unit price simplex into a finite number of pieces which are in turn simplices. It starts at the corner of the simplex and evaluates the excess demands at that point. Movement is to neighbouring smaller simplices. A no-cycling argument together with the limit to the number of smaller simplices that can be examined guarantees eventual convergence to an approximate equilibrium solution. However, this can take a considerable amount of time, and involves the computation of many sets of excess demands. Merril (1972) Kuhn and MacKinnon (1975), and van der Laan and Talman (1979) have developed alternative algorithms which overcome these problems, whilst still guaranteeing convergence.

The procedure most commonly used to select parameter values for a model has come to be known as 'calibration'. In order to simulate a general equilibrium model an initial 'benchmark set' of data must be obtained. The assumption that an economy is in equilibrium, implicit in all these models, implies that in the benchmark data set all equilibrium conditions are satisfied. Demands must equal supplies in all markets and there must be non-positive profits made in all industries. In order to ensure this, adjustments must be made to the data obtained from the National Accounts and other sources. This is partly because these different sources are not always mutually consistent with one another, for example payments to labour by firms will not equal household income. But also important, perhaps even more so, is that the real world is seldom if ever in equilibrium, and thus data from the real world needs to be doctored to fit this hypothetical world. Paramaters are chosen so that the model can reproduce this data set as an equilibrium solution.

Calibration is typically based on one year's observation. Ballard, Fullerton, Shoven and Whalley (1985) for example use data for 1973 in analysing the United States economy. This reliance on a single set of data means that all the parameters of the model need not be uniquely defined. This will be the case for the CES production function, although the parameters of the Cobb–Douglas production function would be uniquely defined from a single observation. Instead particular values for relevant elasticities are chosen on the basis of other research. Typically this involves a literature search, but as Shoven and Whalley (1984) note, the literature is frequently sparse and sometimes contradictory. Thus the validity of any model and the conclusions reached by it must be treated with some caution. Many econometricians are troubled by this somewhat cavalier approach to parameter estimation. But frequently the number of parameters to be estimated run into thousands and there is inevitably a lack of sufficient data for estimation. There are also difficulties in formulating a maximum-likelihood expression which incorporates equilibrium constraints.

Policy evaluation then consists of examining the impact of a policy change on the general equilibrium solution. Thus two equilibrium situations are being considered. There is a potential problem in that the uniqueness of these solutions has rarely been established, but a counter example of non-uniqueness has not yet been found and most modellers accept that uniqueness can be assumed. Most of the models are static one-period ones, although recent work is beginning to incorporate time specifically. For example, the Ballard, Fullerton, Shoven and Whalley model of the United States has saving determining the demand for capital goods in any one period, and therefore affecting intertemporal behaviour by changing future consumption possibilities.

Although most of the initial work has been limited to tax and trade applications, recent research has begun to extend this into other areas. Nguyen (1985) for example, considers the problem of resource allocation and price controls from a computational general equilibrium framework. Whilst James (1985) reviews some applied general equilibrium models to economic history. The main criticism which has been levelled at applied general equilibrium modelling is that too much has to be guessed at in setting up the model. Thus the net result of so many guesses is hardly reliable. There is some validity in this. But what is the alternative? Partial equilibrium analysis can hardly be thought of as giving better results. Modellers can rightly claim that what they have developed is the best available tool at the present time for analysing tax and trade policies. There is also some validity in the argument that the modelling techniques should be developed now rather than waiting until data availability and econometric techniques have advanced sufficiently to allow more satisfactory parameter estimation.

More serious are the same genre of criticisms that I have already levelled at the Walrasian approach in general. The world is seldom, if ever, in equilibrium. What is of interest is not so much how tax changes affect equilibrium states, but disequilibrium ones, and the speed with which equilibrium is approached. For example the impact of a cut in company taxation on an economy with a labour market characterised by severe excess supply is currently of much more interest to most policy makers, then sterile questions about any impact on an equilibrium position the economy is not in and may not ever reach. Will equilibrium be approached more rapidly after such a cut? Will it be approached at all? If so, how do the two disequilibrium paths compare? These are the types of question which should be of interest to the policy maker.

A further point is that the models are still highly aggregative. Dixon, Parmenter, Sutton and Vincent (1982) develop a trade model of Australia with 114 commodities and 112 industries but effectively just one household. This is an extreme case, although by no means unique. Piggot and Whalley (1985) in a UK tax model based on 33 industries have a 100 socio-economic household groupings, they also model public sector spending, investment and external sectors. None the less within these groups there is still only one representative household and in each industry effectively just one firm. Thus, the same criticisms which have been levied at macromodels concerning aggregation also apply here. It is partly because of this that many aspects of disequilibrium states simply cannot be analysed, thus effectively ruling out the analysis of many of the most interesting economic problems. These include how firms compete with one another, bankruptcies and the impact on individual firms of tax changes. Neither can Schumpeterian themes of the business cycle which centre on the life cycle of individual firms be readily handled. For consumers the individual impact of tax changes cannot be examined nor inter-generational transmission of wealth or changes in the age structure of the population. Many other problems can only be examined in an approximate manner. The labour market is a prime example of this. Labour market flows for each industry can be modelled, although to date most modellers have paid scant attention to the labour market to the extent that they have treated labour as homogeneous. But the individual flow of labour between firms and perhaps between industries is more difficult, whilst it is simply not possible to model individual experiences in the labour market. Who are the unemployed? Do the same people suffer repeated and possibly extended spells of unemployment in these models or is it more evenly spread throughout the population? This is an important distinction, as demand-based policies may well be more effective in tackling the latter type of unemployment than the former.

TOWARDS A NEW EMPIRICAL APPROACH

Both macroeconomic models and applied general equilibrium models are attempts to model actual economies in a similar way as an engineer will attempt to model the behaviour of some structure under different conditions. In the rest of this book I propose to extend this in two ways. First, to build computer models of a hypothetical economy rather than a real world one, to be used in much the same way as mathematical models are currently used to examine the properties of a hypothetical system under different conditions and assumptions. The advantages of the computer model over the mathematical one is its flexibility. One is not limited to what can be solved using calculus or other analytical techniques. This is particularly important when attempting to model the discontinuities brought about by capital scrapping, the switching from a supply constrained regime to a demand one or the impact of the product cycle across industries. Secondly, I propose to build a computer model based on individual agents rather than groups of agents as has traditionally been done.

We shall illustrate how the first of these objectives can be achieved by developing a simplified form of the model set out in chapter 2. A distinctive feature of this model is that there will be different vintages of capital. In more sophisticated versions of the model this feature will enable us to have differing capital output and capital labour ratios, but in this model these are assumed to remain fixed and unchanged over time. This therefore corresponds to a clay-clay model. However, capital is assumed to be specific to each industry and there can be no switching of capital from one industry to another. There are five such industries, four supplying the consumer and one producing capital goods. The only impact of the vintage model is therefore the capital stock will depreciate at an uneven rate depending upon the time pattern of the vintage model is therefore that capital stock will period, however after 40 periods that vintage of capital becomes redundant.

A listing of the computer program is given at the end of this chapter. It is written in BASIC and should be readily portable to other computers. Lines 100–1000 define the variables used in the program. The initialisation section follows in lines 1000-2000. This sets the initial value of variables such as each industry's capital stock, financial reserves, etc. The simulation part of the program begins at line 2000. The investment decision for each industry is shown in lines 2300-2440. Investment is proportional to the gap between twice the level of demand in the previous period and current stocks, plus replacement investment. The rate of adjustment depends upon the difference between the profit rate and the rate of interest plus the depreciation rate. If current industry profits are less than this indicator of the cost of capital no investment occurs. Expenditure on investment is bounded by the industry's reserves, and there is a minimum viable level of capital stock which firms have to maintain. Finally, if the industry's planned investment exceeds the stocks of the capital goods industry, then actual investment is reduced to this limit.

Demand for consumer goods at current prices is given by

$$D_{j1} = D_{j2}(WL + X + S) \qquad (4.3)$$

where D_{j2} is the proportion of demand going to the ith good, W is the wage rate, L, the employed labour force, X, exogenous demand and S previously accumulated savings. D_{j2}

in the basic model is an unchanging function of relative prices, although in one of the simulations it varies over time, proxying the product cycle (lines 2020-2080). Exogenous demand can be positive or negative, and in the program is used to proxy the government's counter-cylical policies. This is cumulated over the simulation to give the value, positive or negative, of the national debt. As consumers are assumed to spend all their current income and accumulated wealth in each period, the only way they can accumulate savings is if they are forced to by supply constraints. In an open economy, these savings would probably be spent on imported goods, but this is a model of a closed economy, and thus these forced savings play an important role in returning the model to full employment when it is constrained by supply.

The labour force each industry wishes to employ is the minimum (line 2180) of what it would wish to employ from consideration of demand (line 2640) and the maximum it can employ given its current level of capital stock (line 2160). If the total desired labour force is greater than the number of workers (N) then each industry is rationed in equal proportion (line 2230). There is a common wage paid by all industries to all workers. This responds to the rate of unemployment as in the Phillips curve (line 2280). Prices vary according to the ratio of industry demand to stocks. However, there is a lower and upper bound which is linked to the wage rate to prevent firms setting prices which result in excessive profits or losses (lines 2620–2630). Reserves in excess of a given minimum level are distributed to consumers (lines 2570–2580). A bankruptcy occurs when the industry's reserves are negative (line 5040). There are two systems of bankruptcy. In the first, which approximates the British system, all the capital stock is lost. A new firm is set up to replace it immediately with an initial level of capital stock, of the most-up-to-date vintage, set at 15, and reserves equal to three times its wage bill. The consumers have both to incur the cost of setting the firm up plus meeting any debts the bankrupt firm had built up (lines 5090, 5130 and 5180). In the second system, which is meant to approximate the US system, the bankrupt firm is rescued in its entirety, thus the only cost to the consumer is that of meeting any debts, plus giving it reserves equal to three times the current wage bill. The final part of the program reinitialises certain variables.

The results from the various simulations are shown in Table 4.1. Simulation 1 is of the basic model with flexible wages, an operative fiscal policy and the UK system of bankruptcy. Column 1c indicates to what degree the economy is constrained by demand or supply. A value of -5 indicates that all five industries are constrained by demand, -3 four industries, -1 three industries, $+1$ two industries, $+3$ one industry and $+5$ indicates that all are constrained by supply. To begin with the economy is constrained by supply, but by period 25 all industries are constrained by demand, which remains the case for most of the remaining

Table 4.1: Model Simulations

Period	Column									
	1	1b	1c	2	3	4	4c	5	6	7
5	2500	-126	-1	2500	2500	2500	-1	2500	2500	2500
10	1731	1662	5	1716	1731	1714	5	1731	1391	1595
15	1738	2995	5	1724	1738	1695	5	1738	1763	1704
20	2384	2836	3	2500	2384	2500	3	2384	2500	2247
25	2431	641	-5	2500	2431	2500	-5	2431	2014	2500
30	1392	1392	-5	1600	1392	1630	-5	1392	1993	1980
35	2348	2666	-3	2078	2348	1779	-1	2348	2317	2057
40	2337	716	-3	2428	2337	2091	-1	2337	1384	2167
45	1722	1716	-5	1957	1722	2500	-1	1722	2500	2500
50	2500	1956	-5	2174	2500	1443	1	2500	2389	2220
55	2347	206	-5	2400	2347	2500	1	2347	1228	2166
60	1759	1706	-5	1648	1759	2500	-1	1759	2471	2380
65	2303	1717	-1	2125	2030	1657	1	1527	2500	2400
70	2499	346	-3	2282	2456	1892	-1	2470	2286	2500
75	1837	-154	-5	2182	2062	2408	3	1764	1647	1945
80	1886	2048	-3	1750	1669	2163	-1	1855	2404	800
85	2500	752	-5	2290	2470	1336	-1	2396	2230	595
90	2355	-725	-5	2409	2358	2500	-1	1999	1615	1948
95	1654	274	-5	2190	2116	2433	3	1619	2500	2135
100	2500	1078	-5	1837	2044	981	-1	2041	2298	2455
Average	2136			2114	2119	2036		2041	2096	1932

Key: Columns 1-7 show unemployment in the seven simulations. Columns 1b the national debt and 1c and 4c regime indicators for simulations 1 and 4.

periods. After the initial periods, unemployment is generally at a level of 80 per cent or more of its ceiling of 2500. Although there are some occasions when it falls sharply. This is when imposed upper bounds on industries' stocks force drastic cuts in employment (line 2650). However, the fiscal policy response generally results in a rapid return to full employment. There is just one bankruptcy in period 5 to industry 5, which is the investment goods industry.

Simulation 2 shows the impact of the product cycle with gradually changing market shares. There is no marked difference between the two simulations and it would appear that this hypothetical economy can easily adjust to moderate changes. Whether this would still be the case with regionally concentrated industries and a skill specific labour force is something which will be explored in later versions of the model. The third simulation is of the basic model with an imposed, permanent demand shock in period 60. Demand for good 3 is halved, with a corresponding increase for good 4 (line 2070). The immediate impact is to reduce employment and industry 4 becomes constrained by supply. By period 70, however, the economy appears to have adjusted and employment is close to what it was in the original simulation. However, the pattern of investment has been disturbed. In the first instance, the decline in investment in industry 3 is more than compensated for by the increase in industry 4, and thus the capital goods industry also expands. However, once industry 4 has increased its capacity sufficiently, there is a decline in investment and the over-expanded capital goods industry goes bankrupt in period 95.

The fourth simulation is of the basic model with rigid wages. On average employment is 100 per period less than in the model with flexible wages. In addition fiscal policy is having to be much more expansionary. There is only a limited deflationary demand effect in the basic model of a cut in wages, because the decline in labour income will be largely matched by an increase in distributed profits. The stabilising effect of falling wages comes largely through its effect on investment by increasing or potentially increasing reserves. This is reflected in the regime indicator which shows the model much more constrained by the supply side than in the original simulation. Indeed, this would appear to be the reason for the final very low figure on unemployment. The effect of a forced bankruptcy on industry 4 in period 60 (line 5010) is shown in simulation 5. This has an immediate impact on employment which by period 65 has declined to 1527, despite an expansionary fiscal policy which has increased the national debt to 3391. However, by period 70 employment has recovered. The re-expansion of industry 4 results in a massive increase in investment demand which is accompanied by a rapid expansion in the investment industry. However, by period 71 investment demand suddenly drops to zero, and in the following period the capital goods industry also goes bankrupt. The same simulation with the US bankruptcy system is much better able to deal with the disruption. This is shown in simulation 6. The bankruptcy in the capital goods industry in period 5 which occurs in the basic model has further knock on effects under the US system. This is because during the bankruptcy the industry's reserves are increased to a level equal to three times the labour force. Under the US system this labour force is the pre-bankruptcy one, which at this early stage of the simulation is very large. There is therefore a large reduction in consumer spending power, with the result that in the early stages of the simulation all the consumer goods industries go bankrupt. In the basic model with the UK bankruptcy system the labour force is severely reduced and hence the reduction in consumers savings is much less. However, by period 20 full employment has been achieved and over the simulation as a whole employment is at a considerably higher level, and the national debt at a lower level, than with the UK bankruptcy system.

The final simulation shows the impact of no fiscal stabilisation policy. Surprisingly enough for much of the simulation this appears to be remarkably successful and by period 70 employment has tended to be higher than in the basic model with stabilisation policies operative. However, there is then a very sharp fall in employment and although by the end of the period it has recovered the average level of employment is on average 204 less than in the basic model. In addition, the capital goods goes bankrupt several times. The purpose of demand management in the model is twofold, first, to prevent the economy overheating and therefore building up excess capacity, and secondly to provide a stimulus to the economy when it is in recession. This severe recession was caused by the failure of *laissez-faire* policy to prevent the first and its inability to provide the second. None the less, the early success of this policy suggests either that the fiscal policy rule followed by the model is too strong or that fiscal policy should be confined to periods of severe overheating and recession.

The model is of a simple closed economy with no regional differences, technical progress or skill differences between labour. Each of these would make recovery from a reduction in supply-side capacity more difficult. In an open economy, for example, consumers when unable to buy all they want are not forced to save but can buy imported goods. Thus there will not be a build up of demand during a supply-constrained regime to help ensure a fairly easy return to full employment. None the less, the simulations have yielded some interesting, if tentative, results. Apart from suggesting the importance of forced saving in a closed economy, they have also emphasised that bankruptcies have demand-side effects, they entail losses to creditors, as well as supply-side ones. The importance of wage flexibility and a bankruptcy system which preserves productive potential in maintaining high levels of employment have also been confirmed. The results also suggest that gradual changes in demand brought about by the product cycle do not pose a serious threat to full employment, but that more sudden changes do pose problems. Finally, going back to Keynes, the need for some form of stabilisation policy is reaffirmed as is the singular nature of the capital goods industry which is particularly subject to booms and slumps. But the most important contribution of the simulations is to illustrate how computer models can be usefully used to determine the dynamic properties of systems which cannot be analysed using standard mathematical techniques.

CONCLUSION

This chapter has been concerned with the empirical approach economists adopt. The traditional mode of analysis is to set up a system of, generally linear, equations, and use mathematical techniques to analyse the properties of these equations. I have argued that this is too simplistic due to the large number of restrictive assumptions which mathematical tractability imposes. Computers have been used to model economies, but these are generally either large scale macroeconomic models or applied general equilibrium models. The former, are almost always models of real economies, as are frequently the latter. Seldom have computer models been used to analyse the properties of theoretical systems. I have tried to show how such models can be simulated to analyse systems under conditions and assumptions which are not conducive to conventional mathematical analysis.

The next chapter will advance this process one step further and set up a computer model of a hypothetical economy with individual consumers, workers and firms based in different regions of the country. Not all consumers will be workers as some will have retired. Consumers will maximise utility functions, based on several different goods including housing, subject to wealth constraints. The parameters of these utility functions will be unique to each individual consumer. Firms will maximise profits subject to information uncertainties and a production function with non-homogeneous labour and capital. I shall develop several versions of the model with varying degrees of factor substitution. It will be a dynamic one, with the basic period being a month. This will entail modelling each individual's life cycle from birth to death. Similarly new firms will be incorporated and existing ones close down. There will be a government sector engaged in three different activities, health, education and general services. A fully-developed banking system will provide loans to consumers for house purchases, and to industry. Individuals will be able to buy and sell shares in the largest of the firms. And as our major concern is with unemployment, particular attention will be devoted to modelling the labour market, which will be done in a search theoretic manner. But the potential uses of the model extend far wider than this, and considerable effort will be made to model other aspects of an economy such as the education system, housing markets, and foreign trade.

Macroeconomic variables, such as unemployment and consumption will be found by summing together the number of unemployed people and each individual's consumption. Using such a model it will be possible to analyse the impact of supply and demand shocks on the system, under varying institutional frameworks, and in particular to determine how quickly the economy returns to equilibrium both when wages are inflexible downwards and when they are not. This will allow us to build a much more complex model of the macroeconomy which more closely approximates the real world than models based on aggregates, and at the same time is firmly grounded in microeconomic theory. This solid theoretical foundation should allow us to overcome the problems raised by Lucas. If we have can correctly model the individual's decision-making process, then changes in the state of the world should not affect the validity of any predictions. The model should be able to predict how individuals respond to such changes. We will also be able to absorb within macroeconomics those arguments which have occurred within microeconomic theory, such as theories of search and the product cycle, but have not been fully absorbed into macroeconomic theory.

DISEQUILIBRIUM MODEL USED IN SIMULATIONS

```
10 DIM Z(10),K(10,40,3),L(10,3),S(10,3),D(10,5),P(10,4),R(10,4)
100 REM d1=demand d2=share of expenditure to industry d3=sales =min(S,D)
110 REM s1=production, s2=stocks, s3=total capital stock
120 REM l1=desired labour force from capital stock, l2=actual labour force
130 REM l3=desired labour force from profits
140 REM k(i,j,1)=cap stock of i'th firm, vintage j
150 REM k(i,j,2)=cap output ratio of i'th firm vintage j
160 REM k(i,j,3)=cap labour ratio of i'th firm vintage j
170 REM r1 =industry revenue r2= profits r3= reserves
180 REM p1=industry price, p2=last period's price
190 REM c=supply/demand constrained regime indicator
200 REM s=savings, r=interest rate, b=national debt
210 REM w=wage rate, t=time
500 REM
510 REM *********INITIALISATION*********
520 REM
530 D(1,2)=.2
540 D(2,2)=.1
550 D(3,2)=.3
560 D(4,2)=1-D(1,2)-D(2,2)-D(3,2)
570 D(5,5)=1
580 B=0
590 W=1
```

```
600 R=.025
610 N=2500
620 T=1
630 FOR I=1 TO 5
640 R(I,2)=200
650 R(I,3)=W*500*(1+4*D(I,5))
660 FOR J=1 TO 40
670 IF I < 5 THEN K(I,J,1)=(100-2*J)*D(I,2) ELSE K(I,J,1)=30-.8*J
680 K(I,J,2)=1
690 K(I,J,3)=1.5
700 L(I,1)=L(I,1)+K(I,J,1)/K(I,J,3)
710 S(I,2)=S(I,2)+K(I,J,1)/K(I,J,2)
720 L=L+L(I,1)
730 NEXT J
740 L(I,2)=L(I,1)
750 L(I,3)=L(I,1)
760 L(I,1)=0
770 P(I,1)=W*K(I,1,2)/K(I,1,3)*1.2
780 NEXT I
790 FOR I=1 TO 4
800 D(I,1)=D(I,2)*W*L+D(I,2)*X
810 NEXT I
2000 REM
2010 REM *********PROGRAM SIMULATIONS***********
2020 D(1,2)=(P(1,1)/(P(1,1)+P(2,1)+P(3,1)+P(4,1)))*.8
2030 D(2,2)=(P(2,1)/(P(1,1)+P(2,1)+P(3,1)+P(4,1)))*.6
2040 D(3,2)=(P(3,1)/(P(1,1)+P(2,1)+P(3,1)+P(4,1)))*1.2
2050 REM D(1,2)=(P(1,1)/(P(1,1)+P(2,1)+P(3,1)+P(4,1)))*(.6+SIN(T/20)/2.25)
2060 REM D(2,2)=(P(2,1)/(P(1,1)+P(2,1)+P(3,1)+P(4,1)))*(.4+SIN(.5+T/20)/2.25)
2070 REM IF T>60 THEN D(3,2)=D(3,2)*.5
2080 D(4,2)=1-D(1,2)-D(2,2)-D(3,2)
2090 L=0
2100 FOR I=1 TO 5
2110 FOR J= 40 TO 2 STEP -1
2120 IF J>1 THEN K(I,J,1)=K(I,J-1,1)*.975 ELSE K(I,J,1)=K(I,J-1,1)
2130 K(I,J,2)=K(I,J-1,2)
2140 K(I,J,3)=K(I,J-1,3)
2150 S(I,3)=S(I,3)+(K(I,J,1)/K(I,J,2))*K(I,1,2)
2160 L(I,1)=L(I,1)+K(I,J,1)/K(I,J,3)
2170 NEXT J
2180 IF L(I,3)>L(I,1) THEN L(I,2)=L(I,1) ELSE L(I,2)=L(I,3)
2190 C=C+SGN(L(I,3)-L(I,1))
2200 L=L+L(I,2)
2210 NEXT I
2220 FOR I=1 TO 5
2230 IF L>N THEN L(I,2)=L(I,2)*N/L
2240 S(I,1)=L(I,2)*K(I,1,3)/K(I,1,2)
2250 NEXT I
2260 REM X=INT((2250-L)/250)*250
2270 REM IF 1.1+(L-N)/N>1 THEN W=(1.1+(L-N)/N)*W*.1+W*.9
2280 W=(1.1+(L-N)/N)*W*.1+W*.9
2290 IF L>N THEN L=N
2300 FOR I=5 TO 1 STEP -1
2310 S(I,2)=S(I,2)+S(I,1)
2320 Z(I)=((R(I,2)/(S(I,3)*P(5,1)))-R-.025)*4
2330 IF L=N THEN K(I,1,1)=0 ELSE IF Z(I)<.75 THEN K(I,1,1)=((2*D(I,1)/P(I,1)-S(I
,2))*K(I,1,2))*Z(I)+S(I,3)*.025 ELSE K(I,1,1)=.75*(2*D(I,1)/P(I,1)-S(I,2))*K(I,1
,2)+.025*S(I,3)
2340 D(I,1)=0
2350 IF K(I,1,1)*P(5,1)>R(I,3) THEN K(I,1,1)=R(I,3)/P(5,1)
2360 IF K(I,1,1)<0 OR Z(I)<0 THEN K(I,1,1)=0
2370 IF S(I,3)<50 THEN IF K(I,1,1)=0 THEN K(I,1,1)=10
2380 D(5,1)=K(I,1,1)*P(5,1)+D(5,1)
2390 IF K(I,1,1)>S(5,2)-15 THEN K(I,1,1)=S(5,2)-15
2400 K(I,1,3)=K(I,2,3)
2410 S(5,2)=S(5,2)-K(I,1,1)
2420 D(5,3)=D(5,3)+K(I,1,1)*P(5,1)
```

```
2430 K(I,1,2)=K(I,2,2)
2440 NEXT I
2450 FOR I=1 TO 4
2460 D(I,1)=D(I,2)*(W*L+X+S)
2470 IF D(I,1)>S(I,2)*P(I,1) THEN D(I,3)=S(I,2)*P(I,1) ELSE D(I,3)=D(I,1)
2480 S(I,2)=S(I,2)-D(I,3)/P(I,1)
2490 S=S-S*D(I,2)*D(I,3)/D(I,1)+W*L*D(I,2)*(1-D(I,3)/D(I,1))
2500 B=B+X*D(I,2)*D(I,3)/D(I,1)
2510 NEXT I
2520 FOR I=1 TO 5
2530 R(I,1)=D(I,3)
2540 R(I,2)=R(I,1)-W*L(I,2)
2550 R(I,3)=R(I,3)+R(I,2)
2560 R(I,3)=R(I,3)-P(5,1)*K(I,1,1)
2570 IF R(I,3)>W*500*(1+4*D(I,5)) THEN IF R(I,2)>0 THEN S=S+R(I,3)-W*500*(1+4*D(
I,5))
2580 IF R(I,3)>W*500*(1+4*D(I,5)) THEN R(I,3)=W*500*(1+4*D(I,5))
2590 P(I,2)=P(I,1)
2600 IF S(I,2) > 0 THEN IF D(I,1) > 0 THEN P(I,1)=P(I,1)*((D(I,1)*2/(S(I,2)*P(I,
1)))^.05) ELSE P(I,1)=.95*P(I,1) ELSE P(I,1)=1.1*P(I,1)
2610 IF P(I,1)>1.1*P(I,2) THEN P(I,1)=1.1*P(I,2) ELSE IF P(I,1)<.95*P(I,2) THEN
P(I,1)=.95*P(I,2)
2620 IF P(I,1)>W*K(I,1,2)/K(I,1,3)*2.5 THEN P(I,1)=W*K(I,1,2)/K(I,1,3)*2.5
2630 IF P(I,1)<W*K(I,1,2)/K(I,1,3)*.9 THEN P(I,1)=W*K(I,1,2)/K(I,1,3)*.9
2640 L(I,3)=D(I,1)*K(I,1,2)/K(I,1,3)*.2+L(I,2)*.8
2650 IF S(I,2) > 3*S(I,1) THEN IF P(I,1)*S(I,2)>3*D(I,1) THEN IF L(I,2)>20 THEN
L(I,3)=L(I,2)*.5
2660 REM IF Z(I)<0 THEN IF P(I,1)<1.1*P(I,2) THEN P(I,1)=1.1*P(I,2)
2670 REM IF D(I,1)=0 THEN P(I,1)=P(I,2)*.5
2680 NEXT I
2690 P=0
2700 FOR I=1 TO 4
2710 P=P+((P(I,1)-P(I,2))/P(I,2))*D(I,2)
2720 NEXT I
2730 IF T/5-INT(T/5)=0 THEN PRINT T;" ";L,W,P,B;" ";C
5000 REM ************BANKRUPTCY**************
5010 REM IF T=60 THEN R(4,3)=-S/10
5020 REM GOTO 5210
5030 FOR I=1 TO 5
5040 IF R(I,3)>0 THEN GOTO 5190
5050 PRINT "bankrupt",I,T
5060 FOR J=2 TO 39
5070 K(I,J,1)=0
5080 NEXT J
5090 S=S+R(I,3)
5100 K(I,1,1)=15
5110 IF K(I,1,1)>S(5,2) THEN K(I,1,1)=S(5,2)
5120 S(5,2)=S(5,2)-K(I,1,1)
5130 S=S-P(5,1)*K(I,1,1)
5140 R(5,3)=R(5,3)+P(5,1)*K(I,1,1)
5150 S(I,2)=0
5160 L(I,2)=K(I,1,1)/K(I,1,3)
5170 R(I,3)=W*L(I,2)*3
5180 S=S-W*L(I,2)*3
5190 NEXT I
5200 GOTO 6000
5210 FOR I=1 TO 5
5220 IF R(I,3)>0 THEN GOTO 5270
5230 PRINT "bankrupt",I,T
5240 S=S+R(I,3)
5250 R(I,3)=W*L(I,2)*3
5260 S=S-R(I,3)
5270 NEXT I
6000 REM ************REINITIALISATION**********
6010 FOR I=1 TO 5
6020 S(I,1)=0
6030 S(I,3)=0
```

```
6040 L(I,1)=0
6050 NEXT I
6060 D(5,3)=0
6070 T=T+1
6080 C=0
6090 IF T<101 THEN GOTO 2010
6100 STOP
```

5 An Agent-Based Applied General Disequilibrium Model

The model was written on an ICL Estriel mainframe computer in standard Fortran 77 and should be readily portable to other mainframes. It can either be copied directly from the listing given in Appendix 1 of this book, or obtained from the author on magnetic tape or floppy disk. The listing has a large complement of comment statements which it is hoped will help in comprehending the more detailed aspects of the program which space prevents a full discussion of in this chapter. Each line is numbered, and these are referred to throughout the chapter. (For those not familiar with Fortran 77 a useful text is that by Balfour and Marwick (1979).)

The program can be divided into two main sections. The first sets the initial values of the variables, for example individual wealth, and the values of parameters, such as those in the production function. Initially there are 1100 consumer units, and 50 firms distributed across 3 regions and 12 industries. These are food, cars, retailers, consumer durables, clothes, drink, construction, computers, machines, mining, agriculture and intermediate goods respectively. Thus in the program when industry 2 is referred to, it is understood to mean cars. These firms are of varying size and in addition there are 'firms' 51, 52 and 53 representing health, education and general government services respectively. These firms are classified as being in 'industry 13'. In the program the unemployed are classified as working for 'firm 54' and the retired for 'firm 55'. The initial probability of a worker being unemployed is 5 per cent.

The simulations were carried out in three separate stages.

First, the model was set up with an initial set of values for the variables apportioned in an arbitrary, frequently random, manner. The model was then simulated for 120 periods or ten years, to attempt to remove the arbitrariness of the initial allocations. The simulation proper was then begun for another ten years, under a variety of different scenarios and assumptions.

INITIAL ALLOCATIONS

Households

Individual's characteristics are stored in matrix $X(I,J)$, where I refers to the individual, and J the characteristic. For example, the 100th individual's total wealth is stored as entry $X(100,1)$ and his utility parameter with respect to automobiles is stored as entry $X(100,22)$. A key to the relevant J value of each characteristic is given in lines 40–60 of the program. The following outlines how some of these key attributes were initially allocated.

Population: Fathers were allocated randomly to sons in lines 370–94 of the program using NAG library routines G05EBF and G05EYF. These, along with other NAG library routines, are explained in Appendix 2 (see pp. 234-5). The restriction was made that no father could have more than three sons. This reference to fathers and sons should have alerted the reader to the fact this is a single-sex model. To do otherwise might well prove interesting but is not of core interest to the problem at hand and would add significantly to the size of the model.

Educational Status: $X(J,9)$. This was also allocated randomly, using the NAG subroutines G05EXF and G05EYF. This was done in lines 413–30 of the program. There were three levels of status: leave school at 16, at 18 or a college graduate, the relative probabilities of these being 0.5, 0.35 and 0.15 respectively.

Ability: Inherent or natural abilities ($X(J,6)$) were allocated in lines 433–59 using NAG library subroutine GO5DDF. It was assumed that intelligence was distributed normally around a mean of 110, with a standard deviation of 75 and a lower bound of 50 imposed. The actual ability or skill of the individual (X(J,29)) is then a function of both natural ability and educational level (lines 558–9).

Age: X(J,5): This is measured in months and is allocated in lines 351–68 non-randomly so that individual 1 is the youngest, and individual 1100 the oldest. This is the only variable for which this method of allocation was followed.

Occupation: X(J,10). There are in addition to managing directors just four types of workers—unskilled, skilled, white-collar workers and executives. A worker was allocated to be an executive if he went to university, a white-collar worker if he left school at 18, a skilled worker if his natural ability is greater than 120 and he left school at 16, and an unskilled worker otherwise. In this part of the program those initially unemployed are also chosen (lines 528–82).

Fathers and Sons: Lines 371–94. This was decided by allocating sons to fathers, rather than the other way round. It was assumed that the father of anybody aged over 600 months was dead (line 374). Apart from this it had to be ensured that the ages matched, i.e. that one ruled out the possibility of a 25-year-old son having a 30-year-old father. This was achieved by previously allocating individuals to age groups in the matrix AGE(I,J), which denotes the Jth member of the Ith age group. The maximum number of sons is three.

Region: X(J,8). Workers were allocated to the same region as the firm for which they work (line 553). In the case of firms 51–53, i.e. education, health and general government services, workers were allocated to the regions randomly using NAG subroutine GO5EYF (line 551). The relative probabilities of public employees being assigned to the three regions were 0.3, 0.3 and 0.4 respectively, as the third region is considered the administrative centre of the country.

Unemployed workers were treated in a similar manner, with the same relative probabilities being 0.5, 0.3 and 0.2 (line 552).

Income: X(J,2). Income was allocated in accordance with status. Managing directors were initially given monthly salaries of $2000, executives $1500, white-collar workers $700, skilled workers $800 and unskilled workers $600. All workers are assumed to work the same hours, so the wage rate is the same as earnings. The unemployed and retired received a fixed government grant of $400 and $500 respectively (lines 645–8 and 650–2). Personal disposable income, X(J,12), is determined by the application of tax bands and rates. There are just three rates. The first at 30 per cent begins at an income level of $6000 per annum, the second at 40 per cent begins at $16,000 and the top rate is 60 per cent and becomes operative at $40,000. Both tax bands and rates are adjusted in the simulation part of the program to reflect changing economic conditions (lines 614–60).

Wealth: X(J,1). This is set as a stochastic function of disposable income and inherited wealth. The latter depends upon the age at which they left full-time education, and whether their parent is still alive, it being assumed that the wealthier the family the longer the individual stays in education (lines 644, 648 and 652).

Bank Deposits and Share Holdings: X(J,33) and X(J,32) respectively. The individual has two options open to him in storing his wealth. He can either keep it all deposited in the one bank, or he can have part of it in company shares. The initial decision is entirely mechanical. If his initial wealth is greater than $6000 or he is a company director, he becomes a shareholder (line 667). He is then apportioned the same number of shares in all quoted firms, which is initially the same number as all other shareholders. The maximum number of shareholders (SHRH) is limited to 100.

Consumers' Capital Stocks: Consumers' initial stocks of cars, durables and home computers (X(J,25), X(J,24) and

X(J,26) respectively) are also allocated randomly using NAG library subroutine GO5DDF. The measure of stocks we are using is a fraction of the initial industry quality level (lines 664–84).

Consumers' Utility Function: The parameters of the utility function, discussed later, are also allocated randomly again using subroutine GO5DDF. Thus the basic form of the utility function is standard for all consumers, but its parameters do differ between them. A future possibility might be to link in these variations to demographic factors such as age and family size (lines 705–20).

Housing: Each individual is allocated a house. The matrix HSE(I,J) stores information on the Ith house. For example HSE(I,1) represents the owner of the Ith house. Whereas X(K,3) represents the Kth individual's house number. It is assumed that all individuals are home-owners, thus there is no rented sector (lines 688–702).

Firms

Firms' characteristics are stored in matrix Y(I,J), where I refers to the firm, and J the characteristic or attribute. For example, the 10th firm's wage to skilled workers is stored as entry Y(10,30). A key to the relevant J value of each characteristic is given in lines 151–78 of the program. The following outlines how some of these key attributes were initially allocated.

Firm Size and Industry: The initial size of firms was decided non-randomly. The first 26 firms were assumed to be small, the next 15 medium and the final 9 large. Firms were allocated to industries in a non-random manner in lines 246–8. Thus the first firm was allocated to industry 1 (food) and the second to industry 3 (shops). Education, health and general government service were placed in industry 13. Education and health were both assumed to employ approximately 5 per cent of the labour force, whilst 20 per cent were employed in general government service. These probabilities being set in lines 407–9.

Regions: Y(J,1). Firms were also allocated to the regions in a non-random manner. It was assumed that the first region was characterised by declining industries with higher unemployment than the other two areas. The second was a relatively prosperous industrial and agricultural region, whilst the third was the prosperous administrative and commercial capital of the country. This allocation was done in lines 242–3, and it can be seen that the first three firms are all based in the first region.

Managing Directors: Y(J,2). The managing directors of the smallest firms were allocated randomly from those with IQs greater than 140, of medium-sized firms from those who went to university and are more than 40 years old and of large firms from university graduates, over 40 with an IQ in excess of 140. The managing directors of medium and small firms are also the sole owners. Large firms are quoted on the stock exchange, and are owned by shareholders (lines 462–501).

The Workforce: Workers were allocated to firms in a random manner using NAG library subroutines GO5EYF and GO5EXF in lines 528 and 582. Workers were allocated to firms randomly in accordance with the firms size, i.e. whether it was a small, medium or large firm. The probability of a worker being allocated to a specific large firm was 0.085, to a specific medium-sized firm 0.016 and to a specific small firm 0.004. These probabilities are set in lines 400–10. The Jth executive of the Ith firm is stored as EXEC(I,J). The Ith firm's Jth white-collar, skilled and unskilled workers are stored in WC(I,J), SK(I,J) and UNS(I,J) respectively. These are initially set in lines 564–7.

Prices: Y(J,16). Potential prices are initially set equal to the ratio of total labour costs to potential production multiplied by a mark-up factor (lines 734–5).

Capital Stock: There are three types of capital stock; machines (Y(J,10)), buildings (Y(J,36)) and computers (Y(J,37)). These are a function of the total number of workers in the firm adjusted by an initial approximation to the capital intensity of the industry (lines 724–6).

Industry Variables
There are several industry variables and coefficients in the program stored in the matrix $Z(I,J)$. For example $Z(3,7)$ represents the number of firms in industry 3 (retailing). A key to the interpretation of different values for J can be found in lines 69–80 of the program.

THE SIMULATION PART OF THE PROGRAM: THE CONSUMER

The simulation part of the program begins at line 750. The basic time-period is a month, and the value of CLOCK, which varies between 1 and 12, represents the current month. This plays an important role in the program, because some variables (e.g. wage rates) are set just once a year. TIME represents the current number of periods simulated. Because the program is starting from an arbitrary beginning a number of iterations are allowed before the full simulation is followed. For example line 1217 causes the bankruptcy part of the program to be omitted for the first 55 periods. This is because the initial starting values may have been so far away from any long-run value as to lead to viable firms going into bankruptcy. Similarly in lines 1830–32 wages are set every period during the first 36 periods of the simulation, and from then onwards just once a year. This is to allow a more rapid iteration to a mutually consistent set of prices and wages.

Demographic Factors
The first major section of this program deals with demographic factors and is found in lines 763–977. This deals with the actual life-cycle of individual agents. All children are assumed to go to school immediately following their birth. Until they leave school the attributes of the child are stored in the matrix $SON(I,J)$, see lines 63–4. The child's ability develops in accordance with the 'output' of the education sector and the number of children/students being educated (line 769). This is done in such a way that there is an upper bound on ability of 3, regardless of how much is spent on education. The decision on whether to go on to

upper school or enter the labour market is taken once a year in month 9, by those who are aged 16. This depends simply upon ability, DEM(2) represents the ability level above which young people automatically transfer to upper school. A similar mechanism determines whether the student goes on to university. When the student leaves full-time education he leaves the SON matrix and is allocated a place in the X one. If there are any vacant places in this matrix, due to the death of a previous individual, then he will fill one of these slots, alternatively he will be given a new entry. He is then allocated the same utility coefficients as his father. He also immediately enters the labour market and begins looking for work and a house. Retirement is automatic at the age of 60 years, except for chief executives of firms. The individual is then in receipt of a pension from the central government.

More stochastic in nature are the processes of births and deaths. Births are programmed in lines 834–50 of the program. No person is assumed to have more than three children in total and no individual is assumed to have children after the age of 340 months. The probability of an eligible parent having a son in any one period is 0.009. The son is then allocated the *inherent ability* of his father. He is immediately placed into lower school, his initial current ability is at birth set equal to his inherent ability. The probability that an individual dies is linked stochasticaly to age (lines 886–8). No individual is assumed to die before the age of 640 months. The probability of an eligible individual dying then increases with age. His net wealth is then shared equally between his surviving sons (lines 889–918). This involves the sale of his house and any shares. If the individual has no sons then the next individual in the X matrix is allocated his wealth. If the individual is the owner/chief executive of a firm, then the most senior of the executive workers succeeds him. Upon death the individual's entry in the consumer/worker matrix, X, becomes vacant, and all the relevant entries need to be re-initialised to zero (lines 975–6). This information is stored in the vector BLANK. At any one time there are BLN entries void in the X matrix, and BLANK(BLN) represents the final one. If BLN is not zero then when a young person enters the labour force he is allocated this position in the X matrix. If

BLN is zero, and there are no vacant positions in the X matrix, he will be allocated as individual NCON + 1 in the X matrix. If the deceased individual was not retired then he will need to be deleted from either his firm's list of employers or the list of unemployed. The former is done through the calling of the LOSS subroutine in lines 971–4.

The Consumer's Problem
The next major part of the program deals with the consumer's problem (lines 984–1178). Each consumer is assumed to maximise a utility function in each time-period subject to a wealth constraint, rather than an income constraint. There are six goods the consumer can buy, three necessities: food, drink and clothing, and three luxuries: consumer durables, computers and cars. In addition, wealth is entered as a good. That part of the utility function relating to necessities is a simple additive one. The utility parameters are set randomly for each consumer using NAG library routines as already described when discussing initial allocations. Ideally one would want to make explicit the intertemporal nature of the problem by setting up a lifetime utility-maximisation problem to be solved in every period. But that is considerably more complex and will have to wait for the future. In the present model this is achieved by the inclusion of wealth. The amount of necessities and saving 'brought' are found by differentiating the Lagrangean formed by combining the utility function with a budget constraint, by each good and setting to zero. For food this gives:

$$F = [\lambda Pf/a](1/(a-1)) \tag{5.1}$$

where λ is the Lagrangean multiplier, Pf the price of food, F the amount of food bought and a the utility coefficient. These are calculated in lines 1069–75, except for λ. Subroutine SPEND is called at line 1078 to ensure that the total amount spent, including savings, just equals wealth.

The luxury goods pose a different, more 'lumpy' problem. Many consumers will already have a car, a 'durable', and possibly a computer too, each of which is deteriorating at a given rate. The problem for them therefore is whether to replace these. The utilities associated with four possible states of the world are calculated: (a) none of these goods is bought, (b) a new car is bought, (c) a new durable is bought, (d) a new computer is bought (lines 1080–104). These calculations are not based on the full utility function, but that part of it relating to wealth and the three luxury goods. Thus in this part of the program the individual is deciding whether to buy a new car, computer or durable out of his net wealth after the necessities have been bought. The outcome which yields the highest utility is followed.

There are several aspects of the consumer's problem we have to model which are not found in the macro literature. For example, the consumer needs to decide which retailer to buy his goods from, and which brand or make. We have made the assumption that all retailers sell all the goods in our model. The choice of shop is made randomly, with the probability of a shop being chosen in proportion to the size of the shop (line 995). In future versions of the program it is planned to base this decision on a combination of size, price-competitiveness and quality. The choice of shop, which must be in the same region as the consumer, is made in lines 1060–62. The decision on which firm's make or brand to buy is made in subroutine CHOICE (lines 2158-71). Each individual is given a 'quality preference coefficient', $X(J,17)$, which varies between 0.4 and 1.6 (set in lines 618–20) the greater this is, the more important the individual rates quality over price. The consumer will choose that firm whose quality level, $Y(I,19)$ (set in lines 255–8) is closest to his quality preference coefficient. Each consumer will not make the same decision due to differences in the importance individuals attach to quality.

Housing
The decision on whether to enter the housing market is taken on a different, more mechanistic, basis to other expenditure decisions taken by the consumer. Young people who have just entered the labour market on leaving full-time education are assumed to buy a house immediately on obtaining full-time employment. This simplifies a great deal. It ignores the possibility that the young person may choose to live with his parents, and it also ignores the possibility of a rented sector.

Once the individual has a house, the decision to change to a better type of house is taken when his annual gross income is greater than the value of his current house multiplied by 0.2 plus the real interest rate (line 1034–39). This is fairly arbitrary, but at least does link the housing market to the business-cycle. In particular when real interest rates rise activity in housing will decline.

Each house has a value index HSE(J,3) which is assumed to deteriorate at a rate of 0.1 per cent per month. The actual value of a house is equal to the product of this index and the cost of a new house of the given type in that region. The maximum value this index can take is 1. Once it falls below 0.2 and its inhabitant dies the house is demolished (lines 896–900). HSESAL(J,I) represents the Ith house for sale in the Jth region. The buying and selling of houses is done in subroutine HOUSE (lines 2263–322). When an individual decides to sell his house he does so directly to the bank. The bank acts as a super house agent buying and selling houses. All houses which are on the market have to be placed with the bank. This is, of course, a gross simplification, but again it simplifies the problem considerably and removes the need to model chains of house buyers, where all have to be in a position to move house before anybody in the chain can. For this service the bank gets 1 per cent of the selling price as a fee. Each individual has a desired price he wishes to pay and of the houses the bank has for sale he chooses that which is nearest this price. If no house is within a range of − 10 per cent to + 20 per cent of this desired price, the individual does not buy in the current period. Once a house is sold the individual obtains a mortgage equal to the difference between the receipts from the sale of his old house and the cost of the new one plus any outstanding amount on the old mortgage. Houses are placed on the market at several points in the program, and use is then made of subroutine HOUSE. A key to the various variables relating to the housing market and the construction industry can be found in lines 125–38 and 1524–38.

The construction industry builds houses in response to regional demand. Provided the number of houses of a given type it has in the process of construction is less than 10 and it has no unsold houses of this type, then it will begin construction on a new one in that period (lines 1578–83). Construction work on all houses and factories the firm is building proceeds at the same pace, which is a function of the number of houses and factories under construction and its current output (line 1544–45). Factories are completed in 40 per cent of the time of a small house. It is assumed that a medium-sized house takes twice as long to build as a small house, and a large house three times as long. Upon completion a new house will be offered to the bank, who if they accept it will buy it from the builders and place it on the market. The bank will accept it provided the number of new houses of this type it has on sale in the region is no more than 75 per cent of the total number of new houses it has for sale, or alternatively if it has no more than three new houses of this type on sale in the region (lines 2311–20 of subroutine HOUSE). The price of all houses is linked to the price of new houses in their region via their value index. The price of new houses is determined in a two-stage process. First, the standard price based on costs is calculated as with firms in other industries (line 1633–37). This is then adjusted upwards or downwards according to the state of the regional housing market, rather than unsold stocks as with other industries. If there are more buyers than sellers then prices are adjusted upwards, and vice versa (line 2076).

Portfolio Decisions
The individual's choice on what medium to store his wealth is limited to just two options, bank deposits and shareholdings in public quoted companies. Shareholding is restricted to those whose wealth is greater than the national average by a ratio of 2.5 plus some adjustment for the return on shares *vis-à-vis* that of bank deposits (lines 1862–67). The amount such an individual wants to hold in shares is equal to 0.25 of his wealth, again with some adjustment for the relative return on shares. If his current holdings of shares exceeds this amount, then he becomes a seller (lines 1881–86), if it is less he becomes a buyer (lines 1887–93). The buying and selling of shares is programmed on lines 1900–43. If there are more buyers than sellers, then buyers will all be

rationed by the same proportion, whilst if there are more sellers than buyers, then all sellers will be rationed and each only be able to sell the same proportion of shares that he wanted. Individuals in the market are constrained to holding the same proportion of shares in all firms, which rules out speculative buying, but also considerably simplifies the programming problem. Shareholders receive dividends once a year (lines 1203–9), where 50 per cent of the firms net profits are distributed to shareholders, with the rest being added to reserves. If the firm is not publicly quoted, than the profits all accrue to the single owner (lines 1205–9).

THE FIRM

Each firm is assumed to pursue maximum profits in each time-period subject to a production function constraint, given stocks of capital and labour, and some degree of uncertainty. Because of the potential importance of whether labour is or is not substitutable for capital in determining whether the economy is self-adjusting we shall work with two models characterised by a standard Cobb–Douglas production function, with several types of labour and capital, and one where output is effectively limited by building stock. The production function is programmed as a special function (lines 2105–54) which can be called from within the main program. The labour input in all of these will, as mentioned in the previous chapter, be based not simply on the number of workers as such, but also their ability. Each worker is assumed to have a given level of ability, $X(J,29)$, based on his initial ability and amount and quality of schooling. Particularly important is the efficiency of management, especially the managing director or in the case of a small firm the owner. When using a production function based on several different types of labour, problems can arise for a small firm who may not have a white-collar worker, for example. In this case, all the other workers, including the managing director, share equally in doing white-collar work.

Many models of wage determination are possible. For

private sector workers, we shall be using one in which contracts are set once a year, with a common wage for each type of worker, which increases in proportion to the ratio between regional vacancies and unemployment for that skill (line 1820–37). This is therefore a search-theoretic model in which wages are not directly set to marginal revenue product. However, the number of vacancies reflects such pressures and is set at the level at which the marginal revenue product of an additional worker of a specific skill is equal to his wage (line 1869–710). Additional workers can be hired after a process of search, or the labour force can be contracted by either failing to make good workers who leave, or by firing workers. Apart from construction and retail firms, the pricing decision, which is taken in every period, is based, within a partial adjustment framework, upon the mark-up basis programmed in lines 1633–37 of the program. Total labour costs are added to the current value of capital stock multiplied by the rate of interest plus a risk factor and then divided by the level of output. This gives the average cost of current production, which is adjusted by the deviance of the firm's own stock output ratio from a desired ratio of 2. The net effect of this is that if the firm's stocks of its own product exceed this desired ratio then the price will exceed average cost by less than the desired mark-up, and the firm may even be making a loss. Firms in industries 10–12, i.e. mining, agriculture and intermediate goods, face a common industry price.

Investment decisions, for all firms other than shops, are made in a similar manner to that which determines vacancies. However, if the firm's unsold stocks of its own product are greater than its sales by a factor of 2.5, no investment will take place (line 1351). Firms also face a financial constraint in this line. Apart from this, the firm will expand its capital stock of either machines, computers or buildings if their marginal revenue product exceeds their cost, which is related to the interest rate, by a desired margin which is initially 10 per cent. Because of uncertainty about the effects of an expansion in supply this desired margin increases exponentially as the number of capital units being bought increases (lines 1364–65, 1388–89 and 1417–18). The choice of which firm to order the investment good from is made in a random manner (lines 1343–48). An alternative which will later be explored would be to do this in a manner which reflected quality, price and distance factors. If the chosen supplier does not have sufficient stocks to meet the order, then an alternative one is tried. If no domestic supplier can meet the order, the goods are imported. For machines this whole process is shown in lines 1353–83.

The firm also has to decide at what level of quality to produce. There is a trade-off between quality and output per man so firms will not simply aim for the highest quality level available. An important factor in this is the divergent tastes of consumers. Initially the firm's quality level $Y(J,19)$ is assigned randomly. Firms are given a quality index which varies between 0.5 and 1.5, with higher numbers indicating higher quality. This quality index is then one of the factors which determine a firms output lines (2146–50). This quality index is adjusted towards 1 in the simulation if the firm has stocks above the desired level of twice its monthly output.

Many of these processes are again not ones which are adequately, if at all, discussed in the literature. Another problem which falls under this heading concerns the chain linking retail sales to manufacturing firms sales and then to raw materials sales. As indicated above inventories play an important role here. If a shop's inventories of a particular brand of good fall below a given proportion of their sales then they will be increased to that level (lines 1447–59). Similarly if a manufacturer's stocks of any intermediate or raw material fall below twice that of the amount used in the present period they will be increased to that level. This is done for the raw materials supplied by the mining industry in lines 1484–96, where again the choice of which potential supplier firm is made randomly using NAG subroutine G05EYF. In future versions of the program it is planned to develop some measure of continuity in choice of supplier, as well as basing the decision on price, quality and distance considerations. In addition to mining there are two other supplier industries, agriculture and intermediate goods. Thus a reduction in retail sales will have a double effect on new orders. First, the rate at which inventories are falling will decline, but secondly the desired level of inventories will also decline.

Apart from investment and pricing, retailers are treated differently from other firms and are modelled in lines 1444–59. This is because 'total production' cannot be determined in advance of sales. In other firms goods can be produced, then stocked until sold. A retailer's production is by definition the act of selling goods. Hence we shall need to distinguish between potential production and actual production. A distinction that will not, initially at least, be made for other industries. In the initial part of this section of the program stocks and sales are calculated. If stocks fall below a critical level, they are re-ordered as discussed above.

Bankruptcies
Bankruptcies are programmed in lines 1220–27. The condition for bankruptcy is that the firm's net indebtedness, i.e. their bank loan less any reserves, should be greater, in absolute terms, then three times the value of current output (line 1220). For construction firms this figure is greater by a factor of 2.5. Once a firm becomes bankrupt, the bank loses its loan, but the firm does stay in business. The owner/chairman is retrained, so that his ability is increased by 20 per cent (line 1224). Alternatively, one could view this as replacing the entrepreneur with another of greater ability. He is also assumed to put half of his liquid assets into the reformed firm. Thus, this has a greater affinity with the American system than the UK one, although it is planned to develop a UK version at a later stage. Similarly, the part of the program dealing with the birth of new companies is not operative in this version of the model.

THE LABOUR MARKET

Labour market variables are defined in lines 118–23 and 182–4. In many respects this is the most important part of the model for the present purpose. The book is concerned with unemployment and this is to a considerable extent a labour market phenomenon. There are several different parts of the labour market which we shall model. First, there are labour market flows: hires, fires and quits. The basic approach will be a search-theoretic one as laid out in Chapter 1. Search is restricted to the unemployed, hence a worker dissatisfied with his current wage will have to quite in order to engage in full-time search. Job searchers are assumed to have a reservation wage. If they are offered a job with a wage at least equal to this then they will take it, otherwise they will reject it. For workers who quite their previous job this is initially set equal to the average wage for their type of job. After an unsuccessful interview the reservation wage will be revised downwards in proportion to the difference between the current reservation wage (R) and that offered by the employer at the interview (E):

$$R_{t+1} = R_t + \delta(E_t - R_t) \tag{5.2}$$

where δ is the coefficient of adjustment which we shall assume to depend upon the ratio of unemployment benefit to the current reservation wage (lines 1750–51). This latter term represents a measure of the opportunity cost of search and the greater this is the more rapid the reservation wage will fall. It does not matter whether this adjustment takes place before the individual evaluates the employer's offer or after, as unless δ equals one, the new reservation wage will still be higher than the employer's offer.

This differs from the standard analysis in several ways. First, it is assumed that adjustment takes place after every interview, rather than mechanistically at each time-period. Thus the more interviews take place the more rapidly will wages get adjusted downwards, whilst if no interviews take place, no adjustment will occur. Secondly, the rate of adjustment also depends on the gap between the prior expectation of the old reservation wage and the new information provided by the employer's offer. More in line with standard theory is that the rate of adjustment will depend upon the ratio of the reservation wage to the unemployment benefit the worker receives. There are a number of implications of these assumptions which have not been widely realised. First, the reservation wage will decline more rapidly in periods or areas of high vacancies where job interviews are frequent.

Secondly, because unemployment benefit in this model is paid at a standard rate to all the unemployed, the gap between the reservation wage of workers previously employed in high-wage occupations and unemployment benefit will be greater than that for workers previously employed in low-wage occupations. Because of this one would expect the former's reservation wage to decline more rapidly than the latter's. However, this will not be the case in a system where unemployment benefit is related to previous earnings.

Workers who are fired are assumed to set their initial reservation wage equal to that in their previous employment, this too gets revised every period in a similar manner. Employers are assumed not to revise their wage offer every period in line with search conditions. Instead their offer is equal to the standard wage they pay all their workers, this then is revised once a year in light of search conditions as well as other considerations as already discussed. Workers may be fired for two reasons. First, they may be unsatisfactory, in the sense that their marginal revenue product is less than their wage, due to relatively low ability. Given an unchanged state of the cycle, this is most likely for workers who have been recently hired, and whose ability is less than anticipated. This corresponds to the concept of mismatch found in the literature. In theory mismatches could also arise if the worker found his non-pecuniary working conditions unsatisfactory. But these are not taken account of in the model, hence mismatches can only arise in this asymmetric form. Workers may also be fired in a downswing of the economy. Conceptually, this is different to the first case in that workers who were previously satisfactory are no longer so. In practice, however, this condition is identical to the first case, a worker will be fired if his marginal revenue product is less than his wage.

Quits are determined in lines 1805–16. An individual worker will quit if his current wage is less than a proportion of the average wage for his occupation. This proportion varies with the number of unemployed (line 1810). Once the worker quits he needs to be taken off the firm's payroll, as well as added to the number of unemployed in his region for his occupation. This is done in subroutine QUITS (lines 2227–42). Fires are determined in lines 1711–26. If an average worker's marginal productivity is less than 90 per cent of the wage rate, then workers are dismissed. This differential is to allow for firing and hiring costs. The identity of the fired worker is determined in a separate subroutine. The rule followed is that the least able go first. In fact this will give similar, but not identical, results to a 'last-in first-out' practice by which the most recently hired workers are the first to be dismissed. As with quits, once the worker is dismissed he needs to be taken off the firm's payroll, as well as added to the number of unemployed in his region for his occupation. This is done in subroutine FIRES (lines 2202–24).

The hiring process is theoretically the most difficult to analyse, as it depends upon the interaction of two different sets of decision-makers. We shall assume that each interview results in a job offer which will be accepted or rejected as indicated previously. The problem is approached from the point of view of the firm rather than the individual. The number of interviews in a given labour market, i.e. for a particular skill in a given region, that a firm will get in a single period depends upon the ratio of the number of job vacancies to the number of unemployed. It is also assumed that the more vacancies of this type the firm itself has, the more interviews will take place (line 1742) where J1, in this part of the program, represents the number of interviews. The applicant for each interview is chosen randomly from the unemployed of that category in the region, although one could easily introduce greater sophistiction, so that the more able are likely to get more interviews, for example. The number of vacancies the firm has is revised each period in line with current market conditions as discussed earlier, thus an unfilled vacancy in one period may not carry over to the next period. However, the unemployed do carry over to the next period of course.

THE FOREIGN SECTOR

Exports

Exports are a function of the competitiveness of the firm's

price compared with foreign competitors, which in turn is a function of the exchange rate M(18), the firm's price Y(J,16) and quality Y(J,19), the price of foreign competition Z(D6,22) and a scale factor representing the size of the industry. This is programmed in lines 1473–81. It can be seen that for each industry exports are in fact assumed to be determined by a partial adjustment model, as changes in competitiveness will not have an immediate impact on exports. For example, if the firm becomes more competitive, it will take time to find new customers. Similarly, a loss in competitiveness will not be immediately accompanied by a withdrawal of all its current customers. The stock constraint is operational for exports as with the home market, and if exports were to fall because of an inability to meet them via a lack of stocks, this would also affect further export sales via the partial adjustment mechanism. The retail and construction industries are assumed to have no exports.

Imports
Consumers are limited in the conscious decision of buying foreign goods to consumer durables, cars and computers. Other goods may be imported, but only if domestic stocks are insufficient to meet demand. The consumer's decision is a function of the competitiveness of domestic goods compared with foreign competitors plus a 'patriotic factor', i.e. consumers prefer to buy home-produced goods than goods produced abroad. The variable measuring this is X(J,30), and is initially defined to vary stochastically for each consumer around a mean of 0.65. It has a lower bound of 0.1 and the larger it becomes the stronger is the patriotic factor and the less likely the individual is to buy imported goods. The decision on whether to buy an imported car, for example, is taken in lines 1109–11 of the main program and lines 2412–13 of subroutine CHSP, and depends upon the relative price of domestic to imported cars and the patriotic factor (line 1109). For cars, consumer durables and computers, if the individual wishes to buy from a domestic producer and the shop of his choice has no stock he is assumed not to buy in that period. However, X(J,30), the patriotic variable, will decline. So that in the next period he may then decide to buy

an imported good. It will also decline every time he actually buys an imported good and increase every time he buys a home-produced good.

Firms too can buy imported goods. However, with respect to investment goods other than building structures, they will buy domestically-produced goods if possible. If no domestic supplier has sufficient stocks to meet the order, then they will be imported. (For machines this is shown in lines 1372–79). A similar process is followed for the ordering of stocks of goods from the intermediate industries 10–12 (lines 1483–1521). Finally, in all production there is a minimum content of raw materials which have to be imported. In the current version of the model this minimum is fixed and does not respond to changes in relative prices, although this will be changed in later versions. For other consumer purchases on clothes, food and drink; if the shop does not have the consumer's choice in stock then the desired quantity is automatically imported.

The Exchange Rate
For the US, for example, the exchange rate represents the number of marks for which one US dollar can be exchanged. It is determined in lines 1669–70. It adjusts upwards (downwards) if exports are greater (less) than imports. The exchange rate is also influenced by its purchasing power parity level, which is indeed the equilibrium level for the exchange rate.

THE GOVERNMENT SECTOR

A definition of all government variables, including those related to taxes, can be found in lines 98–105. There are several types of taxation included in the model—income tax, profits tax, value added tax and taxes on bank interest payments. Income tax is progressive and is determined by a combination of three sets of rates and bands, in lines 2000–11. Those with an annual income of less than the lower band, which is initially set at $6000, pay nothing, while the middle and upper bands are set at $16,000 and $40,000 respectively. The bands are adjusted once a year so as to equal unemployment benefit, and three and five times this. The three tax rates corresponding to these bands initially are 0.3, 0.4, 0.6. These are increased if the government is in deficit, subject to a maximum rate of 95 per cent for the highest tax rate (lines 2047–49). Total government revenue from direct taxes is calculated in line 2012. The rate of value added tax M(19) is initially set at 15 per cent, this is included in the price of all goods sold to the final consumer at several points in the part of the program which determines consumer spending, e.g. lines 1069–74. In subsequent periods this is set equal to the lowest rate of direct tax. Total government revenue from indirect taxes is calculated in line 1149. Profits are taxed at a fixed initial rate of 40 per cent for all firms and subsequently at a rate equal to that of the middle rate of direct tax (line 1191). Total government revenue (GOV(3)) from this is calculated in lines 1187. All government tax rates are revised once a year in line with the government deficit, the aim being to move towards a balanced budget (lines 2043–51).

Current government expenditure can be divided into three main categories, expenditure on wages and salaries, grants and benefits, and subsidies to the central bank which may be positive or negative. Wages are determined in a separate subroutine (lines 2194–99), called from line 2065. Occupational wages are a proportion of the average in the private sector. Both pensions and unemployment benefits are set at 80 per cent of the lowest wage paid in any regional-occupational labour market (lines 2053–58).

Vacancies in the government sector are determined in lines 1678–86. GRR(I,K) represents the desired labour force per head of population for the Ith branch of government service, i.e. education, health and general government service, for occupation K. The desired number of vacancies for each occupation in each region is simply found by multiplying this by the population in that region. This is a very basic approach and it is planned to introduce technical progress and, e.g., link health spending to the age structure of the population, in future versions of the model.

THE MONETARY SECTOR AND OTHER
MACROECONOMIC VARIABLES

The variables relating to the bank are defined on lines
107–11. There is just one bank in the system, which performs
the roles of both central and private bank. It also performs
the more unusual role of the only house agent. It employs no
workers directly, these are included under general government, nor does it have any direct capital. Thus its operating
costs are all subsumed under the general government budget.
Total deposits are represented by BANK(2), and are deposits
by both individuals (line 2020) and firms (line 1339). Loans
to firms (BANK(5)) are made automatically upon request, up
to the point at which the firm goes bankrupt (lines 1220 and
1268–72). An individual firm will ask for a loan if its reserves
are less than the value of one period's output (line 1266). Existing loans for house purchase (BANK(4)) are calculated at
lines 1030. New loans are calculated in line 2292 of
subroutine HOUSE. Net current revenue (BANK(7)) is
calculated at several points throughout the program and can
be either positive or negative depending upon whether income exceeds expenditure, or vice versa. The total money
supply (BANK(3)) increases by 2 per cent per period (line
2337) after the first 30 periods. All cash is in the hands of the
bank, none is in the hands of the public. All private transac-
tions being financed by the transfer of bank funds. The sole
purpose of 'cash' in this model is to provide a check on the
level of borrowing. This is done in line 2340 where the rate
of interest (M(1)) adjusts according to the ratio of deposits
to the money supply and the bank's holdings of treasury bills
(BANK(1)). There is a lower bound of 3 per cent for the
nominal interest rate and an upper bound of 60 per cent. The
real rate of interest (M(30)) is the difference between the
nominal rate and the rate of inflation (line 2343). There is a
lower bound on this of 1 per cent which prevents it from being negative. There will be no change in the interest rate when
this ratio is 3. The central bank is the only holder of treasury
bills, which it automatically buys from the government on
need. Any profits the bank makes are a source of revenue to
the government, similarly any losses are subsidised.

Some macroeconomic variables are determined in a standard macroeconomic way, such as the exchange rate responding to the difference between imports and exports. Others, however, are the sum of individual decisions. Total consumers' expenditure is an example of such a variable. This is programmed in line 1148 as the sum of total consumers' expenditure on clothes, drink, food, cars, consumer durables and computers. These totals in turn are found by aggregating individuals' expenditures on these goods. Unemployment and vacancies are further examples of such variables. This distinction in the way macro variables are formed matches a similar one in real economies. In general, variables whose values are set by some central agency, or even a small group of agents, respond to aggregate forces. Interest rates set by central banks are a good example. Other variables, like investment and unemployment are the outcome of many individual decisions or events. The distinction between the nature of these two types of variables has not been fully perceived. Yet I believe it is a crucial one. Much of macroeconomics in the past 30 years has been devoted to finding suitable aggregate proxies for this micro-based decision process. To a significant extent this model has broken with this tradition, and offers a way forward in directions where such traditional attempts have failed to make progress.

6 Model Simulations

This chapter analyses several simulations of the agent-based model described in the previous chapter and listed at the end of the book, under a number of alternative scenarios. First, it is intended that the standard model will be simulated for 20 years with no shocks. This will provide a benchmark against which the other simulations can be compared. These alternative simulations will all be characterised by a supply-side shock beginning in period 121 and lasting for one year. The form that this shock takes is of a sudden speeding-up in the rate of technical advance of new consumer durables. For this 12-month period the quality index relating to consumer durables increases by 50 per cent per period. This index reflects the usefulness of consumer durables to consumers. The shock will result in the existing stock of consumer durables held by households becoming quickly dated, and lead to a rapid increase in the demand for consumer durables. This increase will be permanent as by period 132 consumer durables are much more useful than previously and will therefore be replaced more rapidly. Thus we are not here dealing with exogenous shocks to the level of aggregate demand, but changes to the structure of demand, and we shall be interested in how successfully the economy reacts to this change.

We shall simulate two variations of the standard model, as well as the standard model itself. These entail (i) imposing downward wage rigidity, and (ii) a fixed coefficient production function. It is expected that all models will eventually restore an economy to full employment following a supply-side shock, but the timescale is all-important. How long will it take the fixed coefficient model with inflexible wages to return to equilibrium following a supply-side shock compared with the standard version of the model? In addition we shall be simulating the standard model, but with the demographic part of the program bypassed. This will give information as to what degree any cyclical behaviour in the model is due to a changing population and a changing population structure.

SIMULATING THE BASIC MODEL

The simulation relating to the standard model is shown in Table 6.1. Nominal GDP is initially $1,301,850, but then declines. This is not GDP as usually measured in western countries, but the total value of output from all the production industries. It therefore omits any contribution from the public sector and retailing. By period 30 this measure of output is increasing again, and by period 120 it has reached $1,469,234. Consumer spending follows a roughly similar pattern, with an initial decline and then increase so that by period 120 it is roughly what it was at the beginning of the simulation. Unemployment follows a more steady downward trend, but with some hint of a cycle in the adjustment path. At the beginning of the simulation 79 people are unemployed. This rapidly declines, until the ninth period, when there are just 28 people unemployed. This is again the level of unemployment in period 48, but there is then a steady decline so that by the end of the initial simulation in period 120 there is no unemployment. The first period sees a considerable redistribution of labour. Sixty-nine workers are fired, and some 29 are hired. By the second period this shake-out seems to have ended and there are no more redundancies, but 44 workers are hired. This suggests that the labour market adjusts quickly to any arbitrary allocation of workers imposed on firms. There are no figures on the rate of inflation for the first 30 periods as it is restricted to be 8 per cent. However, from the 36th period on it fluctuates around 11 per cent. There is also a hint of a Phillips curve relationship

Table 6.1: Standard simulation of the basic model with no shocks

Period	GDP	Unemployment	Consumer spending	Inflation	Durable spending	Imports	Population
1	1301850	79	542050	..	42791	34696	1100
2	1239156	44	848802	..	329381	89659	1100
3	1244968	35	818164	..	83330	123712	1100
6	1224444	34	707068	..	21075	301850	1098
9	1156954	28	728443	..	13374	422982	1095
12	1129176	25	737072	..	16243	474137	1095
18	1082268	24	750390	..	20033	506993	1087
24	1081092	19	634579	..	24121	448991	1080
30	1089102	18	481111	..	38086	220393	1073
36	1116923	19	519266	8.9	30614	248161	1065
48	1137763	28	731975	10.8	44975	506308	1056
60	1166858	15	771053	11.9	45206	534318	1043
72	1185353	13	761687	15.4	27063	538096	1029
84	1233469	19	843142	5.6	33079	553651	1011
96	1332790	7	714422	16.3	43455	477876	994
108	1393080	0	713129	10.6	50595	441592	978
120	1469234	0	832186	12.5	58386	521453	983
123	1463837	0	1040843	17.1	52371	609461	980
126	1459065	0	915916	19.2	44934	552750	977
129	1459311	0	978552	18.4	54655	530280	976
132	1518985	0	909197	18.3	59810	526359	984
138	1535218	0	1226281	11.6	43172	606568	977
144	1558496	0	1017657	16.7	81858	582802	986
156	1604904	0	1414920	11.2	93512	840900	992
168	1617118	0	1083510	5.7	106719	649582	990
180	1588334	1	1635633	8.2	58292	1014155	996
192	1785953	0	1678945	15.2	103500	1051392	997
204	1783248	0	2431805	18.6	123609	1735050	987
216	1958371	3	1586792	18.3	50586	1151481	983

between inflation and unemployment and the rate of change of unemployment. Imports follow a similar pattern to GDP, and the final column shows that for the first 120 periods the population is declining.

The second phase of the simulation sees a more stable population structure, which by period 216 is at the same level as it was in period 120. The fact that the final period is 216, rather than 240 as originally intended, is because the run for the full 20 years exceeded the maximum time allowed on the SWURCC computer. Despite the fact that this represents a benchmark set of data, where the program is unchanged from that which generated the initial set of data, many of the variables are somewhat different from this initial period. Inflation, for example is running at a considerably higher level than before, and is characterised by a cyclical pattern. In most of these periods there is no unemployment, although it does begin to re-emerge towards the end of the simulation. Both of these developments are a reflection of the fact that the economy is running at a very high level, mainly due to high exports. This is shown by the figures for GDP, consumer spending and consumer durable spending. The figures for consumer spending, particularly on durables, but cars and computers as well, are fairly volatile. Because of this it will probably be necessary in future versions of the program to program higher desired stock levels for these three industries. There are periodic bankruptcies in all the simulations, but under the American-type system prevailing the firms are rescued. They mostly concern retailers and suggests the possible need to revise the mechanism governing the mark-up charged by retailers.

Table 6.2 shows the distribution of wages at various points

Table 6.2: Wage rates during the basic simulation with no shocks

Period	2	12	36	60	120
Executive					
Region 1	1501	1525	1535	1537	287
Region 2	1500	1508	1519	1521	367
Region 3	1500	1504	1506	1507	249
White-collar					
Region 1	700	709	714	716	724
Region 2	700	701	704	705	585
Region 3	700	703	705	705	663
Skilled					
Region 1	802	816	828	830	565
Region 2	800	805	813	814	397
Region 3	800	804	808	809	369
Unskilled					
Region 1	702	713	722	723	570
Region 2	701	704	712	712	592
Region 3	700	704	707	707	420

throughout the initial simulation. It can be seen that there is some change in the first 60 periods, with the first region emerging as the area of highest pay. This distinction is much less clear by period 120, when there is considerably greater degree of adjustment to market conditions. However, the first region still emerges as the highest paid region for white-collar and skilled workers, and it is probably correct to regard this as being the most prosperous region. The biggest surprise in this simulation is the wages of executives, who were the highest paid workers in the first 60 periods, but finish the lowest by some margin. This might reflect either the coefficient relating to them in the production function being too low, or that there are simply too many executives, perhaps due to an imbalance in the occupational structure of school-leavers. In the real world this should lead to a shift in executive workers to white-collar occupations, and this is something which must be built into future versions of the program.

Table 6.3 shows the distribution of prices at various points throughout this initial simulation. There is a fairly clear pattern of prices falling throughout the first year, but by the 36th period having recovered. By the end of this initial simulation prices are very much higher than they were at the beginning, which reflects the economy wide rise in prices shown by the inflation figures in Table 6.1. The final column of this table shows the proportionate increase between period 2 and 120, where it can be seen that agricultural goods have

Table 6.3: Prices in the basic simulation with no supply-side shocks

Period	2	12	36	60	120	% change
Food	1.1	0.9	1.0	1.5	2.7	245
Cars	2261.0	2237.0	2763.0	3518.8	5692.0	252
Durables	408.0	398.4	359.1	404.4	1060.8	260
Clothes	201.0	165.1	253.6	224.1	356.5	177
Drink	1.8	1.8	1.8	2.5	4.9	272
Construction	3477.0	3008.0	4048.0	4392.0	6439.4	185
Computers	221.0	233.2	268.0	326.2	591.9	267
Machines	280.0	250.9	294.8	399.0	693.0	248
Mining	20.5	19.5	22.6	27.0	31.2	152
Agriculture	16.0	13.7	17.3	22.9	45.3	283
Intermediate goods	16.5	16.2	19.2	23.4	37.3	226

Table 6.4: Output in the basic simulation with no supply-side shocks

Period	2	12	36	60	120
Food	83 292	75 613	62 204	65 059	64 100
Cars	111	98	76	59	36
Durables	193	188	144	113	124
Clothes	278	262	295	347	448
Drink	16 067	21 073	16 407	20 837	13 592
Construction	33	32	28	25	18
Computers	408	378	289	222	131
Machines	260	249	199	135	79
Mining	6 535	7 106	5 922	4 936	3 250
Agriculture	7 447	7 756	6 800	5 805	4 708
Intermediate goods	12 317	12 296	9 839	7 794	4 341

increased most in price and mining the least. Table 6.4 shows the changes in production over the first 120 periods. There is a general decline in production, with the sole exception of the clothes industry, although food and drink hold their original position quite well. This change is partly a reflection of the redistribution of the initial labour allocations towards the public and retail sectors. The size of the workforce too is declining over time. But also important is the decline in capital stock, which was originally set 'too high'. An important task for the future is to assess, the performance of the model starting from different initial allocations, such as that for capital stock.

SIMULATING ALTERNATIVE VERSIONS OF THE MODEL

Table 6.5 contains the results of simulating the basic model, but with a supply-side shock increasing the quality of consumer durables by 50 per cent each period for 12 successive periods beginning in period 121. This is done by removing the comment statement in line 2380 of the program. The effects on nominal GDP and unemployment are minimal. More marked is the impact on inflation which is generally substantially below what it was in the previous simulation. Thus by the end of the simulation, the consumer price index stands at

Table 6.5: Simulation with supply-side shock in period 120 of the basic model

Period	GDP	Unemployment	Consumer spending	Inflation	Durable spending	Imports	Population
120	1469234	0	832186	12.5	58386	521453	983
123	1461839	0	1058448	17.0	204670	627334	980
126	1459904	0	781103	18.8	304696	467262	977
129	1459446	0	761673	18.7	290530	477527	976
132	1523400	0	745917	20.0	280444	459543	984
138	1550402	0	770131	15.0	288316	521389	977
144	1558816	0	677899	11.4	169313	450674	986
156	1589832	0	756528	11.5	227735	512452	992
168	1611815	0	891554	1.8	331764	591641	990
180	1566840	2	883391	9.2	299681	523290	996
192	1717251	0	1077766	19.9	509498	709150	997
204	1797533	0	1215043	17.8	521323	832545	987
216	2027757	0	1290355	10.6	716132	895631	983

1450 compared to 1590 in the original simulation. This is the main reason consumer spending has fallen. However, there is also a slight decline in real consumer spending which is partly why prices are lower. Much more marked is the increase in spending on durables, an increase which is maintained throughout the simulation.

The impact of a supply shock on this basic model, but with an unchanging population structure, is shown in Table 6.6. There are a number of differences between this and the basic model simulation. With respect to production there are two influences at work. The decline in the population, and therefore the labour force too, will result in less production. However, new entrants into the labour force will be of a different level of ability to existing workers, due to differences in education standards. On balance this would appear to have reduced the productive capacity of the economy. In period 120 only drink, construction, machines and intermediate goods are producing at a higher level. The decline in food production is particularly sharp, from 64,100 units to 44,273. This would appear to have had a significant impact on the rate of inflation, and by period 120 the retail price index stands at 680 compared to 560 in the original simulation. This trend is continued throughout the simulation, and by period 216 the relative price indices are 1786 and 1450 re-

Table 6.6: Simulation with supply-side shock in period 120 of the model with an unchanging population structure

Period	GDP	Unemployment	Consumer spending	Inflation	Durable spending	Imports
1	1301634	80	543944	..	43136	33535
2	1240934	45	843589	..	321114	93057
3	1241800	38	819613	..	85597	133283
6	1222777	38	705745	..	21809	320482
9	1164846	31	732337	..	19451	425659
12	1119046	31	737295	..	19687	482551
18	1080273	29	720095	..	17336	490680
24	1093764	23	686624	..	19726	471939
30	1096037	23	438671	..	15148	202179
36	1114917	23	521025	10.0	31773	256376
48	1131614	22	764381	12.2	38894	538936
60	1161505	10	811888	11.9	44244	572925
72	1193159	2	821605	19.1	68384	532281
84	1233064	0	723554	8.0	39842	515318
96	1255694	0	657248	14.3	14952	399440
108	1295513	0	854314	16.5	24996	507763
120	1284045	0	1049087	15.3	120132	559158
123	1271765	0	863761	15.2	262268	487721
126	1270531	0	839400	14.2	311978	504811
129	1264345	0	912107	14.7	394186	528346
132	1262730	0	846438	16.6	324336	518650
138	1254977	0	732352	14.6	243623	482425
144	1207263	0	841553	10.2	302201	570291
156	1202012	0	789355	10.0	226534	559855
168	1226496	0	874387	7.7	240119	598493
180	1216505	0	1027240	12.2	425597	643365
192	1241257	0	1125149	12.3	537027	759933
204	1307119	0	1295015	19.1	686649	851977
216	1269694	0	1399213	14.9	768025	959236

spectively. A further factor affecting the price levels is that the model with a constant population structure is more rigid and less responsive to change. Extra workers in one industry have to be attracted from others, which is more difficult and more inflationary than attracting them direct from school. Imports and consumer spending, both generally and on durables, are all slightly greater in this simulation than previously, but with a higher population this is only to be expected. Apart from any effects on levels, the simulation with an unchanging population structure has damped any cycle in both inflation and unemployment, for example, and would suggest that an important source of cyclical variation does come from demographic factors.

The basic model was also simulated with both a supply-side shock and downward inflexibility of nominal wages. This was achieved by removing the comment state from line 1834. However, there was no difference between this model simulation and that done without the restriction on wages. At first sight this was somewhat surprising, but the context of the simulation is of a supply-side shock altering the pattern of demand within a buoyant economy. One cannot conclude from this that wage inflexibility would have no impact in all possible scenarios, and initial simulations with a less buoyant economy suggest that in some cases rigid wages do reduce the allocative efficiency of the economy and therefore increase unemployment. More of an impact in the current set of simulations was achieved by using a fixed coefficient production function. The model was simulated for 120 periods as in the basic model, and the ratio of output to building stock pertaining in the 120th period was taken to represent the output:capital ratio for this type of capital. This was then used to impose an upper bound on production, which was achieved by removing the comment statements on lines 2151–53 of the program. Thus this is only a limited type of fixed coefficient model, with there being substitution possibilities between machines, and computers and the different types of labour.

The results of this simulation are shown in Table 6.7. The most striking feature of this simulation is that for the first time unemployment appears as a problem during the second part of the simulation, with it being concentrated in the third region. Moreover, there is a distinct cyclical pattern of unemployment with there being one peak in period 129 and a second in 204. Despite this increase in unemployment there is also a rise in the average rate of inflation, reflecting the poorer allocative performance of economies characterised by fixed-technology production possibilities. The economy is less responsive to changing conditions, resulting in both

Table 6.7: Simulation with supply-side shock in period 120 of the model with a fixed coefficient production function

Period	GDP	Unemployment	Consumer spending	Inflation	Durable spending	Imports
120	1469234	0	832186	12.5	58386	521543
123	1453721	8	987950	18.7	275559	499955
126	1430036	13	942138	19.5	363322	514151
129	1424109	33	761287	17.4	302818	426082
132	1489433	23	758015	17.2	290296	440066
138	1466874	31	765198	15.6	305341	484564
144	1515942	13	704551	18.9	225357	507455
156	1452875	37	814095	8.0	296343	489333
168	1560074	4	830403	7.8	254193	570274
180	1593039	31	1041202	13.8	414094	703312
192	1641739	45	925186	13.4	358392	595531
204	1673653	65	1077628	20.3	505786	661741
216	1717539	57	1099575	21.1	517787	638945

higher unemployment and inflation. The effect of this takes some time to feed through to output and consumers expenditure, but by period 192 these are both below the corresponding figures in Table 6.5, as are imports.

CONCLUSIONS

The main purpose of this part of the book has been to demonstrate that it is feasible to construct an agent-based model of the economy, which can be used in theoretical analysis, providing an alternative to current modes of analysis which are based on unrealistic assumptions and are inadequate to the needs of the time. That purpose has been achieved. In addition, despite the relative simplicity of the model, it has yielded valuable insights in both its construction and simulation. In building such a model one is forced to come to grips with problems which have previously been avoided. Thus, when modelling the search process in the labour market it became apparent that the reservation wage should fall after each unsuccessful interview, rather than by a given amount each period. This implies that it will fall at a different rate depending upon local labour market conditions which can be expected to differ across time and space. The simulation process emphasised the interactive nature of the macroeconomy, where a change in one industry has repercussions across a wide range of others. This may seem obvious enough, but it is something which has tended to be forgotten in Keynesian analysis, with its emphasis on aggregates in general and aggregate demand in particular. The simulations also indicated that if there is perfect substitutability of factors of production and wage flexibility, then supply-side shocks, at least, can be absorbed by the economy without causing excessive unemployment. However, once one moves towards a fixed coefficient production function, this conclusion changes, unemployment follows in the wake of supply-side shocks as the economy struggles to adjust towards a new equilibrium. Finally, the simulations suggest the importance of demographic factors in determining the cyclical behaviour of an economy.

There are many more questions to be asked and answered, and considerable refinements to make to the model. The financial and government sectors are still primitive. The monetary sector is not simulating that well, with the rate of interest tending to drift towards its boundary points. The model needs to be made larger, with more consumers, firms and industries. Concepts of technical change and the product cycle need to be introduced. Further consideration needs to be given to such problems as how the consumer chooses between products of differing quality and price, and the role of 'patriotism' in this decision. The labour market needs to be made more flexible with workers having the opportunity to retrain for other occupations or migrate to other regions. It also needs to be simulated for longer time-periods, of say up to 100 years in order for the full impact of shocks and policy changes to become apparent. This will also be necessary to assess the dynamic properties of the model, whether it is stable and whether it is subject to cycles. Also of interest are the adjustment paths to an initial equilibrium given different starting points. Finally, there is the hope that eventually it will be possible to use an agent-based model for policy analysis of an actual economy.

7 Policy and Other Conclusions

GENERAL POLICY CONCLUSIONS

Implicit in the *General Theory* and much of subsequent Keynesian analysis is Keynes' law, analogous to Say's law, that demand creates its own supply. Thus if there is a problem of high unemployment, one only needs to expand demand to solve it. To a large extent it does not even matter how the expansion is targeted, any increase will serve. It does not seem to have occurred to the Keynesians that the economy may not have the capacity to meet the expansion in demand. Perhaps with mass unemployment this is deemed an irrelevant consideration. I have argued that it is not, that when an economy moves into a recession, supply-side capacity is likely to fall due to the contraction of some firms and the complete disappearance of others. A firm which has closed down, scrapped its capital and disbanded its workforce cannot suddenly start producing again once demand for its product revives. The research on company failures clearly showed how they vary with the business cycle. When one gets large numbers of companies failing, and even more contracting, then the capital stock of the economy also inevitably declines. The fact that official figures of capital stock do not show this is a reflection of just how poor these figures are in both the US and the UK. It is very important that they are revised to take account of capital destruction as well as capital creation and depreciation for an accurate picture of the supply side of the economy to be obtained.

Many economists would like to view this process of capital

contraction as one of creative destruction, in which the old and the inefficient are swept away in a recession by the dynamic and the new. Our analysis of company failures showed that this view is difficult to sustain. Firms in all industries and at all ages are at risk during a slump. Whether the reduction of supply side capacity leads to large scale unemployment or not depends upon the nature of capital. Traditionally, it is treated as malleable jelly, and in this case full employment can be restored, albeit at a lower level of output, by either a fall in wages or a Keynesian-based policy of fiscal expansion. However, the empirical evidence would appear to favour the view that capital is predominantly putty-clay in which case these familiar and comfortable conclusions no longer hold. Neither Keynesian policies of fiscal expansion nor cuts in wages will be sufficient to restore full employment. Equally, policies aimed at stimulating the supply side, if pursued in isolation, are doomed to failure. To successfully emerge from a depression both demand and supply side policies need to be followed. I believe that this assumption concerning the nature of capital is as important as that relating to the flexibility of wages and prices. Given unexpected shocks to the economic system which result in bankruptcies and capital scrapping an economy with a putty-clay capital stock will experience a prolonged period of unemployment, regardless of whether or not wages are flexible downwards.

Although, it is the case that demand-based policies are not always appropriate, they still have an important role to play, particularly in the early stages of a recession before capital contraction has occurred on a serious scale. Indeed it still seems to be the case that, appropriately handled, demand management policies can prevent serious recessions altogether so that the following steps should not be necessary. However, to the extent that a recession may be unavoidable, care should be taken to preserve effective supply as near as possible to the full employment level. This means that bankrupt companies should to a large extent be saved, although not necessarily their management or shareholders. Inefficient management should not be shielded from the consequences of their actions, or even events outside their control. The profit motive can be an effective mechanism for promoting efficiency and innovation only if it is accompanied by the fear of failure. But this is no reason why the productive capacity of potentially profitable firms should be lost to the economy.

The American system seems far more effective in reconciling these objectives than its British counterpart, despite recent changes in the UK insolvency law. However even in the US, it may be necessary for the government to act more directly to prevent firms from closing down. This might involve subsidising temporarily loss-making industries until with the recovery from a recession they become profitable again. In doing this the full costs of letting a firm disappear should be borne in mind, including the monetary costs to the state of welfare benefits and reduced tax revenue, as well as the health costs to the families of the unemployed. These costs are likely to vary with the business cycle and the speed with which an unemployed worker can expect to find alternative employment. It is possibly more difficult for governments to interfere with the decisions of troubled, but solvent firms who wish to reduce their capacity. But, the same arguments which were used to argue that the market place would not save the optimal number of liquidated firms can be used to argue that what is good for an individual company is not necessarily good for the economy as a whole. Companies have responsibilities to the communities within which they operate, and the costs to these communities should be a factor in any closure decision. One way of doing this would be to make firms pay separation payments to communities in the same way as they do to individuals. One potential source of rescue for troubled firms comes from large foreign, or multinational, firms. On the face of it this is wholly beneficial, bringing with it not only new sources of finance but also management and technical expertise. However, the analysis of the British car industry in Chapter 3 shows that often such a development is succeeded by the decline of domestic capacity, to be replaced by imports from plants in other countries.

On the wider question of international trade it is clear that most economists have traditionally been against restrictions.

Such views are based upon comparisons of general equilibrium positions. But severe disequilibrium is far from unusual. Industries faced with large-scale shocks, necessitating a radically different pattern of production, need time to adjust to that pattern. Faced with such a situation following the 1973–74 oil price increases British car firms, many already in difficulties, were not given that time. Disequilibrium states are not just restricted to individual sectors of the economy, many European countries are constrained from re-expanding their economies by the effects of such an expansion on their balance of trade. In both these cases trade restrictions would be to the short-term benefit of the domestic economy, and eventually to the world economy as well. Yet there is no provision for their implementation. Such provisions, detailing the circumstances in which they can be invoked and the form they can take, must be agreed by the international community. If they are not, if the rules remain inflexible, then they risk being broken, and with them the whole structure of free trade built up over the last 40 years. One possibility would be to use the level of unemployment as a trigger allowing such restrictions to be introduced and dictating their removal.

Skilled labour has also emerged as an important supply-side constraint. Again, with the onset of a recession firms will be laying off skilled workers, not taking on new workers or closing down altogether. Given the onset of a recovery skilled labour constraints might then hamper the return to previous levels of employment. It is therefore essential that governments provide full training to new entrants to the labour force who cannot find work and retraining to existing workers who have become unemployed.

The situation is much more difficult for an economy already in recession attempting to return to full employment. This has always been seen as a difficult task, but with the recognition that many such economies have supply- as well as demand-side constraints on the expansion of output the prospects seem doubly difficult. When an industry is constrained by supply factors as well as demand, then expanding only one side of the economy will do nothing for employment. If demand is increased through an expansionary fiscal policy then imports and inflation will simply rise as happened in the UK in 1973/74 and France more recently. Similarly for the supply side alone to be increased is also futile. This might possibly be achieved by retraining programmes or investment incentives, but this increase in potential output would remain unused. Faced with such a situation effective supply and demand need to be increased simultaneously.

Effective demand can be increased through all the tools that Keynes gave us. Increased government expenditure will to an extent increase employment opportunities directly, from then on the multiplier will be operative. Reducing tax rates will increase consumer spending and to the extent that this is spent on home-produced goods the multiplier will work again. However, the multipliers will not be operative unless effective supply is simultaneously increased. Policies aimed at increasing investment, such as differential tax policies and low interest rate policies, will increase both effective demand and supply, although not always in the same industry. For example if the car industry invests more this will increase its own effective supply, but effective demand in the investment industries. Such a policy would therefore need to be accompanied by others aimed at increasing the demand for cars and ensuring the investment industries expanded their capacity to be able to supply the increased demand. Moreover, the timing would have to be such that this increased demand occurred once the increased supply became effective.

On the supply side, our analysis of company births showed that the unemployed appear more likely to start up new firms than employed people. Superficially, this would appear to be beneficial both to the economy and the unemployed alike. However, further research also showed that, in both the UK and the USA, such firms appear more likely to fail. The majority of firms who fail appear to do so through incompetence or inexperience. To reduce this probability of failure with its potential harmful effects on other firms, compulsory training schemes should be set up, not just for the entrepreneur who was previously unemployed, but for all who wish to start a new business. At least one director from every newly incorporated business seeking to claim the benefit of limited liability should attend a short course on running a business. Thus providing an optimal climate in which new businesses can prosper does not necessarily go hand in hand with deregulation of the market-place. In some cases government control needs to be increased.

In building the agent-based model it became clear how crucial the entrepreneur, and others in positions of authority, are in determining the level of output and efficiency of a country. Increasing the efficiency with which a relatively small number of key people operate could make a very significant difference to the prosperity of the whole country. This has several implications. First, it should be an explicit aim of policy that those most naturally gifted should rise to the most important positions in business and the state. In this, as in many more areas, the US seems more successful than the UK. Secondly, it should also be ensured that the optimal amount is being spent on their training, and that they are taught courses relevant to their needs. Oxbridge classics graduates are not really what is required to fill top jobs in commerce and government, yet too often in the UK they are in those jobs.

The analysis has throughout stressed the importance of the firm in determining living standards and the manner and the speed with which the economy adjusts in disequilibrium. This realisation naturally leads to considerations as to why the firm should be taxed. Such taxes are placed on entrepreneurship and hit hardest at the most efficient firms. Those which make no profits pay no taxes. It is difficult to make the case on distributional grounds, as these concern the distribution of income and wealth amongst individuals not firms. If one argues that it is the rich who own most shares, this is still no justification for taxing the firms rather than the individuals on the income they receive including income from shares. It may be that it is easier on collection grounds to hide the full extent of taxes by having them come from as many diverse sources as possible. But arguments based on fooling the public have never had that strong an appeal to the economist. In any case these gains, if any, must be set against the potential reduction in efficiency by having taxes on firms. All taxes have efficiency implications, and any change in the tax structure should be made gradually, so that the implications of a new structure can be evaluated and adjustments made if necessary. Such a policy would have the added attraction of stimulating both the supply and demand sides of the economy together.

THE UNITED STATES

Unemployment in the United States appeared to be on a long-term upward trend until the most recent downswing beginning in 1983 saw unemployment fall rapidly. Reagan's supply-side strategy has given precedence to lower tax rates, but simultaneously increased effective demand. The effective rate of household tax has fallen by about 1.5 per cent since 1980. More spectacular has been the cut in corporation taxation. At the same time, largely because of rising defence expenditure, public expenditure has also increased. Thus by the 1984 fiscal year the budget deficit had risen to 5 per cent of GNP. Therefore in some circumstances at least, Keynesian policies still appear to be effective. Unfortunately, this lesson seems to have been lost on Congress who have passed legislation to move the budget automatically to a balanced position by 1991. This is probably an overreaction to what in international terms is a relatively low budget deficit.

The reason unemployment fell so sharply in response to the Keynesian stimulus, when in other countries it has been much more sluggish, lies in the flexibility of the economic system. The US has far fewer legal, regulatory and financial restrictions on the hiring and firing of labour than most European countries. The practice of temporarily laying off workers in a downswing is more common and collective bargaining less important than in the UK. Because of this there is much greater real wage flexibility in the face of demand- and supply-side shocks. Of course such flexibility is not without its costs. The potential for exploitation of the workforce is also greater in the US than in the UK, and the case for more legal rights for employees and their organisations can be made. None the less, it must be recognised that this is a factor in the responsiveness of the system to changes in demand, and consequently the relatively low levels of unemployment.

The US system of bankruptcy is a further, although relatively unnoticed, factor in determining the speed with which the economy can respond to demand and supply-side changes. The new code introduced in 1978/79 places much more emphasis on the rescue of troubled firms than do the British and most other European systems. This allows troubled firms to reorganise and renegotiate contracts with workers and other firms. The essence of the reorganisation process is a plan for which the code gives the firm or its trustees exclusive right for 120 days to file and a further 180 days to gain acceptances. If agreement is not reached voluntarily then the courts can impose a settlement by use of the 'cramdown' procedure. The net result of this is that more of the productive capacity of bankrupt firms is likely to be retained than in the UK. Thus a recession, which results in a large number of bankruptcies, is not likely to be accompanied by such a sharp contraction in effective supply. The economy is therefore able to respond more readily to any expansion in demand.

It would be wrong, however, for this to lead to complacency amongst policy-makers. The probability is that unemployment will increase in the latter half of the 1980s. The investment boom is bound to decline somewhat, following the short-term stimulus given by corporate tax cuts, although this may be modified by falling interest rates. The misjudged move towards a balanced budget will also tend to reduce demand in the economy. Thus unemployment is likely to remain one of the major economic issues in the USA. Despite the US's commitment to a private enterprise economy, and the rewards this has reaped, there is still a need for a more active industrial policy to meet this problem. US administrations have in the recent past been willing to subsidise and even nationalise failing firms. But this has always been done on an *ad hoc* basis, in response to sudden crises, and always amid a great deal of controversy. It needs to be written into government policy, and provision also needs to be made to save small firms which play an important role in local communities. The bankruptcy system too can be improved. The position of unsecured creditors, often other firms, needs at a minimum to be made equal to that of secured and privileged creditors, in the distribution of an insolvent company's assets. This will make the banks more responsible in deciding who to lend to, and reduce the knock on effects of insolvencies.

The competitive problems posed by Japan and the emerging economies of the Far East pose a new threat to the US economy. Can the US continue to compete with Japan's more centralised approach to economic development, especially as the fruits of its commitment to the fifth generation of computers become evident in the 1990s? The US has been predominantly the major computer producer and it seems almost unthinkable that it could slip from this position. Yet the benefits of the Japanese approach could give them a considerable technical advantage which individual American firms will find hard to compete against. A co-ordinated approach to research in this field can avoid unnecessary duplication and yield economies of scale, the results from which even the largest of US firms might find difficult to match. Thus, it may be that a greater involvement in the co-ordination of advanced research will have to develop along the Japanese mould.

THE UNITED KINGDOM

The US economy is basically a strong one, although there must be some concern as to how it will develop in the future. The British economy, on the other hand, is in a parlous position. Economic decline is not a threat it is a reality. Social decay is not a possibility for the future it is here in the present. The reasons for the economic decline are numerous, and it should be remembered that this decline has been going on for decades, rather than years. But the perverse policies of the Thatcher government have turned a rather gentle decline into an avalanche. By pursuing a restrictive monetary policy interest rates were pushed up to record levels. This was largely responsible for the sharp decline in investment which followed. High interest rates together with North Sea oil pushed the pound up to levels at which British industry could not compete and large sections of it declined and some disappeared altogether. As we have seen in Chapter 3, this led to large numbers of liquidations amongst all firms in all industries and of all ages.

In the USA it is possible that this sequence of events would not have had such a dramatic impact on unemployment. But in the UK, labour markets are not as flexible and the insolvency legislation aims at merely securing the maximum dividend for creditors—and a limited class of creditors at that—rather than the rescue of troubled firms. The government has introduced legislation to deal with both of these problems. In the case of the labour market there may be some eventual improvement. However, the insolvency legislation will do little to improve the chances of a bankrupt company being saved. Clearly this needs to be changed. Further new legislation needs to be brought in to move the British system closer to the American one in this respect. The government should also take the opportunity of improving the position of unsecured creditors. As in the US, these are often other firms, and the losses they suffer through bad debts can also cause them to close. At the very least the unsecured creditors needs to be placed in the same position as preferential creditors (largely government bodies) and secured creditors (generally the banks).

The effect of reforming the institutional framework in this way will make the economy more resilient in the face of a recession. However, further steps need to be taken to move the economy out of the recession it is now in. Simply expanding demand will not be effective in reducing unemployment. The loss of capital is such that there are no longer sufficient firms of sufficient size to employ them, nor the factories and the offices for them to work in, or the machines for them to work with. Having so readily reduced the capital stock of the country it cannot be suddenly conjured back into existence. Thus coupled with a steady expansion of demand should go an expansion of supply. Training and retraining play an important role here, not just for skilled workers and scientists, but also for those in key administrative and management positions. Viable new firms need to be encouraged and a proper environment created to ensure they survive the hazardous initial years. Existing firms need to be encouraged to expand. In both cases a regime of low real interest rates, which have not been seen since 1979, needs to be followed together with cuts in corporate taxation. Care needs to be taken so that the expansion in demand matches at an industry level that in supply. Increased consumer demand, for example, needs to be matched by an increase in the productive capacity of the consumer goods' industries, otherwise the only result will be an increase in imports. Import controls may also have an important role to play in permitting a more rapid expansion than would otherwise be the case. But such controls need to be introduced in an internationally agreed manner, and there also needs to be prior agreement on when they are to be removed.

COMPUTER MODELLING OF THEORETICAL ECONOMIC SYSTEMS

The small-scale computer model presented in Chapter 4 represents one of the relatively few examples where computers have been used to analyse the dynamic properties of a theoretical economic system. It has traditionally been the case that such models have been analysed mathematically, with computers being restricted to the analysis of large-scale models of actual economies. But this methodology enforces simplifying assumptions which distort the real world and bias conclusions. It is simplest to assume functional continuity, which in the production function, for example, results in putty–putty models of capital, and perfect competition with continuously clearing markets. No one doubts that in such models there are few economic problems, the doubts concern whether this is an acceptable representation of real-world economies. Given the widespread use of computers to simulate theoretical models in other sciences, their relative lack of use in economics is something I find surprising. I would not argue that they should replace mathematical models. But surely they are a valuable additional tool for the theorist which can be used in the analysis of theoretical systems which are unsuited to conventional mathematical analysis.

The computer model of the economy which has been described in Chapter 5 is a much more ambitious affair altogether. It is based on individual agents, rather than aggregates, hence the term 'agent-based modelling', and as the world is nearly always in disequilibrium it, too, is primarily concerned with disequilibrium states rather than equilibrium ones. Although there are forces in the model moving it towards equilibrium and as with the real world it may even get quite close. It is in a sense the logical development of existing thought. To a large extent the model has been constructed on well-known micro-economic foundations. There have also been other attempts to explain macroeconomic phenomena from a microeconomic base in recent years, but none have been true microeconomic in the sense of capturing the results of individual's actions. They attempted to model the results of people's actions, but not the actions themselves. Simply to go down to industry and consumer group levels is still to be dealing with aggregates, and thus has more in common with macroeconomic analysis then microeconomics. One is still forced to approximate the overall result of individual agents' actions, rather than model those actions themselves. The version developed in chapters 5 and 6 is at the moment the prototype of a theoretical tool rather than a fully-fledged empirical one. It, or developments of it, can be used in a full economy-wide framework to analyse virtually any aspect of economics. In the field of general equilibrium/disequilibrium analysis, variations on it can be used to analyse the stability properties of non-tattonement or non-perfect competition economies. In the field of taxation and distribution one could analyse the long-term effects of income tax changes on equality and output or the effects of changing company taxation on investment. The intergenerational transmission of wealth, patterns of saving behaviour, the unemployment vacancies relationship, the impact of technical change are all better analysed within an economy-wide approach using an agent-based model. One could also use it in the wider area of the social sciences, for example building into it voting behaviour and analysing the electoral cycle.

Much of this work can be validly be done, with a theoretical model of the kind developed here which is meant to be representative of a modern economic system, rather than a representation of any one economy. In this it parallels the standard theoretical approach of setting up a model of a theoretical economy, to gain insights on how such an economy behaves and what impact different parameter values have on such an economy. But it should also be possible to build an agent-based applied general disequilibrium model of an actual economy. This would be an enormously ambitious undertaking. First, it would require a model with many more actors than have been used in this model. To model the US economy for example, would require us to model firms within the main industries, and consumer units in the principal ethnic/age/family size groups. Each industry would have its own production function, each region its own characteristics and each ethnic/age/family size group its own basic utility function. These would all have to be estimated or modelled. The number of firms would probably run into thousands and the number of consumers into tens or even hundreds of thousands. The first problem, may be one of computer power. But this is unlikely to be a binding constraint for long, if at all. Computers are likely to become increasingly more powerful and easily keep pace with the economist's demands upon them.

More daunting is the estimation of the hundreds of behavioural equations which would go to make such a model. This will undoubtedly take many man-hours to complete. But much of the data are available now, for example cross-section expenditure surveys can be used to estimate the standard utility functions for different consumer groups. In addition these can also provide information on the variance–covariance matrix of error terms which can be used in calling the random number generators to get a distribution of consumption expenditures within groups which also matches that in the economy. This availability of data is in stark contrast to the scenario which accompanied the *General Theory*. There were no national accounts data of the kind which are currently used to estimate aggregate relationships such as the consumption function, nor any ready access to large-memory computers. To this extent the job would be much easier than that facing early macro-model builders.

In other respects, however, the task is more difficult than that which they faced. Some of the relationships which have been included in this model and should also figure predominantly in any other model have not before been estimated. Indeed it is debatable if any serious consideration has ever been given to them. For example, the unit of labour in the production function is not based on men or man-hours, but on man-skill, the total amount of labour in terms of ability available to the firm. This is of crucial importance for policy purposes in evaluating the long-run effects of increased expenditure on schooling, for example, labour productivity and effective supply. But it requires us to have a measure either by industry or firm of the skill levels of different groups of workers. Concentrating economists' minds on these problems may eventually turn out to be one of the most important contributions of the model. For too long what cannot be conveniently estimated in aggregate form has been left out of models and then forgotten. There may be a temptation for this to happen in agent-based models. But I would hope that where information is not available, models, even those used for planning, will be simulated under a number of differing plausible assumptions.

Appendix 1: Program Listing

```
1  C   •••••••••••••••••••••••••••••••••••••••••••••••••••••••••••••••••••••••••••
2  C       A PROGRAM TO MODEL A MICRO MACRO ECONOMY.X DENOTES THE CONSUMER
3  C       THERE ARE INITIALLY ELEVEN HUNDRED. Y DENOTES THE FIRM, Z THE
4  C       INDUSTRY. THESE ARE:1=FOOD, 2=CARS, 3=SHOPS, 4=CONSUMER
5  C       DURABLES, 5=CLOTHES, 6=DRINK, 7=CONSTRUCTION, 8=COMPUTERS
6  C       9=MACHINES, 10=MINING, 11=AGRICULTURE, 12=INTERMEDIATE GOODS
7  C   •••••••••••••••••••••••••••••••••••••••••••••••••••••••••••••••••••••••••••
8  C
9          LOGICAL D20,D21,G05DZF
10         DOUBLE PRECISION P(55),R(81),P2(4),R2(10),P3(4),R3(10),P4(4),D25
11         DOUBLE PRECISION P5(10),P6(10),P7(10),R5(70),R6(200),R7(650)
12         DOUBLE PRECISION P8(10),P9(10),P10(10),R8(10),R9(10),R10(10)
13         DOUBLE PRECISION R12(200),R13(200),R14(200),R15(200),R16(200)
14         DOUBLE PRECISION R4(10),R11(50),P17(4),R17(12),G05DDF,P18(10)
15         DOUBLE PRECISION R18(14)
16         REAL X(1200,36),Y(65,60),Z(20,30),M(30),FLAG,FLAG1,UT(5),RPI(12)
17         REAL MRPEX,MRPSK,MRPUNS,MRPWC,INF,INF1,EXPT,IMPT,RPIL,BANK(20)
18         REAL INC,W(10),L1,L2,L3,L4,LL1,LL2,LL3,LL4,SALES,D14,D22,D27
19         REAL FLD,DUM1,FLD1,FLD2,FLD3,STOK1,WAGE(3,4),GRR(3,7),GDP
20         REAL QF(5),QC(5),QD(5),QW(5),U(5),SHARE1(60,100,2),GOV(20)
21         REAL Y12,HSE(1400,5),REGFA(3),SHARE(60,100,2),GOVW(3,8,3),EXW
22         REAL FACB(10,3,100),SON(400,5),HSEB(10,6,100),BUY,SELL,PROF,PROFR
23         REAL INCOME,WEALT2,FOOD,DRINK,CLOTHE,CARS,CONSD,COMPS,EXP2,SAVE
24         INTEGER I,SHOP,IFAIL,G05EYF,S2,S3,S4,S1,S5,S6,S7,D4,VACAN,D26
25         INTEGER D5,D6,D7,D8,D9,Y8,Y9,Y10,Y5,Y6,Y7,D10,D11,D12,DUMSE
26         INTEGER MACH(10),MN(10),AGR(10),INM(10),COMP(10),CONS(10),SH(10)
27         INTEGER EXEC(65,100),WC(65,100),SK(65,100),UNS(65,100),UN(5)
28         INTEGER UNE(200,3,4),VAC(65,3,4),REG(3,17),S(7,450),TP(40),TI,YP
29         INTEGER STOCK(65,65),STOCK1(65,20),SALE(65,60),AGE(16,120),TIME
30         INTEGER STOK,CLOCK,SHRH,DEM(5),FLA,FL,BLN,FB
31         INTEGER SCHL(3,4),BLANK(200),NCONA(3),GVAC(3,4)
32         INTEGER FIRB(20),NFAB(10),CONSAL(10,3,20),HSEBLN(100),DEMHS
33         INTEGER HSESAL(3,350),REGHS(3,10),NHSB(10,3),CONSN(10,3),NHSE(4)
34         CHARACTER*6 IND(20)
35 C
36 C          ••••••••••••••••••••••••••••••••••••••••••
37 C          •  VARIABLE & PARAMETER DEFINITIONS   •
38 C          ••••••••••••••••••••••••••••••••••••••••••
39 C
40 C       X1=TOTAL WEALTH, X2=WAGE RATE OR RESERVATION WAGE FOR UNEMPLOYED
41 C       X3=NUMBER OF HOUSE X4 AMOUNT LEFT ON MORTGAGE
42 C       X5=AGE, X6=INHERENT ABILITY
```

189

```
43 C    X7=FIRM, PENSIONER OR UNEMPLOYED, X8=REGION
44 C    X9=STAGE AT WHICH LEFT FULL TIME EDUCATION
45 C    X10=STATUS OF WORKER:5=MAN DIRECTOR, 1=EXECUTIVE, 2=WHITE COLLAR,
46 C    3=SKILLED, 4=UNSKILLED.
47 C    X12=AFTER TAX EARNINGS, X11=IDENTITY OF PARENT=0 IF DEAD
48 C    X13=IDENTITY OF FIRST SON=0 IF NONE, X14 2ND SON, X15 3RD SON
49 C    X16=NUMBER OF SONS AT SCHOOL
50 C    X17=QUALITY PREFERENCE FACTOR:0-1
51 C    X18=UTILITY PARAMETER FOR FOOD, X19=UTILITY PARAMETER FOR DRINK
52 C    X20=UTILITY PARAMETER FOR CLOTHES, X21=  "        "    CONS DURS
53 C    X22=  "      "     "      "   CARS, X23=   "         "   HOME COMPUTERS
54 C    X24=STOCK OF CONSUMER DUR'S, X25=STOCK OF CAR, X26=STOCK OF HOME COMP
55 C    X27=UTILITY,X28=UTILITY PARAMETER FOR WEALTH
56 C    X29=SKILL/EFFICIENCY OF WORKER, X30=PREFERENCE FOR BUYING
57 C    FOREIGN GOODS, THE HIGHER IT IS THE LESS LIKELY TO BUY
58 C    X31=SHAREHOLDER NUMBER, X32=VALUE OF SHARES, X33=BANK DEPOSITS
59 C    X34=INITIAL PRICE OF HOUSE USED IN CALCULATING MORTGAGE PAYMENTS
60 C    X35=NUMBER IN UNEMPLOYMENT MATRIX IF UNEMPLOYED.
61 C
62 C    AGE(I,J) THE JTH PERSON OF AGE I, AGED=NUMBER OVER 60
63 C    SON1=IDENTITY OF PARENT, SON2=INHERENT ABILITY, SON3=AGE
64 C    SON4=CURRENT ABILITY,SON5=CURRENT SCHOOL LEVEL.
65 C    DEM1=NUMBER OF SCHOOL CHILDREN/STUDENTS, DEM2=INTELLIGENCE LEVEL
66 C    REQUIRED TO GO TO UPPER SCHOOL, DEM3=INTELLIGENCE LEVEL REQUIRED
67 C    TO GO TO UNIVERSITY
68 C
69 C    Z1=PROPN OF AVERAGE WAGE INDUSTRY PAYS, Z2=CAPITAL INTENSITY INDEX
70 C    Z3=IO COEFFICIENT FOR MINING/STEEL/PLASTIC, Z4=DITTO AGRICULTURE
71 C    Z5=DITTO FOR INTERMEDIATE GOODS, Z6=QUALITY LEVEL FOR INDUSTRY
72 C    Z7=NUMBER OF FIRMS IN INDUSTRY, Z8=PRICE IN PREVIOUS PERIOD,
73 C    Z9=IMPORTED RAW MATERIALS PER UNIT OF OUTPUT
74 C    Z10=INDUSTRY OUTPUT, Z11=INDUSTRY PRICE, Z12=A IN PRODN FN.
75 C    Z13=COEFF ON EXEC, Z14=COEFF ON WHITE COLLAR, Z15=COEFF ON SKILLED
76 C    Z16=COEFF ON UNSKILLED, Z17=COEFF ON MAN DIR,Z18=COEFF ON CAPITAL,
77 C    Z19=COEFF ON COMPUTERS, Z20=COEFF ON BUILDINGS/PLANT
78 C    Z21=IMPORTS OF THIS GOOD, Z22=IMPORT PRICE, EXCLUDING EFFECT OF
79 C    EXCHANGE RATE, Z23=EXPORTS OF GOOD, Z24=INDUSTRY PROFIT/CAPITAL RATIO
80 C    Z25=WEIGHTING OF PRICE IN RPI
81 C
82 C    NCON=NUMBER OF CONSUMER UNITS,NWORK=NUMBER IN LABOUR FORCE
83 C    NFIRM=NUMBER OF FIRMS
84 C
85 C    MACRO VARIABLES: M1=RATE OF INTEREST, M2=AVERAGE WAGE FOR EXECUTIVE
86 C    M3=AVERAGE WAGE FOR WHITE COLLAR WORKER, M4=AVERAGE WAGE FOR SKILLED
87 C    WORKER, M5=AVERAGE WAGE FOR UNSKILLED WORKER
88 C    M6=LOWER RATE TAX BAND,M7=MIDDLE RATE TAX BAND,M8=UPPER RATE TAX BAND
89 C    M9=LOWER RATE OF TAX,M10=MIDDLE RATE OF TAX,M11=UPPER RATE OF TAX
90 C    M12=RATE OF DEATH DUTIES, M13=UNEM BEN PROPORTION OF AFTER TAX INCOME
91 C    OF FIRST THREE INCOME GROUPS, M14=NUMBER OF EXECUTIVES IN PRIVATE
92 C    IND,M15 DITTO WHITE COLLAR, M16 DITTO SKILLED, M17 DITTO UNSKILLED
93 C    M18=EXCHANGE RATE, M19=INDIRECT TAX RATE, M20=CORPORATE TAX RATE
94 C    M21-M24= AVERAGE ABILITY FOR EXEC, WC, SK AND UNS WORKERS
95 C    M26-29=NUMBERS OF WORKERS EMP AND UNEMP FOR EXEC,WC,SK and UNS
96 C    M30=REAL INTEREST RATE
97 C
98 C    GOV1 DIRECT TAXES GOV2 INDIRECT TAXES GOV3 PROFITS AND INTEREST TAXES
```

```
 99 C    GOV4=DEATH DUTIES, GOV5=TOTAL CAPITAL EXPENDITURE, GOV6=BORROWING
100 C    GOV7=NET TOTAL REVENUE, GOV8=CURRENT EXPENDITURE, GOV9=TOTAL WAGES
101 C    GOV10=TOTAL UNEMPLOYMENT BENEFITS, GOV11=TOTAL PENSIONS
102 C    REQUIREMENT, COV19=NATIONAL DEBT, GOV20= CURRENT PERIOD DEFICIT
103 C    GOVW(I,J,K):I'TH REGION, J=1,4,K=1 EDUCATION WORKERS, K=2 HEALTH
104 C    WORKERS, K=3 GENERAL SERVICE WORKERS, J=5,8 LAB FORCE SKILL TERMS
105 C    GRR(I,J) DESIRED WORKERS PER HEAD I'TH PUBLIC SECTOR INDUSTRY J'TH
106 C
107 C    BANK1=BANKS HOLDING OF TREASURY BILLS,BANK2=TOTAL DEPOSITS,
108 C    BANK3=TOTAL MONEY, BANK4=LOANS FOR HOUSE PURCHASE, BANK5=LOANS TO
109 C    INDUSTRY, BANK6=OTHER LOANS TO INDIVIDUALS, BANK7=CURRENT REVENUE
110 C    BANK8=CASH IN HANDS OF PUBLIC, BANK9=BANK PROFITS
111 C    BANK10=OLD HOUSE ACCOUNT, BANK11=HOUSE ACCOUNT
112 C    SHARE(I,J,K):K=1->PROPORTION OF I'TH FIRM J'TH SHAREHOLDER OWNS
113 C              K=2->IDENTITY OF OWNER
114 C    SHARE1(I,J,K)=(FOR K=1)->PROPORTION OF I'TH FIRM J'TH SHAREHOLDER
115 C    WISHES TO SELL, (FORK=2)->PROPORTION OF I'TH FIRM J'TH SHAREHOLDER
116 C    WISHES TO BUY
117 C
118 C    FURTHER MACRO TYPE VARIABLES: REG(J,I) J'TH REGION I=1-4 VACANCIES
119 C    FOR EXEC, WC,SK, UNSKILLED, I=5-8, UNEMPLOYED IN THESE CATEGORIES.
120 C    I=9-12 TOTAL WORKERS OF I'TH SKILL, I=13-16 AVERAGE WAGE I'TH SKILL
121 C    UNE(J,I,K) J'TH PERSON UNEMPLOYED IN I'TH REGION, K'TH SKILL
122 C    VAC(J,I,K) NUMBER OF J'TH FIRM'S VACANCIES IN I'TH REGION FOR K'TH
123 C    SKILL
124 C
125 C    HSESAL(I,J) IDENTITY OF J'TH HOUSE FOR SALE IN I'TH REGION
126 C    IDENTITY OF HOUSEOWNER IN BUYHS(I,K,J), I.E. K
127 C    HSE1=OWNER, HSE2=VALUE INDEX, HSE3=TYPE(1=BASIC,2=MEDIUM,3=LARGE)
128 C    HSE4=1 IF FOR SALE, 0 IF NOT,=2 IF UNSOLD TO BANK, HSE5=REGION
129 C    REGHS(J,I)=(I=1..3)PRICE OF NEW HOUSE OF TYPE I IN J'TH REGION,
130 C    REGHS(J,I)=(I=4)NUMBER OF HOUSES FOR SALE IN J'TH REGION
131 C    REGHS(J,I)=(I=5)NUMBER OF BUYERS IN J'TH REGION
132 C    REGHS(J,I)=(I=6)PREVIOUS PERIOD'S NUMBER OF HOUSES FOR SALE
133 C    REGHS(J,I)=(I=7-9) NUMBER OF NEW HOUSES OF TYPE I IN REGION J
134 C    REGHS(J,I)=(I=10)TOTAL NUMBER OF NEW HOUSES BANK HAS FOR SALE
135 C    REGFA(J)=PRICE OF NEW FACTORY IN J'TH REGION
136 C    FACB(I,1,J) J'TH FACTORY I'TH CONSTRUCTION FIRM STAGE OF COMPLETION
137 C    FACB(I,2,J) DITTO COST SO FAR INCURRED IN BUILDING IT
138 C    FACB(I,3,J) DITTO OWNER
139 C
140 C    W1,W2,W3= DEPRECIATION RATES FOR MACHINES, BUILDINGS AND COMPUTERS
141 C
142 C    S1=THOSE WHO WENT TO UNIVERSITY, S2=THOSE WITH IQ'S>140
143 C    S3=THOSE WHO WENT TO UNIVERSITY, ARE AGED 40+ AND HAVE IQ'S>140
144 C    S4=THOSE WHO WENT TO UNIVERSITY AND ARE AGED 40+.
145 C    S5=THOSE WHO LEFT SCHOOL AT 18
146 C    S6=THOSE WHO LEFT SCHOOL AT 16 & IQ>=120
147 C    S7=THOSE WHO LEFT SCHOOL AT 16 & IQ<120
148 C    SCHL(I,J) J=1 NUMBER IN JUNIOR SCHOOL, J=2 NUMBER IN HIGH SCHOOL
149 C    J=3 NUMBER IN UNIVERSITY, I=REGIONS
150 C
151 C    FOR THE FIRM: Y1=REGION OF THE FIRM, Y2=IDENTITY OF MANAGING DIRECTOR
152 C    AND FOR SMALL FIRMS OWNER
153 C    Y3=INDUSTRY OF THE FIRM, Y4=ADAPTIVE AVERAGE OF PAST OUTPUT
154 C    Y5=NUMBER OF EXECUTIVE EMPLOYEES+COUNT ON UNEMPLOYED FOR 'FIRM 54'
```

```
155 C      Y6=DITTO.... WHITE COLLAR.....
156 C      Y7=DITTO.... SKILLED.....
157 C      Y8=DITTO.... UNSKILLED.....
158 C      Y9=AGE OF FIRM, Y10= MACHINE CAPITAL STOCK OF FIRM
159 C      Y11=TOTAL REVENUE, Y12=IMPORTED RAW MATERIAL COST
160 C      Y13=TOTAL NUMBER OF FIRM'S WORKERS, Y14=TOTAL WAGES BILL OF FIRM
161 C      Y15=TOTAL POTENTIAL PRODUCTION OF FIRM, Y16=FIRM'S PRICE
162 C      Y17=FIRM'S MARK UP ON COSTS,
163 C      Y18=STOCK EXCHANGE VALUE OF FIRM =-1 IF NOT QUOTED, Y19=INDEX OF
164 C      FIRM'S QUALITY VARIES BETWEEN 0.5 AND 1.5, Y20=CURRENT EXPENDITURE
165 C      Y21=CASH RESERVES,Y22=1 IF EXTRA BUILDINGS BEING CONSTRUCTED ELSE 0
166 C      Y23=IDENTITY OF FIRM IN OWN INDUSTRY MATRIX, Y25-27, Y40=VOLUME SALES
167 C      Y24=DISTRIBUTED PROFITS,
168 C      Y28=WAGE TO EXEC,Y29=WAGE TO WHITE COLLAR, Y30=WAGE TO SKILLED
169 C      Y31=WAGE TO UNSKILLED, Y32=WAGE TO MAN DIRECTOR,
170 C      Y33=WAGE BARGAIN COUNTER,Y41=FIRM'S IMPORTS OF RAW MATERIALS
171 C      Y34=PROFITS, Y35=ACTUAL OUTPUT, Y36=BUILDING STOCK OF FIRM
172 C      Y37=COMPUTER STOCK, Y38=ADAPTIVE AVERAGE OF PROFIT CAPITAL RATIO
173 C      Y39=MONTH IN WHICH INVESTMENT PLANS ARE MADE,Y40=VOLUME OF SALES
174 C      Y41=BUILDINGS INPUT OUTPUT RATIO IN FIXED COEFFICIENT PRODN FUNCTION
175 C      Y42=FIRM'S CAPITAL EXPENDITURE, Y43=SUM OF ALL EXECUTIVE'S ABILITY
176 C      Y44=DITTO FOR WHITE COLLAR WORKERS, Y45=DITTO FOR SKILLED
177 C      Y46=DITTO FOR UNSKILLED, Y47=FIRM'S EXPORTS VOLUME TERMS
178 C      Y48=BANKLOAN, Y49=BANK DEPOSITS, Y50=RAW MATERIAL COSTS
179 C
180 C      MIN(I),AGR,MACH,INM,COMP,CONS=I'TH FIRM IN MINING, AGRICULTURE, ETC.
181 C
182 C      EXEC(I,J) JTH EXECUTIVE OF THE ITH FIRM, WC(I,J), SK(I,J),UNS(I,J)
183 C      UN(I) NUMBER OF UNEMPLOYED OF ITH SKILL
184 C      SIMILAR FOR WHITE COLLAR, SKILLED, AND UNSKILLED
185 C
186 C      SALE(J,I)=SALES OF ITH FIRM'S PRODUCT BY JTH SHOP IN VOLUME TERMS
187 C      STOCK(J,I)=JTH FIRM'S STOCK OF ITH FIRM'S PRODUCT
188 C      STOCK1(J,I)=JTH FIRM'S STOCK OF THE I'TH INDUSTRY'S PRODUCT
189 C
190 C      ************************************************************
191 C      *   INITIALISING VARIABLES & ASSIGNING PARAMETER VALUES   *
192 C      ************************************************************
193 C
194 C      INDUSTRY DATA
195        DATA(Z(J,2),J=1,13)/5,10,2,8,4,5,4,9,8,7,4,7,7/
196        DATA(Z(J,3),J=1,12)/0.0,.05,0.0,.04,0.0,0.0,0.0,.02,.04,0.0,0.0,
197       &0.3/
198        DATA(Z(J,4),J=1,12)/.05,0.0,0.1,0.0,0.0,.05,0.0,0.0,0.0,0.0,0.0,
199       &0.1/
200        DATA(Z(J,5),J=1,12)/.001,0.2,.04,0.1,.05,.001,.05,.1,.03,.1,.02,
201       &0.0/
202        DATA(Z(J,6),J=1,12)/12*1.0/
203        DATA(Z(J,9),J=1,12)/0.002,0.03,0.0,0.002,0.03,0.02,0.0,0.02,0.01
204       &,0.02,0.04,0.04/
205        DATA(Z(J,11),J=1,12)/1.0,3000,3.0,100,60,1.0,20000,1000,5000,500,
206       &500,500/
207        DATA(Z(J,12),J=1,13)/2000,0.50,1200,5,12,1200,0.8,7,4,100,200,
208       &100,75.0/
209        DATA(Z(J,13),J=1,13)/0.20,0.20,0.20,0.20,0.20,0.20,0.20,0.20,0.20,
210       &0.20,0.1,0.20,0.20/
```

```
211        DATA(Z(J,14),J=1,13)/.19,0.21,0.23,0.21,0.18,0.19,0.18,0.21,
212        &0.21,.19,0.17,0.21,0.24/
213        DATA(Z(J,15),J=1,13)/0.20,0.21,0.17,0.21,0.20,0.18,0.20,0.23,
214        &0.22,0.19,0.22,0.21,0.18/
215        DATA(Z(J,16),J=1,13)/0.20,0.15,0.22,0.15,0.20,0.20,0.21,0.14,
216        &0.19,0.19,0.17,0.17,0.18/
217        DATA(Z(J,17),J=1,13)/.09,.09,.09,.09,.09,.09,.09,.09,.09,.09,.09,
218        &.09,.09/
219        DATA(Z(J,18),J=1,13)/0.20,0.25,0.15,0.22,0.20,0.20,0.18,
220        &0.22,0.23,0.21,0.23,0.24,0.15/
221        DATA(Z(J,19),J=1,13)/0.08,0.13,0.08,0.13,0.04,0.06,0.02,
222        &0.16,0.13,0.08,0.08,0.11,0.15/
223        DATA(Z(J,20),J=1,13)/0.01,0.01,0.015,0.01,0.008,0.01,0.02,
224        &0.01,0.01,0.008,0.01,0.01,0.015/
225        DATA(Z(J,21),J=1,12)/12*0.0/
226        DATA(Z(J,23),J=1,12)/12*0.0/
227        DATA(Z(J,24),J=1,13)/12*0.4,0.0/
228        DO 1 J=1,12
229        Z(J,9)=0.1*Z(J,9)*Z(10,12)/Z(J,12)
230        Z(J,5)=0.1*Z(J,5)*Z(12,12)/Z(J,12)
231        Z(J,4)=0.1*Z(J,4)*Z(11,12)/Z(J,12)
232        Z(J,3)=0.1*Z(J,3)*Z(10,12)/Z(J,12)
233        Z(J,10)=0
234        Z(J,25)=0
235  1     Z(J,22)=Z(J,11)
236  C
237  C     SETTING INITIAL DATA FOR FIRM************************
238  C     REGION
239  C     REGION 3= PROSPEROUS CENTRAL ADMINISTRATIVE COMMERCIAL CAPITAL,
240  C     REGION 2=RELATIVELY PROSPEROUS INDUSTRIAL & AGRICULTURAL REGION,
241  C     REGION 1=AGEING INDUSTRIAL REGION, DEPRESSED.
242        DATA(Y(J,1),J=1,50)/1,1,1,3,1,3,2,1,2,3,2,2,2,3,2,3,2,1,3,1,3,2,3,
243        &1,1,1,2,3,2,2,2,1,1,1,2,1,3,3,3,1,2,1,3,1,3,2,3,2,2,1/
244  C
245  C     INDUSTRY
246        DATA(Y(J,3),J=1,65)/1,3,5,7,11,6,8,12,1,3,5,7,11,4,8,1,3,5,7,11,8,
247        &3,7,11,3,11,1,3,5,7,11,4,6,8,10,12,1,3,7,11,3,2,8,10,4,2,4,9,12,
248        &12,13,13,13,12*0.0/
249  C     AGE OF FIRM IN MONTHS
250        DATA(Y(J,9),J=1,50)/48,27,120,9,18,28,48,60,72,14,36,24,36,72,
251        &14,12,60,50,115,100,24,25,80,84,150,48,96,80,100,120,240,120,
252        &100,75,200,175,150,95,84,200,200,360,130,300,200,300,240,330,
253        &250,150/
254  C     QUALITY INDEX OF FIRM
255        DATA(Y(J,19),J=1,53)/1.3,.8,.8,1.5,1.0,.8,1.3,.7,1.4,1.4,1.4,0.9,
256        & 1.0,1.3,1.4,0.6,0.7,1.2,1.2,1.0,1.2,1.3,1.1,1.0,1.2,1.0,1.2,0.9,
257        & 1.0,1.0,1.0,1.4,1.0,0.8,0.8,1.3,0.8,1.0,1.0,1.0,1.2,1.0,1.1,
258        & 1.2,0.8,0.8,1.1,1.2,0.8,3*1.0/
259  C
260  C     MISCELLANEOUS INITIALISATION************************
261        DATA A1,A2,A3,A4,CARS,CLOTHE,DRINK,CONSD,FOOD/9*0.0/
262        DATA CLOCK,COMPS,CONSD,D1,D2,D4,D5,D6,EXPA,EXPA2,FLAG/11*0.0/
263        DATA I,I1,IFAIL,INC,INCG1,INCG2,INCG3,INCOME,VACAN/9*0/
264        DATA J1,J3,J6,J7,K,K1,K2,K3,K4,K5,L1,L2,L3,L4/14*0/
265        DATA LL1,LL2,LL3,LL4,M1,M2,M3,M4,M5,M6,MAKE1,MAKE2/12*0/
266        DATA MAKE3,MAKE5,MAKE6,MAKE7,MRPEX,MRPSK,MRPUNS,MRPWC/8*0/
```

```
267         DATA N7,NR2,NR3,NR4,NR5,NR6,NR7,RDUMMY,S1,S2,S3,S4,S5,S6,S7/15*0/
268         DATA SALES,SAVE,SHOP,TOTAL,TOTSKL,WEAL,WEALT2,WEALT/8*0/
269         DATA Y1,Y10,Y11,Y12,Y13,Y5,Y6,Y7,Y8,Y9/10*0/
270         DATA EXPT,IMPT,FB,DEMHS,BUY,SELL,FLAG1,FLAG/8*0/
271         DATA NCON,NWORK,NFIRM,TIME,BLN,TI/1100,0,50,1,0,1/
272         DATA(TP(J),J=1,33)/1,2,3,6,9,12,18,24,30,36,48,60,72,84,96,
273       &108,120,121,122,123,126,129,132,138,144,156,168,180,192,204,
274       &216,228,240/
275         DATA(M(J),J=1,30)/0.1,4*0.0,6000,16000,40000,0.3,0.4,0.6,
276       &0.0,0.8,4*0.0,1,0.2,0.4,5*1.0,4*0,0.05/
277         DATA(GOV(J),J=1,20)/20*0.0/
278         DATA(DEM(J),J=1,5)/5*0.0/
279         DATA(BANK(J),J=1,20)/2*0.0,100000,17*0.0/
280         DATA(NFAB(J),J=1,10)/10*0.0/
281         DATA(NCONA(I),I=1,3)/3*0/
282         DATA(GRR(1,I),I=1,4)/0.008,0.015,0.1,0.015/
283         DATA(GRR(2,I),I=1,4)/0.01,0.015,0.01,0.01/
284         DATA(GRR(3,I),I=1,4)/0.015,0.02,0.015,0.02/
285         DATA(W(J),J=1,3)/0.98,0.99,0.96/
286         DATA INF1,INF,SHARET/0.64,8.0,2700/
287         DATA SHARE/12000*0.0/
288         DATA SHARE1/12000*0.0/
289         DATA CONSN/30*0.0/
290         DATA NHSB/30*0.0/
291         DATA NHSE/4*0/
292         DATA REG/51*0/
293         DATA GVAC/12*0/
294         DATA WAGE/12*0.0/
295         DO 18 I=1,3
296         REGFA(I)=10*12*3*3
297         NFAB(I)=0.0
298         DO 878 J=1,10
299  878    REGHS(I,J)=0
300         DO 18 J=1,3
301         REGHS(I,J)=70*12*3*J
302         SCHL(I,J)=0
303         DO 18 K=1,8
304  18     GOVW(I,K,J)=0
305         DATA(RPI(J),J=1,12)/12*100./
306         DATA UNE/2400*0/
307         DATA VAC/780*0/
308         DATA(UN(J),J=1,5)/5*0/
309         DATA X/43200*0.0/
310         DO 3 J=1,65
311         DO 6 I=1,60
312         IF(I .LE. 20)STOCK1(J,I)=0
313         SALE(J,I)=0
314         IF(Y(I,3) .NE. 0)STOCK(J,I)=NINT(Z(NINT(Y(I,3)),12)+1)*12
315         Y(J,18)=0
316         IF(J .GE. 42 .AND. J .LE. 50)Y(J,18)=30000
317         IF(J .LT. 42)Y(J,18)=-1
318         IF(I .EQ. 1 .OR. I .EQ. 3 .OR. I .EQ. 9 .OR. I .EQ. 19
319       & .OR. I .EQ. 18)GO TO 6
320         Y(J,I)=0.0
321  6      CONTINUE
322         Y(J,28)=1500
```

```
323        IF(J .LE. 50)Y(J,47)=Z(NINT(Y(J,3)),12)/10
324        Y(J,29)=700
325        Y(J,30)=800
326        Y(J,31)=700
327 3      CONTINUE
328 C
329 C      SETTING INDUSTRY NAMES
330        IND(1)='  FOOD'
331        IND(2)='  CARS'
332        IND(3)='SERVIC'
333        IND(4)='CON DU'
334        IND(5)='CLOTHE'
335        IND(6)=' DRINK'
336        IND(7)='CONSTN'
337        IND(8)='COMPUT'
338        IND(9)='MACHNS'
339        IND(10)=' MINES'
340        IND(11)='  AGRI'
341        IND(12)='INT GD'
342 C
343 C      TO SET MONTHLY CLOCK INITIALLY 1 FOR ALL FIRMS AND WAGE BARGAIN
344 C      COUNTER INITIALLY = 11.
345        J1=0
346        DO 22 J=1,NFIRM+5
347        J1=J1+1
348        IF(J1 .GT. 12)J1=1
349        Y(J,39)=J1
350 22     Y(J,33)=J1
351 C      TO ALLOCATE PEOPLE'S AGE
352        DO 14 J=1,16
353 14     AGE(J,1)=1
354        DO 10 J=1,39
355 10     X(J,5)=AINT(192.0+(J/2.0))
356        DO 20 J=40,131
357 20     X(J,5)=AINT(212+((J-39)/1.95))
358        DO 30 J=132,670
359 30     X(J,5)=AINT(259+((J-131)/1.90))
360        DO 40 J=671,1100
361 40     X(J,5)=AINT(542+((J-670)/1.20))
362        DO 12 J=1,1100
363        K1=AINT(X(J,5)/60)-2
364        AGE(K1,1)=AGE(K1,1)+1
365        AGE(K1,AGE(K1,1))=J
366        J6=J6+1
367        IF(J6 .GT. 50)J6=0
368 12     CONTINUE
369 C
370 C      TO ALLOCATE FATHERS AND SONS TO EACH OTHER
371        CALL G05CBF(0)
372        J1=1
373        DO 156 J=1,NCON
374        IF(X(J,5) .GT. 600)GO TO 157
375        K1=NINT(X(J,5)/60)+2
376        K3=5+1.4*(AGE(K1,1)-1)
377 154    CALL G05EBF(1,AGE(K1,1),R11,K3,IFAIL)
378        K2=G05EYF(R11,K3)
```

```
379        IF(K2 .EQ. 1)GO TO 157
380        K=AGE(K1,K2)
381        GO TO 150
382 155    IF (X(K,13) .EQ. 0.0) GO TO 151
383        IF (X(K,14) .EQ. 0.0) GO TO 152
384        IF (X(K,15) .EQ. 0.0)GO TO 153
385        GO TO 154
386 151    X(K,13)=J
387        GO TO 150
388 152    X(K,14)=J
389        GO TO 150
390 153    X(K,15)=J
391 150    X(J,11)=K
392        GO TO 156
393 157    X(J,11)=0
394 156    CONTINUE
395 C
396 C      TO ALLOCATE RELATIVE SIZE OF FIRMS IN TERMS OF WORKERS, FOR USE
397 C      WITH G05EXF.
398 C      FIRST 26 FIRMS ARE SMALL, NEXT 15 MEDIUM, NEXT 9 LARGE, 'FIRMS' 51-3
399 C      ARE EDUCATION, HEALTH AND GENERAL GOVERNMENT.
400        P(1)=0
401        DO 60 J=1,26
402 60     P(J+1)=J*0.005*8/10
403        DO 61 J=27,41
404 61     P(J+1)=P(J-1)+0.02*8/10
405        DO 62 J=42,50
406 62     P(J+1)=P(J-1)+0.060000*10/7
407        P(52)=P(51)+0.05
408        P(53)=P(52)+0.05
409        P(54)=P(53)+0.2
410        P(55)=1.0
411 C
412 C      TO ALLOCATE EDUCATIONAL STATUS
413        P2(1)=0
414        P2(2)=0.5
415        P2(3)=0.85
416        P2(4)=1.0
417        CALL G05CBF(0)
418        IFAIL=0
419        CALL G05EXF(P2,4,0, .TRUE. ,R2,10,IFAIL)
420        S1=0
421        S4=0
422        DO 120 J=1,1100
423        X(J,9)=G05EYF(R2,10)
424        IF(X(J,9) .NE. 3.) GO TO 120
425        S(1,S1+1)=J
426        S1=S1+1
427        IF(X(J,5) .LT. 480.)GO TO 120
428        S(4,S4+1)=J
429        S4=S4+1
430 120    CONTINUE
431 C
432 C      TO ALLOCATE INHERENT ABILITIES
433        S2=0
434        S3=0
```

```
435        CALL G05CBF(0)
436        DO 50 J=1,1100
437        X(J,6)=G05DDF(6.0D+01,7.5D+01)
438        IF (X(J,6) .LT. 0) GO TO 52
439        X(J,6)=X(J,6)+50.0
440        IF(X(J,6) .LT. 140)GO TO 121
441        S(2,S2+1)=J
442        IF(X(J,9) .EQ. 3 .AND. X(J,5) .GT. 479) GO TO 53
443        GO TO 54
444 53     S(3,S3+1)=J
445        S3=S3+1
446 54     S2=S2+1
447        GO TO 50
448 52     X(J,6)=50.0
449 121    IF(X(J,9) .NE. 2)GO TO 122
450        S5=S5+1
451        S(5,S5)=J
452        GO TO 50
453 122    IF(X(J,6) .LT. 120)GO TO 123
454        S6=S6+1
455        S(6,S6)=J
456        GO TO 50
457 123    S7=S7+1
458        S(7,S7)=J
459 50     CONTINUE
460 C
461 C      TO ALLOCATE MANAGING DIRECTORS & 1 WORKER OF EACH TYPE TO FIRMS
462        CALL G05CBF(0)
463        IFAIL=0
464        NR3=5+1.4*S3
465        CALL G05EBF(0,S3,R5,NR3,IFAIL)
466        NR4=5+1.4*S4
467        CALL G05EBF(0,S4,R6,NR4,IFAIL)
468        NR2=5+1.4*S2
469        CALL G05EBF(0,S2,R7,NR2,IFAIL)
470        NR5=5+1.4*S5
471        CALL G05EBF(0,S5,R13,NR5,IFAIL)
472        NR6=5+1.4*S6
473        CALL G05EBF(0,S6,R14,NR6,IFAIL)
474        NR7=5+1.4*S7
475        CALL G05EBF(0,S7,R15,NR7,IFAIL)
476        NR8=5+1.4*S1
477        CALL G05EBF(0,S1,R16,NR8,IFAIL)
478        DO 130 J=1,53
479        IF(J .LT. 27)GO TO 131
480        IF(J .LT. 42)GO TO 132
481 134    D4=G05EYF(R5,NR3)
482        IF(D4 .EQ. 0)GO TO 134
483        K=S(3,D4)
484        IF (X(K,7) .NE. 0)GO TO 134
485        Y(J,2)=K
486        GO TO 133
487 131    D4=G05EYF(R7,NR2)
488        IF(D4 .EQ. 0)GO TO 131
489        K=S(2,D4)
490        IF (X(K,7) .NE. 0)GO TO 131
```

```
491        Y(J,2)=K
492        GO TO 133
493  132   D4=G05EYF(R6,NR4)
494        IF(D4 .EQ. 0)GO TO 132
495        K=S(4,D4)
496        IF (X(K,7) .NE. 0)GO TO 132
497        Y(J,2)=K
498  133   X(K,7)=J
499        IF(J .GT. 50)X(K,8)=3
500        IF(J .LE. 50)X(K,8)=Y(J,1)
501        X(K,10)=5
502  139   D4=G05EYF(R16,NR8)
503        IF(D4 .EQ. 0)GO TO 139
504        K=S(1,D4)
505        IF(X(K,7) .NE. 0)GO TO 139
506        CALL INAL(X,J,Y,K,1)
507  135   D4=G05EYF(R13,NR5)
508        IF(D4 .EQ. 0)GO TO 135
509        K=S(5,D4)
510        IF(X(K,7) .NE. 0)GO TO 135
511        CALL INAL(X,J,Y,K,2)
512  136   D4=G05EYF(R14,NR6)
513        IF(D4 .EQ. 0)GO TO 136
514        K=S(6,D4)
515        IF(X(K,7) .NE. 0)GO TO 136
516        CALL INAL(X,J,Y,K,3)
517  137   D4=G05EYF(R15,NR7)
518        IF(D4 .EQ. 0)GO TO 137
519        K=S(7,D4)
520        IF(X(K,7) .NE. 0)GO TO 137
521        CALL INAL(X,J,Y,K,4)
522  130   CONTINUE
523  C
524  C     ALLOCATING FIRMS TO WORKERS & THE STATE OF BEING UNEMPLOYED, INITIAL
525  C     PROBABILITY OF BEING UNEMPLOYED EQUALS 3.0 PER CENT, UNEMPLOYMENT IS
526  C     DISTRIBUTED BETWEEN REGIONS IN RATIO 0.5 0.3 &0.2. ALSO TO FIND
527  C     OUT HOW MANY WORKERS WORK FOR EACH FIRM AND HOW MANY ARE UNEMPLOYED
528        TOTSKL=0
529        CALL G05CBF(0)
530        IFAIL=0
531        P3(1)=0
532        P3(2)=0.5
533        P3(3)=0.8
534        P3(4)=1.0
535        P4(1)=0
536        P4(2)=0.3
537        P4(3)=0.6
538        P4(4)=1.0
539        CALL G05EXF(P,55,0, .TRUE. ,R,81,IFAIL)
540        CALL G05EXF(P3,4,0, .TRUE. ,R3,10,IFAIL)
541        CALL G05EXF(P4,4,0, .TRUE. ,R4,10,IFAIL)
542        DO 80 J=1,1100
543        RDUMMY=1
544        IF(X(J,7) .GT. 0)GO TO 85
545        IF(X(J,5) .GT. 720)X(J,7)=55
546        IF(X(J,5) .GT. 720)Y(55,13)=Y(55,13)+1
```

```
547        IF(X(J,5) .GT. 720)X(J,8)=G05EYF(R4,10)
548        IF(X(J,5) .GT. 720)GO TO 80
549        NWORK=NWORK+1
550        X(J,7)=G05EYF(R,81)
551        IF (X(J,7) .GT. 50)X(J,8)=G05EYF(R4,10)
552        IF(X(J,7) .EQ. 54)X(J,8)=G05EYF(R3,10)
553        IF(X(J,7) .LE. 50)X(J,8)=Y(NINT(X(J,7)),1)
554        IF (X(J,9) .EQ. 3) X(J,10)=1
555        IF (X(J,9) .EQ. 2) X(J,10)=2
556        IF (X(J,6) .GT. 120 .AND. X(J,10) .EQ. 0) X(J,10)=3
557        IF (X(J,10) .EQ. 0) X(J,10)=4
558 85     X(J,29)=X(J,6)*(X(J,9))/100
559        IF(X(J,29) .LT. 1)X(J,29)=1.0
560        TOTSKL=TOTSKL+X(J,29)
561        IF(X(J,7) .EQ. 54)GO TO 801
562        IF(X(J,10) .LE. 4.0)Y(NINT(X(J,7)),NINT(X(J,10))+4)=Y(NINT(X(
563       &J,7)),NINT(X(J,10))+4)+1
564        IF(X(J,10) .EQ. 1) EXEC(NINT(X(J,7)),NINT(Y(NINT(X(J,7)),5)))=J
565        IF(X(J,10) .EQ. 2) WC(NINT(X(J,7)),NINT(Y(NINT(X(J,7)),6)))=J
566        IF(X(J,10) .EQ. 3) SK(NINT(X(J,7)),NINT(Y(NINT(X(J,7)),7)))=J
567        IF(X(J,10) .EQ. 4) UNS(NINT(X(J,7)),NINT(Y(NINT(X(J,7)),8)))=J
568        Y(NINT(X(J,7)),42+NINT(X(J,10)))=Y(NINT(X(J,7)),42+NINT(X(J,10
569       &)))+X(J,29)
570        GO TO 80
571 801    UN(NINT(X(J,10)))=UN(NINT(X(J,10)))+1
572        REG(NINT(X(J,8)),NINT(X(J,10))+4)=REG(NINT(X(J,8)),NINT(X(J,10))+
573       &4)+1
574        UNE(REG(NINT(X(J,8)),NINT(X(J,10))+4),NINT(X(J,8)),NINT(X(J,10)))
575       &=J
576        Y(54,13)=Y(54,13)+1
577        X(J,35)=Y(54,13)
578 80     CONTINUE
579        CALL GOVEMP(GOVW,Y,EXEC,X,5)
580        CALL GOVEMP(GOVW,Y,WC,X,6)
581        CALL GOVEMP(GOVW,Y,SK,X,7)
582        CALL GOVEMP(GOVW,Y,UNS,X,8)
583 C
584 C      TO ALLOCATE SONS AND NUMBERS AT SCHOOL/UNIVERSITY
585        DO 1021 J=1,NCON
586        IF(X(J,5) .GT. 480)GO TO 1021
587        P17(1)=0.45
588        P17(2)=0.3+(ABS(360-X(J,5))/1000)+P17(1)
589        P17(3)=(X(J,5)/1800)+P17(2)
590        IF(P17(3) .GT. 1)P17(3)=1
591        P17(4)=1
592        CALL G05EXF(P17,4,0, .TRUE. , R17,12,IFAIL)
593        K6=G05EYF(R17,12)
594        K6=K6-X(J,13)-X(J,14)-X(J,15)
595        IF(K6 .LE. 0)GO TO 1021
596        DO 1020 I=1,K6
597        DEM(1)=DEM(1)+1
598        J1=DEM(1)
599        X(J,16)=X(J,16)+1
600        SON(J1,1)=J
601        SON(J1,2)=G05DDF(6.0D+01,7.5D+01)+50
602        IF(SON(J1,2) .LT. 50)SON(J1,2)=50
```

```
603        SON(J1,3)=INT(X(J,5)-192)/1.25
604        SON(J1,4)=0.01*SON(J1,2)*(1+SON(J1,3)/252)
605        IF(SON(J1,3) .LE. 195)SON(J1,5)=1
606        IF(SON(J1,3) .GT. 195 .AND. SON(J1,3) .LE. 219)SON(J1,5)=2
607        IF(SON(J1,3) .GT. 219)SON(J1,5)=3
608        SCHL(NINT(X(J,8)),NINT(SON(J1,5)))=SCHL(NINT(X(J,8)),NINT
609       &(SON(J1,5)))+1
610 1020   J1=J1+1
611 1021   CONTINUE
612 C
613 C      TO ALLOCATE WEALTH, INCOME + OTHER ENDOGENOUS CONSUMER VARIABLES
614        CALL G05CBF(0)
615        SHRH=0
616        DO 140,J=1,1100
617        IF(X(J,8) .EQ. 0 .AND. X(J,7) .NE. 55) X(J,8)=Y(NINT(X(J,7)),1)
618        X(J,17)=G05DDF(1.0D0,2.0D-01)
619        IF(X(J,17) .GT. 1.6)X(J,17)=1.6
620        IF(X(J,17) .LT. 0.4)X(J,17)=0.4
621        K4=G05DDF(1.0D+03,5.0D+02)
622        IF(K4 .LT. 0)K4=0
623        D1=0
624        IF(X(J,11) .LT. 1)D1=1
625        IF(X(J,7) .EQ. 55)GO TO 144
626        IF(X(J,10) .NE. 5)GO TO 146
627        X(J,2)=2000
628        X(J,12)=(((X(J,2)*12)-M(7))/12)*(1-M(10))+M(7)/12
629        GO TO 1401
630 146    IF(X(J,10) .NE. 1)GO TO 147
631        X(J,2)=1500
632        X(J,12)=(((X(J,2)*12)-M(7))/12)*(1-M(10))+M(7)/12
633        GO TO 1401
634 147    IF(X(J,10) .NE. 2)GO TO 148
635        X(J,2)=700
636        X(J,12)=(((X(J,2)*12)-M(6))/12)*(1-M(9))+M(6)/12
637        GO TO 1401
638 148    IF(X(J,10) .NE. 3)GO TO 149
639        X(J,2)=800
640        X(J,12)=(((X(J,2)*12)-M(6))/12)*(1-M(9))+M(6)/12
641        GO TO 1401
642 149    X(J,2)=600
643        X(J,12)=(((X(J,2)*12)-M(6))/12)*(1-M(9))+M(6)/12
644 1401   X(J,1)=0.01*D1*K4*X(J,9)*X(J,9)+(X(J,5)-180)*X(J,12)*0.0005
645        IF (X(J,7) .NE. 54) GO TO 1402
646        X(J,2)=400
647        X(J,12)=X(J,2)
648        X(J,1)=X(J,1)*0.9
649        GO TO 1402
650 144    X(J,2)=500
651        X(J,12)=X(J,2)
652        X(J,1)=0.01*D1*K4*X(J,9)*X(J,9)*(1.3-(X(J,5)-780)*0.0005)
653 1402   IF(X(J,10) .EQ. 1 .OR. X(J,1) .GT. 6000)
654       &SHRH=SHRH+1
655        X(J,1)=X(J,1)+X(J,12)
656        X(J,33)=X(J,1)
657        BANK(2)=BANK(2)+X(J,33)
658        WEALT=WEALT+X(J,1)
```

```
659 140   CONTINUE
660       IF(SHRH .GE. 100)SHRH=100
661 C
662 C     TO ALLOCATE CONSUMER'S INITIAL STOCKS OF CARS, CONS DURS & COMPUTERS
663 C     AND INITIAL SHARE ALLOCATION
664       FLA=0
665       DO 920 J=1,NCON
666       WEALT=0
667       IF(X(J,1) .LT. 6000 .AND. X(J,10) .NE. 1)GO TO 921
668       IF(FLA .GE. 100)GO TO 921
669       FLA=FLA+1
670       DO 922 I=42,50
671       SHARE(I,FLA,1)=1.0/SHRH
672       SHARE(I,FLA,2)=J
673       WEALT=WEALT+SHARE(I,FLA,1)*Y(I,18)
674 922   X(J,32)=SHARE(I,FLA,1)*Y(I,18)+X(J,32)
675       X(J,31)=FLA
676       X(J,1)=X(J,1)+WEALT
677 921   DO 920 I=24,26
678       X(J,I)=G05DDF(9.9D-01,4.0D-01)
679       X(J,I)=ABS(1.0-X(J,I))
680       IF(X(J,I) .GT. 1.0)X(J,I)=1.0
681       IF(I .EQ. 24)X(J,I)=X(J,I)*Z(4,6)
682       IF(I .EQ. 25)X(J,I)=X(J,I)*Z(2,6)
683       IF(I .EQ. 26)X(J,I)=X(J,I)*Z(8,6)
684 920   CONTINUE
685 C
686 C     INITIAL ALLOCATION ON HOUSING
687       CALL G05CBF(0)
688       DO 925 J=1,NCON
689       X(J,3)=J
690       HSE(J,1)=J
691       HSE(J,2)=G05DDF(0.0D0,1.0D-1)+0.6
692       IF(HSE(J,2) .LE. 0.1)HSE(J,2)=0.1
693       IF(HSE(J,2) .GE. 1.0)HSE(J,2)=1.0
694       IF(X(J,1) .LT. 20000)HSE(J,3)=1
695       IF(X(J,1) .GE. 20000 .AND. X(J,1) .LT. 50000)HSE(J,3)=2
696       IF(X(J,1) .GE. 50000)HSE(J,3)=3
697       HSE(J,4)=0
698       NHSE(NINT(X(J,8)))=NHSE(NINT(X(J,8)))+1
699       NHSE(4)=NHSE(4)+1
700       X(J,34)=X(J,2)*12*2.5
701       IF(X(J,5) .LE. 600)X(J,4)=X(J,34)*(600-X(J,5))/X(J,5)
702 925   HSE(J,5)=X(J,8)
703 C
704 C     TO ALLOCATE CONSUMER'S UTILITY FUNCTION COEFFICIENTS
705       DO 940 J=1,NCON
706       X(J,30)=G05DDF(0.0D0,2.0D-1)+0.65
707       IF(X(J,30) .LT. 0.1)X(J,30)=0.1
708       X(J,18)=G05DDF(0.0D0,1.0D-1)+0.50
709       X(J,19)=G05DDF(0.0D0,1.0D-1)+0.50
710       X(J,20)=G05DDF(0.0D0,1.0D-1)+0.2
711       X(J,21)=G05DDF(0.0D0,1.0D-1)+0.7
712       X(J,22)=G05DDF(0.0D0,2.0D-1)+0.75
713       X(J,23)=G05DDF(0.0D0,1.0D-1)+0.75
714       DO 941 I=18,23
```

```
715         IF(X(J,I) .GE. 0.90)X(J,I)=0.90
716         IF(X(J,I) .LE. 0.10)X(J,I)=0.10
717  941    CONTINUE
718         X(J,28)=G05DDF(0.0D0,1.0D-02)+0.7
719         IF(X(J,28) .GE. 0.90)X(J,28)=0.90
720  940    CONTINUE
721  C
722  C      TO ALLOCATE FIRM'S INITIAL STOCKS OF MACHINERY, PLANT & COMPUTERS
723         DO 930 J=1,53
724         Y(J,10)=(Z(NINT(Y(J,3)),2)*(Y(J,5)+Y(J,6)+Y(J,7)+Y(J,8)+1)/10)
725         Y(J,36)=(Z(NINT(Y(J,3)),2)*(Y(J,5)+Y(J,6)+Y(J,7)+Y(J,8)+1)/20)
726  930    Y(J,37)=(Z(NINT(Y(J,3)),2)*(Y(J,5)+Y(J,6)+Y(J,7)+Y(J,8)+1)/10)
727  C
728  C TO ALLOCATE POTENTIAL PRODUCTION AND PRICES CHARGED BY FIRMS.
729  C POTENTIAL PRICES = (TOTAL COSTS)*MARKUP/POTENTIAL PRODUCTION
730  C MARKUP ADJUSTS TO MARKET CONDITIONS IN A SEMI STICKY MANNER.
731  C ALSO TO ALLOCATE INITIAL OWN STOCKS
732         DO 160 I=1,NFIRM
733         Y(I,17)=(1.10+Y(I,19)/10)
734         Y(I,16)=(Y(I,5)*Y(I,28)+Y(I,6)*Y(I,29)+Y(I,7)*Y(I,30)+Y(I,8
735        &)*Y(I,31)+Y(I,32))*(2.0+(Z(NINT(Y(I,3)),2)/10))/OUTP(I,Y,Z,X,TIME)
736         Y(I,35)=OUTP(I,Y,Z,X,TIME)
737         Z(NINT(Y(I,3)),10)=Z(NINT(Y(I,3)),10)+Y(I,35)
738         Y(I,4)=Y(I,35)
739         Y(I,49)=Y(I,35)*Y(I,16)*10
740         IF(Y(I,3) .EQ. 7 .OR. Y(I,3) .GT. 9)Y(I,19)=1.0
741         STOCK(I,I)=Y(I,35)*4
742         DO 160 J=10,12
743  160    STOCK1(I,J)=Y(I,35)*Z(NINT(Y(I,3)),J-7)*2
744  C
745  C              ••••••••••••••••••••••••••••••••••••••••
746  C              •    SIMULATION PART OF THE PROGRAM    •
747  C              ••••••••••••••••••••••••••••••••••••••••
748  C
749  C      TO SET THE MONTHLY CLOCK
750  301    CLOCK=CLOCK+1
751         IF(CLOCK .GT. 12)CLOCK=1
752         YP=0
753         IF(TIME .EQ. TP(TI))THEN
754         TI=TI+1
755         YP=1
756         END IF
757         IF(YP .EQ. 1)PRINT *,' '
758         IF(YP .EQ. 1)PRINT *,'•••••••••••••••••••••••••••••••••••••••••••••'
759         IF(YP .EQ. 1)PRINT *,'PERIOD ',TIME
760  C
761  C      DEMOGRAPHIC FACTORS
762  C      GO TO 2001
763         IF(YP .EQ. 1)PRINT *,'NUMBER OF WORKERS',NWORK
764         IF(YP .EQ. 1)PRINT *,'NUMBER OF PEOPLE',NCON
765         TRAIN=OUTP(51,Y,Z,X,TIME)/DEM(1)
766         IF(YP .EQ. 1)PRINT *,'TRAIN',TRAIN
767         I=1
768  1054   D26=X(NINT(SON(I,1)),8)
769         SON(I,4)=(3-(3/(SON(I,4)*TRAIN)))
770         SON(I,3)=SON(I,3)+1
```

```
771        IF(SON(I,3) .LE. 192 .OR. CLOCK .NE. 9)GO TO 1052
772        IF(SON(I,5) .EQ. 1)GO TO 1053
773        IF(SON(I,3) .GT. 216 .AND. SON(I,5) .EQ. 2)GO TO 1053
774        IF(SON(I,3) .GT. 252 .AND. SON(I,5) .EQ. 3)GO TO 1056
775        GO TO 1052
776  1053  IF(SON(I,4) .LT. DEM(1+NINT(SON(I,5))))GO TO 1056
777        SCHL(D26,NINT(SON(I,5)))=SCHL(D26,NINT(SON(I,5)))-1
778        SON(I,5)=SON(I,5)+1
779        SCHL(D26,NINT(SON(I,5)))=SCHL(D26,NINT(SON(I,5)))+1
780        GO TO 1052
781  1056  IF(BLN .EQ. 0)NCON=NCON+1
782        IF(BLN .EQ. 0)FL=NCON
783        IF(BLN .GT. 0)FL=BLANK(BLN)
784        X(NINT(SON(I,1)),16)=X(NINT(SON(I,1)),16)-1
785        IF(X(NINT(SON(I,1)),13) .GT. 0)GO TO 95
786        X(NINT(SON(I,1)),13)=FL
787        GO TO 96
788  95    IF(X(NINT(SON(I,1)),14) .GT. 0)GO TO 97
789        X(NINT(SON(I,1)),14)=FL
790        GO TO 96
791  97    X(NINT(SON(I,1)),15)=FL
792  96    X(FL,9)=SON(I,5)
793        X(FL,5)=SON(I,3)
794        X(FL,10)=X(NINT(SON(I,1)),10)
795        IF(X(FL,10) .EQ. 5)X(FL,10)=1
796        X(FL,29)=SON(I,4)
797        X(FL,6)=SON(I,2)
798        X(FL,11)=SON(I,1)
799        X(FL,8)=X(NINT(SON(I,1)),8)
800        X(FL,2)=REG(NINT(X(FL,8)),NINT(X(FL,10))+12)*0.9
801        X(FL,1)=Y(54,28)
802        X(FL,12)=X(FL,1)
803        X(FL,33)=X(FL,1)
804        BANK(2)=BANK(2)+X(FL,1)
805        GOV(10)=GOV(10)+X(FL,1)
806        SCHL(D26,3)=SCHL(D26,3)-1
807        X(FL,17)=X(NINT(SON(I,1)),17)
808        X(FL,18)=X(NINT(SON(I,1)),18)
809        X(FL,19)=X(NINT(SON(I,1)),19)
810        X(FL,20)=X(NINT(SON(I,1)),20)
811        X(FL,21)=X(NINT(SON(I,1)),21)
812        X(FL,22)=X(NINT(SON(I,1)),22)
813        X(FL,23)=X(NINT(SON(I,1)),23)
814        X(FL,28)=X(NINT(SON(I,1)),28)
815        X(FL,30)=X(NINT(SON(I,1)),30)*0.8
.816       X(FL,7)=54
817        NWORK=NWORK+1
818        IF(BLN .GT. 0)BLN=BLN-1
819        IF(I .EQ. DEM(1))GO TO 1058
820        DO 1059 J=I,DEM(1)-1
821        DO 1059 K=1,5
822  1059  SON(J,K)=SON(J+1,K)
823  1058  DEM(1)=DEM(1)-1
824        REG(NINT(X(FL,8)),4+NINT(X(FL,10)))=REG(NINT(X(FL,8)),4+NINT(X(
825        &FL,10)))+1
826        UNE(REG(NINT(X(FL,8)),4+NINT(X(FL,10))),NINT(X(FL,8)),
```

```
827        &NINT(X(FL,10)))=FL
828        UN(NINT(X(J,10)))=UN(NINT(X(J,10)))+1
829        Y(54,13)=Y(54,13)+1
830        X(FL,35)=Y(54,13)
831 1052   I=I+1
832        IF(I .LE. DEM(1))GO TO 1054
833 C      BIRTH OF CHILDREN
834        D9=0
835        DO 1060 J=1,1200
836        IF(X(J,5) .EQ. 0)GO TO 1060
837        X(J,5)=X(J,5)+1
838        IF(X(J,5) .GT. 400 .OR. X(J,16)+X(J,13)+X(J,14)+X(J,15) .GT.
839        & 3 .OR. DEM(1) .GE. 400)GO TO 1061
840        D25=0.009
841        D20=G05DZF(D25)
842        IF(.NOT. D20)GO TO 1061
843        DEM(1)=DEM(1)+1
844        SON(DEM(1),1)=J
845        SON(DEM(1),2)=X(J,6)
846        SON(DEM(1),3)=1
847        SON(DEM(1),4)=SON(DEM(1),2)/100
848        SON(DEM(1),5)=1
849        X(J,16)=X(J,16)+1
850        SCHL(NINT(X(J,8)),1)=SCHL(NINT(X(J,8)),1)+1
851 C      RETIREMENT
852 1061   IF(X(J,5) .NE. 720 .OR. X(J,10) .EQ. 5)GO TO 1066
853        DUN=0
854        NWORK=NWORK-1
855        IF(X(J,7) .NE. 54)GO TO 1067
856        DUN=1
857        Y(54,13)=Y(54,13)-1
858        REG(NINT(X(J,8)),4+NINT(X(J,10)))=REG(NINT(X(J,8)),4+NINT(X
859        &(J,10)))-1
860        IF(J .EQ. UNE(1+REG(NINT(X(J,8)),4+NINT(X(J,10))),NINT(X(J,8)),
861        &NINT(X(J,10))))GO TO 1065
862        FL=0
863        DO 1069 I=1,REG(NINT(X(J,8)),4+NINT(X(J,10)))
864        IF(UNE(I,NINT(X(J,8)),NINT(X(J,10))) .NE. J)GO TO 1119
865        FL=1
866 1119   IF(FL .EQ. 0)GO TO 1069
867        UNE(I,NINT(X(J,8)),NINT(X(J,10)))=UNE(I+1,NINT(X(J,8)),NINT(X(
868        &J,10)))
869 1069   CONTINUE
870 1065   UNE(1+REG(NINT(X(J,8)),4+NINT(X(J,10))),NINT(X(J,8)),
871        &NINT(X(J,10)))=0
872 1067   X(J,7)=55
873        IF(DUN .EQ. 1)GO TO 1066
874        IF(X(J,10) .EQ. 1)CALL LOSS(EXEC,X,Y,J)
875        IF(X(J,10) .EQ. 2)CALL LOSS(WC,X,Y,J)
876        IF(X(J,10) .EQ. 3)CALL LOSS(SK,X,Y,J)
877        IF(X(J,10) .EQ. 4)CALL LOSS(UNS,X,Y,J)
878        IF(X(J,10) .NE. 5)GO TO 1066
879        Y(J,2)=EXEC(J,1)
880        Y(J,5)=Y(J,5)-1
881        IF(Y(J,5) .EQ. 0)GO TO 1066
882        DO 99 J2 =1,NINT(Y(J,5))
```

```
883 99      EXEC(J,J2)=EXEC(J,J2+1)
884 C       DEATH
885 1066    IF(X(J,5) .LT. 640)GO TO 1060
886         D25=0.00002*(X(J,5)-639)
887         D20=G05DZF(D25)
888         IF(.NOT. D20)GO TO 1060
889         NCON=NCON-1
890         BLN=BLN+1
891         BLANK(BLN)=J
892         SNS=0
893         DO 1064 I=1,3
894         IF(X(J,12+I) .GT. 0)SNS=SNS+1
895 1064    CONTINUE
896         IF(HSE(NINT(X(J,3)),2) .GT. 0.2)GO TO 1115
897         DEMHS=DEMHS+1
898         HSEBLN(DEMHS)=X(J,3)
899         NHSE(4)=NHSE(4)-1
900         GO TO 1116
901 1115    D26=NINT(X(J,8))
902         CALL HOUSE(D26,0.0,REGHS,HSESAL,X,Y,BANK,HSE,J,1)
903 1116    IF(SNS .GT. 0)GO TO 1042
904         J1=J1+1
905 1043    IF(J1 .GT. NCON)J1=1
906         IF(X(J1,5) .GT. 0 .AND. X(J1,8) .EQ. X(J,8) .AND. X(J1,10)
907       & .NE. 5)GO TO 1044
908         J1=J1+1
909         GO TO 1043
910 1044    X(J1,1)=X(J1,1)+X(J,1)
911         X(J1,33)=X(J1,33)+X(J,33)
912         INSH=J1
913         GO TO 1045
914 1042    INSH=X(J,13)
915         DO 1063 I=1,SNS
916         X(NINT(X(J,I+12)),1)=X(NINT(X(J,I+12)),1)+X(J,1)/SNS
917         X(NINT(X(J,I+12)),11)=0
918 1063    X(NINT(X(J,I+12)),33)=X(NINT(X(J,I+12)),33)+X(J,33)/SNS
919 1045    IF(X(J,10) .NE. 5)GO TO 1121
920         IF(X(INSH,10) .EQ. 4)CALL LOSS(UNS,X,Y,INSH)
921         IF(X(INSH,10) .EQ. 3)CALL LOSS(SK,X,Y,INSH)
922         IF(X(INSH,10) .EQ. 2)CALL LOSS(WC,X,Y,INSH)
923         IF(X(INSH,10) .EQ. 1)CALL LOSS(EXEC,X,Y,INSH)
924         X(INSH,7)=X(J,7)
925         Y(NINT(X(J,7)),2)=INSH
926         X(INSH,10)=5
927         X(INSH,2)=Y(NINT(X(INSH,7)),32)
928 1121    IF(X(J,31) .EQ. 0)GO TO 1057
929         IF(X(INSH,31) .EQ. 0)X(INSH,31)=X(J,31)
930 1076    DO 1077 I=1,65
931         IF(Y(I,18) .EQ. -1 .OR. Y(I,3) .EQ. 0 .OR. Y(I,3) .EQ. 13)
932       &GO TO 1077
933         IF(X(INSH,31) .NE. X(J,31))GO TO 1078
934         SHARE(I,NINT(X(INSH,31)),1)=SHARE(I,NINT(X(J,31)),1)
935         GO TO 1089
936 1078    SHARE(I,NINT(X(INSH,31)),1)=SHARE(I,NINT(X(J,31)),1)+
937       &SHARE(I,NINT(X(INSH,31)),1)
938 1089    SHARE(I,NINT(X(INSH,31)),2)=INSH
```

```
939 1077    CONTINUE
940         IF(X(J,31) .EQ. X(INSH,31))GO TO 1057
941         DO 1079 I=1,65
942         IF(Y(I,18) .EQ. -1 .OR. Y(I,3) .EQ. 0 .OR. Y(I,3) .EQ. 13)
943         &GO TO 1079
944         IF(X(J,31) .EQ. SHRH)GO TO 1097
945         DO 1098 K1=NINT(X(J,31)),SHRH-1
946         X(NINT(SHARE(I,K1+1,2)),31)=K1
947         SHARE(I,K1,1)=SHARE(I,K1+1,1)
948 1098    SHARE(I,K1,2)=SHARE(I,K1+1,2)
949 1097    SHARE(I,SHRH,1)=0
950         SHARE(I,SHRH,2)=0
951 1079    CONTINUE
952         SHRH=SHRH-1
953 1057    IF(X(J,7) .EQ. 55)Y(55,13)=Y(55,13)-1
954         IF(X(J,7) .EQ. 55)GO TO 1068
955         NWORK=NWORK-1
956         IF(X(J,7) .NE. 54)GO TO 1046
957         Y(54,13)=Y(54,13)-1
958         REG(NINT(X(J,8)),4+NINT(X(J,10)))=REG(NINT(X(J,8)),4+NINT
959         &(X(J,10)))-1
960         IF(J .EQ. UNE(1+REG(NINT(X(J,8)),4+NINT(X(J,10))),NINT(X(J,8
961         &)),NINT(X(J,10))))GO TO 1047
962         FL=0
963         DO 1049 I=1,REG(NINT(X(J,8)),NINT(X(J,10))+4)
964         IF(UNE(I,NINT(X(J,8)),NINT(X(J,10))) .EQ. J)FL=FL+1
965         IF(FL .NE. 0)UNE(I,NINT(X(J,8)),NINT(X(J,10)))=UNE(I+1,
966         &NINT(X(J,8)),NINT(X(J,10)))
967 1049    CONTINUE
968 1047    UNE(1+REG(NINT(X(J,8)),NINT(X(J,10))+4),NINT(X(J,8)),
969         &NINT(X(J,10)))=0
970         GO TO 1068
971 1046    IF(X(J,10) .EQ. 1)CALL LOSS(EXEC,X,Y,J)
972         IF(X(J,10) .EQ. 2)CALL LOSS(WC,X,Y,J)
973         IF(X(J,10) .EQ. 3)CALL LOSS(SK,X,Y,J)
974         IF(X(J,10) .EQ. 4)CALL LOSS(UNS,X,Y,J)
975 1068    DO 1062 I=1,35
976 1062    X(J,I)=0
977 1060    CONTINUE
978 C
979 C       DETIORATION OF HOUSE
980 2001    DO 306 J=1,REGHS(1,4)+REGHS(2,4)+REGHS(3,4)
981 306     HSE(J,2)=HSE(J,2)*0.99
982 C
983 C THE CONSUMER'S PROBLEM
984         DUM=1
985         Z(3,7)=0
986         DO 308 J=1,65
987         IF(Y(J,3) .NE. 3)GO TO 308
988         Z(3,7)=Z(3,7)+1
989         SH(NINT(Z(3,7)))=J
990         Y(J,23)=Z(3,7)
991         Z(3,10)=Y(J,35)+Z(3,10)
992 308     CONTINUE
993         P18(1)=0.0
994         DO 307 I=1,Z(3,7)
```

```
995          P18(I+1)=Y(SH(I),35)/Z(3,10)+P18(I)
996  307     .IF(P18(I+1) .GT. 1.0)P18(I+1)=1.0
997          P18(NINT(Z(3,7))+1)=1.0
998          CALL G05EXF(P18,NINT(Z(3,7))+1.0, .TRUE. ,R18,NINT(Z(3,7))+4,
999          &IFAIL)
1000         WEALT2=0.0
1001         FOOD=0.0
1002         DRINK=0.0
1003         CLOTHE=0.0
1004         CARS=0.0
1005         CONSD=0.0
1006         COMPS=0.0
1007         EXP2=0.0
1008         SAVE=0.0
1009         RPIL=RPI(CLOCK)
1010         IF(TIME .GT. 1)RPI(CLOCK)=0
1011         DO 300 J=1,1200
1012 C       DECISION TO MOVE HOUSE
1013         IF(X(J,5) .EQ. 0)GO TO 300
1014         NCONA(NINT(X(J,8)))=NCONA(NINT(X(J,8)))+1
1015 C        IF(X(J,12) .EQ. 0)PRINT *,X(J,2),X(J,7),X(J,10),Y(NINT
1016 C       &(X(J,7)),NINT(X(J,10))+27),J
1017         D10=X(J,8)
1018         D11=X(J,3)
1019         MOREP=0
1020         OLD=0
1021         IF(X(J,3) .EQ. 0)GO TO 1003
1022         IF(X(J,4) .EQ. 0)GO TO 1075
1023         OLD=X(J,4)
1024         MOREP=X(J,34)*(M(1)/12)+X(J,12)/20
1025         IF(MOREP .GT. X(J,1)*0.8)MOREP=X(J,1)*0.8
1026         X(J,4)=X(J,4)*(1+(M(1)/12))-MOREP
1027         IF(X(J,4) .GT. 0)GO TO 1075
1028         MOREP=MOREP+X(J,4)
1029         X(J,4)=0
1030 1075    BANK(4)=BANK(4)-OLD+X(J,4)
1031         BANK(7)=BANK(7)+MOREP
1032         X(J,1)=X(J,1)-MOREP
1033         X(J,33)=X(J,33)-MOREP
1034         D14=0.2+M(30)
1035         IF(D14 .LT. 0.2)D14=0.2
1036         IF(D14 .GT. 0.8)D14=0.8
1037         IF(X(J,2)*12 .LT. D14*HSE(D11,2)*REGHS(D10,NINT
1038         &(HSE(D11,3))) .OR. HSE(D11,2)*REGHS(D10,NINT(HSE(D11,3))) .GT.
1039         & 0.95*REGHS(D10,3))GO TO 1071
1040         PR=(X(J,2)*12)/D14
1041         IF(REGHS(D10,4) .GT. 0)CALL HOUSE(D10,PR,REGHS,HSESAL,X,Y,BANK,
1042         &HSE,J,0)
1043 1071    INC=X(J,12)-MOREP
1044 C       NEWLY EMPLOYED YOUNG PEOPLE ENTER HOUSING MARKET
1045 C       AS SOON AS THEY GET A JOB
1046 1003    IF(X(J,3) .GT. 0 .OR. X(J,7) .EQ. 54)GO TO 361
1047         PR=(X(J,2)*12)/(0.2+M(30))
1048         IF(REGHS(D10,4) .GT. 0)CALL HOUSE(D10,PR,REGHS,HSESAL,X,Y,BANK,
1049         &HSE,J,0)
1050 C DEPRECIATION EQUATIONS, NEED TO INITIALISE THESE, IF=0 THEN DOES NOT
```

```
1051 C POSSESS THE GOODS.
1052 361    FLAG1=100000
1053        DO 360 I=1,3
1054        X(J,23+I)=X(J,23+I)*0.950
1055        IF(X(J,23+I) .LE. 0.3)X(J,23+I)=0.0
1056        UT(I)=0.0
1057        IF(X(J,I+23) .NE. 0.)UT(I)=X(J,I+23)**X(J,I+20)
1058 360    CONTINUE
1059 C CHOICE OF SHOP
1060 362    SHOP=G05EYF(R18,Z(3,7)+4)
1061        IF(Z(3,7) .EQ. 1)SHOP=1
1062        IF(Y(SHOP,1) .NE. X(J,8))GO TO 362
1063 C CALCULATE UTILITY FUNCTIONS: BUYS CAR, CON DUR, COMPUTER, NOTHING
1064        DO 335 J1=1,5
1065 335    U(J1)=0.0
1066        CALL CHOICE(1,MAKE5,Y,X,M,10000.0,SHOP,J,DUM,WEAL1)
1067        CALL CHOICE(5,MAKE6,Y,X,M,10000.0,SHOP,J,DUM,WEAL1)
1068        CALL CHOICE(6,MAKE7,Y,X,M,10000.0,SHOP,J,DUM,WEAL1)
1069        QF(5)=((Y(MAKE5,16)*(1+M(19))*Y(SHOP,17))/X(J,18))**(1/(X(J,1
1070        &8)-1))
1071        QC(5)=(((Y(MAKE6,16)*(1+M(19))*Y(SHOP,17))/X(J,20))**(1/(X(J,20
1072        &)-1)))*15
1073        QD(5)=((Y(MAKE7,16)*(1+M(19))*Y(SHOP,17))/X(J,19))**(1/(X(J,19
1074        &)-1))
1075        QW(5)=(1/X(J,28))**(1/(X(J,28)-1))*(1+X(J,36)*10)
1076        EXPA=QF(5)+QC(5)+QD(5)+QW(5)
1077        WEAL=X(J,1)
1078        CALL SPEND(X,QF,QC,QD,QW,WEAL,EXPA,4,J)
1079 C CHOICE OF A CAR
1080        CALL CHOICE(2,MAKE1,Y,X,M,QW(4),SHOP,J,DUM,WEAL1)
1081        IF(WEAL1 .LT. 0.0)GO TO 336
1082        QW(1)=WEAL1
1083        U(1)=WEAL1**X(J,28)+599*(Z(2,6)*Y(MAKE1,19))**X(J,22)
1084        &+299*UT(1)+309*UT(3)
1085 C CHOICE OF A CONSUMER DURABLE
1086 336    CALL CHOICE(4,MAKE2,Y,X,M,QW(4),SHOP,J,DUM,WEAL1)
1087        IF(WEAL1 .LT. 0.0)GO TO 337
1088        QW(2)=WEAL1
1089        U(2)=WEAL1**X(J,28)+299*(Z(4,6)*Y(MAKE2,19))**X(J,21)+599*
1090        &UT(2)+309*UT(3)
1091 C CHOICE OF A COMPUTER
1092 337    CALL CHOICE(8,MAKE3,Y,X,M,QW(4),SHOP,J,DUM,WEAL1)
1093        IF(WEAL1 .LT. 0.0)GO TO 338
1094        QW(3)=WEAL1
1095        U(3)=WEAL1**X(J,28)+309*(Z(8,6)*Y(MAKE3,19))**X(J,23)
1096        &+299*UT(1)+599*UT(2)
1097 C UTILITY IF BUYS NOTHING
1098 338    IF(WEAL .LT. 0)PRINT *,'HI WEAL',J,X(J,1),X(J,12),X(J,7),X(J,10)
1099        &,Y(NINT(X(J,7)),NINT(X(J,10))+26)
1100        IF(QF(4) .LE. 0.0)PRINT *, QF(4),J,WEAL,EXPA
1101        IF(QC(4) .LE. 0.0)PRINT *,'QC',QC(4),J,X(J,5),X(J,1),X(J,12)
1102        IF(QD(4) .LE. 0.0)PRINT *,'QD',QD(4),J
1103        IF(QW(4) .LE. 0.0)PRINT *, 'QW',QW(4),J
1104        U(4)=QW(4)**X(J,28)+599*UT(1)+299*UT(2)+309*UT(3)
1105 C U(1)=UTILITY IF BUYS A CAR, U(2)=UTILITY IF BUYS A CONS DUR
1106 C U(3)=UTILITY IF BUYS A COMPUTER, U4=UTILITY IF BUYS NOTHING
```

```
1107        IF(U(1) .GE. U(2) .AND. U(1) .GE. U(3) .AND. U(1) .GE. U(4))
1108        &THEN
1109        D25=AMIN1(0.05,((M(18)*Z(8,11)/Z(8,22))/((X(J,30)+1)*3.0)))
1110        IF(D25 .GT. 0.5)D25=0.5
1111        D20=G05DZF(D25)
1112        CALL CHSP(2,J,X,M,Z,QW,1,MAKE1,SHOP,Y,CARS,RPI,CLOCK,N7,SALE
1113        &,STOCK,TIME,25,D20)
1114        ELSE IF(U(2) .GE. U(3) .AND. U(2) .GE. U(4))THEN
1115        D25=AMIN1(0.05,((M(18)*Z(8,11)/Z(8,22))/((X(J,30)+1)*3.0)))
1116        IF(D25 ..GT. 0.5)D25=0.5
1117        D20=G05DZF(D25)
1118        CALL CHSP(4,J,X,M,Z,QW,2,
1119        &MAKE2,SHOP,Y,CONSD,RPI,CLOCK,N7,SALE,STOCK,TIME,24,D20)
1120        ELSE IF(U(3) .GE. U(4))THEN
1121        D25=AMIN1(0.05,((M(18)*Z(8,11)/Z(8,22))/((X(J,30)+1)*3.0)))
1122        IF(D25 .GT. 0.5)D25=0.5
1123        D20=G05DZF(D25)
1124        CALL CHSP(8,J,X,M,Z,QW,3,MAKE3,SHOP,Y,COMPS,
1125        &RPI,CLOCK,N7,SALE,STOCK,TIME,26,D20)
1126  326   ELSE
1127        N7=4
1128        END IF
1129  310   EXPA=QF(4)+QC(4)+QD(4)
1130        X(J,33)=X(J,33)-X(J,1)+QW(N7)
1131        OLON=0
1132        IF(X(J,33) .LT. 0)OLON=-X(J,33)
1133        IF(X(J,33) .LT. 0)BANK(6)=BANK(6)+(-X(J,33)-OLON)
1134        X(J,1)=QW(N7)
1135        FOOD=FOOD+QF(4)
1136        CLOTHE=CLOTHE+QC(4)
1137        DRINK=DRINK+QD(4)
1138        INCOME=INCOME+X(J,12)
1139        WEALT2=WEALT2+X(J,1)
1140        Y(SHOP,11)=Y(SHOP,11)+EXPA/(1+M(19))
1141        CALL SHSL(SHOP,MAKE5,SALE,QF,4,Y,M,STOCK,IMPT)
1142        CALL SHSL(SHOP,MAKE6,SALE,QC,4,Y,M,STOCK,IMPT)
1143        CALL SHSL(SHOP,MAKE7,SALE,QD,4,Y,M,STOCK,IMPT)
1144  300   CONTINUE
1145        CARS=CARS*(1+M(19))
1146        CONSD=CONSD*(1+M(19))
1147        COMPS=COMPS*(1+M(19))
1148        EXP2=CLOTHE+DRINK+FOOD+CARS+CONSD+COMPS
1149        GOV(2)=EXP2*(1-(1/(1+M(19))))
1150        IF(TIME .EQ. 1)THEN
1151        Z(1,25)=FOOD/EXP2
1152        Z(2,25)=CARS/EXP2
1153        Z(4,25)=CONSD/EXP2
1154        Z(5,25)=CLOTHE/EXP2
1155        Z(6,25)=DRINK/EXP2
1156        Z(8,25)=COMPS/EXP2
1157        ELSE
1158        DO 374 J=1,8
1159  374   RPI(CLOCK)=RPI(CLOCK)+Z(J,25)*Z(J,11)
1160        END IF
1161        IF(TIME .GE. 36)INF=((RPI(CLOCK)-RPIL)/RPIL)*100
1162        IF(TIME .GE. 36)INF1=INF
```

```
1163      IF(YP .EQ. 1)PRINT *,'RETAIL PRICE INDEX',RPI(CLOCK)
1164      IF(YP .EQ. 1)PRINT *,'ANNUAL INFLATION RATE',INF
1165      IF(YP .EQ. 1)PRINT *,'THE CONSUMER ****'
1166      IF(YP .EQ. 1)PRINT *,'TOTAL INCOME  ',INCOME
1167      IF(YP .EQ. 1)PRINT *,'TOTALWEALTH  ',WEALT2
1168      IF(YP .EQ. 1)PRINT *,'TOTAL FOOD  ',FOOD
1169      IF(YP .EQ. 1)PRINT *,'TOTAL DRINK  ',DRINK
1170      IF(YP .EQ. 1)PRINT *,'TOTAL CLOTHES  ',CLOTHE
1171      IF(YP .EQ. 1)PRINT *,'TOTAL CARS  ',CARS
1172      IF(YP .EQ. 1)PRINT *, 'TOTAL CONS DUR  ',CONSD
1173      IF(YP .EQ. 1)PRINT *,'TOTAL COMPS  ',COMPS
1174      SAVE=1-(EXP2/INCOME)
1175      IF(YP .EQ. 1)PRINT *,'TOTAL EXPENDITURE  ',EXP2
1176      IF(YP .EQ. 1)PRINT *,'SAVING RATIO  ',SAVE
1177      IF(YP .EQ. 1)PRINT *,'INDIRECT TAX REVENUE',GOV(2)
1178      INCOME=0
1179 C
1180 C    BANK LOANS, BANKRUPTCY DECISION - ALL FIRMS
1181      Y(54,42)=0
1182      STOK=0
1183      PROF=0
1184      DO 717 J=1,65
1185      IF(Y(J,3) .EQ. 0 .OR. Y(J,3) .EQ. 13)GO TO 717
1186 C    PROFITS
1187      Y(J,34)=Y(J,11)-(Y(J,5)*Y(J,28)+Y(J,6)*Y(J,29)+Y(J,7)*Y(J,30)
1188     &+Y(J,50)+Y(J,8)*Y(J,31)+Y(J,32)+Y(J,42)+Y(J,48)*M(1)/12
1189     &+Y(J,12))+Y(J,49)*M(1)/12
1190      BANK(7)=BANK(7)-Y(J,49)*M(1)/12
1191      IF(Y(J,34) .GT. 0)GOV(3)=GOV(3)+Y(J,34)*M(20)
1192      IF(Y(J,34) .GT. 0)Y(J,34)=Y(J,34)*(1-M(20))
1193      PROF=PROF+Y(J,34)
1194      Z(NINT(Y(J,3)),24)=Z(NINT(Y(J,3)),24)+Y(J,34)/(Y(J,10)*Z(9,
1195     &11)+Y(J,36)*Z(7,11)+Y(J,37)*Z(8,11))
1196      Y(J,12)=0
1197      Y(J,42)=0
1198      Y(J,11)=0.0
1199      Y(J,50)=0.0
1200      IF(Y(J,34) .GT. 0)Y(J,24)=Y(J,24)+(Y(J,34)/2)
1201      IF(Y(J,34) .GT. 0)Y(J,49)=Y(J,49)+Y(J,34)/2
1202      IF(Y(J,34) .LT. 0)Y(J,49)=Y(J,49)+Y(J,34)
1203      IF(CLOCK .NE. Y(J,39))GO TO 744
1204 C    DISTRIBUTION OF PROFITS
1205      IF(Y(J,18) .NE. -1)GO TO 746
1206      X(NINT(Y(J,2)),1)=X(NINT(Y(J,2)),1)+Y(J,24)
1207      X(NINT(Y(J,2)),33)=X(NINT(Y(J,2)),33)+Y(J,24)
1208      INCOME=INCOME+Y(J,24)
1209      GO TO 755
1210 746  DO 745 I=1,SHRH
1211      X(NINT(SHARE(J,I,2)),1)=X(NINT(SHARE(J,I,2)),1)+SHARE(J,I,1)
1212     &*Y(J,24)
1213      X(NINT(SHARE(J,I,2)),33)=X(NINT(SHARE(J,I,2)),33)+SHARE(J,I,1)
1214     &*Y(J,24)
1215 745  INCOME=INCOME+SHARE(J,I,1)*Y(J,24)
1216 755  Y(J,24)=0
1217 744  IF(TIME .LE. 55)Y(J,49)=Y(J,35)*Y(J,16)*2
1218      DUM1=1.0
```

```
1219        IF(Y(J,3) .EQ. 7)DUM1=2.5
1220        IF(Y(J,49)-Y(J,48) .GE. -Y(J,35)*Y(J,16)*3*DUM1)GO TO 719
1221  C     BANKRUPTCY, FB=NUMBER OF BLANK FIRMS, FIRB(I)=I'TH BLANK FIRM
1222        IF(YP .EQ. 1)PRINT *,'BANKRUPT',J,Y(J,3),Y(J,49),Y(J,48)
1223        BANK(5)=BANK(5)-Y(J,48)
1224        X(NINT(Y(J,2)),29)=X(NINT(Y(J,2)),29)*1.2
1225        Y(J,48)=0
1226        IF(X(NINT(Y(J,2)),33) .GT. 0)Y(J,49)=X(NINT(Y(J,2)),33)/2
1227        IF(X(NINT(Y(J,2)),33) .GT. 0)X(NINT(Y(J,2)),33)=Y(J,49)
1228  C     DO 740 I=1,NINT(Y(J,5))
1229  C     X(EXEC(J,I),7)=54
1230  C     REG(NINT(Y(J,1)),5)=REG(NINT(Y(J,1)),5)+1
1231  C740  UNE(REG(NINT(Y(J,1)),5),NINT(Y(J,1)),1)=EXEC(J,I)
1232  C     DO 741 I=1,NINT(Y(J,6))
1233  C     X(WC(J,I),7)=54
1234  C     REG(NINT(Y(J,1)),6)=REG(NINT(Y(J,1)),6)+1
1235  C741  UNE(REG(NINT(Y(J,1)),6),NINT(Y(J,1)),2)=WC(J,I)
1236  C     DO 742 I=1,NINT(Y(J,7))
1237  C     X(SK(J,I),7)=54
1238  C     REG(NINT(Y(J,1)),7)=REG(NINT(Y(J,1)),7)+1
1239  C742  UNE(REG(NINT(Y(J,1)),7),NINT(Y(J,1)),3)=SK(J,I)
1240  C     DO 743 I=1,NINT(Y(J,8))
1241  C     X(UNS(J,I),7)=54
1242  C     REG(NINT(Y(J,1)),8)=REG(NINT(Y(J,1)),8)+1
1243  C743  UNE(REG(NINT(Y(J,1)),8),NINT(Y(J,1)),4)=UNS(J,I)
1244  C     X(NINT(Y(J,2)),7)=54
1245  C     REG(NINT(Y(J,1)),5)=REG(NINT(Y(J,1)),5)+1
1246  C     UNE(REG(NINT(Y(J,1)),5),NINT(Y(J,1)),1)=Y(J,2)
1247  C     Y(54,13)=Y(54,13)+Y(J,5)+Y(J,6)+Y(J,7)+Y(J,8)+1
1248  C     IF(Y(J,3) .EQ. 3)CALL REMO(J,Y,Z,SH)
1249  C     IF(Y(J,3) .EQ. 7)CALL REMO(J,Y,Z,CONS)
1250  C     IF(Y(J,3) .EQ. 8)CALL REMO(J,Y,Z,COMP)
1251  C     IF(Y(J,3) .EQ. 9)CALL REMO(J,Y,Z,MACH)
1252  C     IF(Y(J,3) .EQ. 10)CALL REMO(J,Y,Z,MN)
1253  C     IF(Y(J,3) .EQ. 11)CALL REMO(J,Y,Z,AGR)
1254  C     IF(Y(J,3) .EQ. 12)CALL REMO(J,Y,Z,INM)
1255  C     Z(NINT(Y(J,3)),7)=Z(NINT(Y(J,3)),7)-1
1256  C     DO 718 I=1,65
1257  C     IF(I .LE. 60)Y(J,I)=0
1258  C718  STOCK(J,I)=0
1259  C     DO 799 I=1,20
1260  C799  STOCK1(J,I)=0
1261  C     FB=FB+1
1262  C     FIRB(FB)=J
1263  C     GO TO 717
1264  719  IF(Y(J,49) .GE. 2*DUM1*Y(J,35)*Y(J,16) .AND. Y(J,48) .GT. 0)
1265        &GO TO 735
1266        IF(Y(J,49) .GE. Y(J,35)*Y(J,16))GO TO 717
1267  C     BANK LOAN
1268        Y(J,48)=Y(J,48)-Y(J,49)+Y(J,35)*Y(J,16)
1269        BANK(5)=BANK(5)-Y(J,49)+Y(J,35)*Y(J,16)
1270        BANK(7)=BANK(7)+Y(J,49)-Y(J,35)*Y(J,16)
1271        Y(J,49)=Y(J,35)*Y(J,16)
1272        GO TO 717
1273  735  BANK(5)=BANK(5)-Y(J,48)
1274        BANK(7)=BANK(7)+Y(J,48)
```

```
1275        Y(J,49)=Y(J,49)-Y(J,48)
1276        Y(J,48)=0
1277 717    CONTINUE
1278 C
1279 C      ALLOCATING PROBABILITIES OF SUPPLIER FIRMS FOR MINING, AGRICULTURE
1280 C      AND INTERMEDIATE GOODS. MN(I), AGR(I) AND INT(I) REPRESENT THE FIRM
1281 C      IDENTITY, I.E. NUMBER, OF THE ITH MINING FIRM ETC. M1, M2, M3= THE
1282 C      NUMBER OF SUCH FIRMS
1283 C      & MACH(I) COMP(I) CONS(I) REPRESENT THE FIRM IDENTITY IN MACHINE
1284 C      INDUSTRY, COMPUTER INDUSTRY AND CONSTRUCTION INDUSTRY, M4, M5 AND
1285 C      M6 THE NUMBER OF SUCH FIRMS
1286        DO 606 I=1,12
1287 606    Z(I,7)=0.0
1288        DO 600 I=1,65
1289        IF(Y(I,3) .EQ. 0 .OR. Y(I,3) .EQ. 13)GO TO 600
1290        Z(NINT(Y(I,3)),7)=Z(NINT(Y(I,3)),7)+1
1291        Y(I,23)=Z(NINT(Y(I,3)),7)
1292        IF(Y(I,3) .EQ. 10)MN(NINT(Z(NINT(Y(I,3)),7)))=I
1293        IF(Y(I,3) .EQ. 11)AGR(NINT(Z(NINT(Y(I,3)),7)))=I
1294        IF(Y(I,3) .EQ. 12)INM(NINT(Z(NINT(Y(I,3)),7)))=I
1295        IF(Y(I,3) .EQ. 9)MACH(NINT(Z(NINT(Y(I,3)),7)))=I
1296        IF(Y(I,3) .EQ. 8)COMP(NINT(Z(NINT(Y(I,3)),7)))=I
1297 600    IF(Y(I,3) .EQ. 7)CONS(NINT(Z(NINT(Y(I,3)),7)))=I
1298        P5(1)=0
1299        P6(1)=0
1300        P7(1)=0
1301        P8(1)=0
1302        P9(1)=0
1303        P10(1)=0
1304        DO 620 I=1,Z(10,7)
1305 620    P5(I+1)=Y(MN(I),35)/Z(10,10)+P5(I)
1306        DO 630 I=1,Z(11,7)
1307 630    P6(I+1)=Y(AGR(I),35)/Z(11,10)+P6(I)
1308        DO 640 I=1,Z(12,7)
1309 640    P7(I+1)=Y(INM(I),35)/Z(12,10)+P7(I)
1310        DO 645 I=1,Z(9,7)
1311 645    P8(I+1)=Y(MACH(I),35)/Z(9,10)+P8(I)
1312        DO 650 I=1,Z(8,7)
1313 650    P9(I+1)=Y(COMP(I),35)/Z(8,10)+P9(I)
1314        DO 655 I=1,Z(7,7)
1315 655    P10(I+1)=Y(CONS(I),35)/Z(7,10)+P10(I)
1316        P5(NINT(Z(10,7))+1)=1.0
1317        P6(NINT(Z(11,7))+1)=1.0
1318        P7(NINT(Z(12,7))+1)=1.0
1319        P8(NINT(Z(9,7))+1)=1.0
1320        P9(NINT(Z(8,7))+1)=1.0
1321        P10(NINT(Z(7,7))+1)=1.0
1322        CALL G05EXF(P5,NINT(Z(10,7))+1,0, .TRUE. ,R5,NINT(Z(10,7))+4,
1323        &IFAIL)
1324        CALL G05EXF(P6,NINT(Z(11,7))+1,0, .TRUE. ,R6,NINT(Z(11,7))+5,
1325        &IFAIL)
1326        CALL G05EXF(P7,NINT(Z(12,7))+1,0, .TRUE. ,R7,NINT(Z(12,7))+4,
1327        &IFAIL)
1328        CALL G05EXF(P8,NINT(Z(9,7))+1,0, .TRUE. ,R8,NINT(Z(9,7))+4,
1329        &IFAIL)
1330        CALL G05EXF(P9,NINT(Z(8,7))+1,0, .TRUE. ,R9,NINT(Z(8,7))+4,
```

```
1331        &IFAIL)
1332        CALL G05EXF(P10,NINT(Z(7,7))+1,0, .TRUE. ,R10,NINT(Z(7,7))+4,
1333        &IFAIL)
1334   C
1335   C    INVESTMENT ALL FIRMS
1336        DO 700 J=1,65
1337        IF(Y(J,3) .EQ. 0 .OR. Y(J,3) .EQ. 13)GO TO 700
1338        Y(J,35)=OUTP(J,Y,Z,X,TIME)
1339        BANK(2)=BANK(2)+Y(J,49)
1340        Y(J,10)=Y(J,10)*W(1)
1341        Y(J,36)=Y(J,36)*W(2)
1342        Y(J,37)=Y(J,37)*W(3)
1343        Y8=G05EYF(R8,Z(9,7)+4)
1344        IF(Z(9,7) .EQ. 1)Y8=1
1345        Y9=G05EYF(R9,Z(8,7)+4)
1346        IF(Z(8,7) .EQ. 1)Y9=1
1347        Y10=G05EYF(R10,Z(7,7)+4)
1348        IF(Z(7,7) .EQ. 1)Y10=1
1349   C    IF(CLOCK .NE. Y(J,39))GO TO 700
1350   C    NEED TO TAKE ABOVE C AWAY IN FUTURE VERSIONS OF PROGRAM
1351        IF(STOCK(J,J)/Y(J,4) .GT. 2.5 .OR. Y(J,48) .GT. Y(J,49))GO TO 700
1352        D5=NINT(Y(J,3))
1353        NMAC=0
1354        NCOMP=0
1355        NBUILD=0
1356        D22=AMIN1(Y(J,36)*4.0-Y(J,10),5.0)
1357        IF(D5 .EQ. 3)THEN
1358        NMAC=AMAX1(0.0,D22)
1359        ELSE
1360        ORIG=Y(J,10)
1361   712  Y11A=OUTP(J,Y,Z,X,TIME)
1362        Y(J,10)=Y(J,10)+Z(9,6)
1363        Y11=(OUTP(J,Y,Z,X,TIME)-Y11A)*(Y(J,16)*(1-Y(J,20)))
1364        IF(Y11 .LE. (M(1))*(1.1**(NMAC+1))*Y(MACH(Y8),16) .OR. N
1365        &MAC*Y(MACH(Y8),16) .GT. Y(J,49)*2)GO TO 711
1366        IF(NMAC .GT. 5 .OR. Y(J,10)/Z(9,6) .GT. 2*NMAC)GO TO 711
1367        NMAC=NMAC+1
1368        GO TO 712
1369        END IF
1370   711  IF(NMAC .EQ. 0)GO TO 710
1371        FL=0
1372   714  IF(STOCK(MACH(Y8),MACH(Y8)) .GE. NMAC)GO TO 713
1373        IF(FL .LT. Z(9,7))GO TO 715
1374        Z(9,21)=Z(9,21)+NMAC*Y(MACH(Y8),16)
1375        GO TO 716
1376   715  FL=FL+1
1377        Y8=Y8+1
1378        IF(Y8 .GT. Z(9,7))Y8=1
1379        GO TO 714
1380   713  STOCK(MACH(Y8),MACH(Y8))=STOCK(MACH(Y8),MACH(Y8))-NMAC
1381        Y(MACH(Y8),11)=Y(MACH(Y8),11)+NMAC*Y(MACH(Y8),16)
1382   716  Y(J,42)=NMAC*Y(MACH(Y8),16)
1383   710  Y(J,10)=Y(J,10)-Z(9,6)
1384        ORIG=Y(J,37)
1385   722  Y12A=OUTP(J,Y,Z,X,TIME)
1386        Y(J,37)=Y(J,37)+Z(8,6)
```

```
1387        Y12=(OUTP(J,Y,Z,X,TIME)-Y12A)*(Y(J,16)*(1-Y(J,20)))
1388        IF(Y12 .LE. (M(1))*(1.1**(NCOMP+1))*Y(COMP(Y9),16) .OR. N
1389       &COMP*Y(COMP(Y9),16) .GT. Y(J,49))GO TO 721
1390        IF(NCOMP .GT. 5 .OR. Y(J,37)/Z(8,6) .GT. 2*NCOMP)GO TO 721
1391        NCOMP=NCOMP+1
1392        GO TO 722
1393 721    IF(NCOMP .EQ. 0)GO TO 720
1394        FL=0
1395 723    IF(STOCK(COMP(Y9),COMP(Y9)) .GE. NCOMP)GO TO 724
1396        IF(FL .LT. Z(8,7))GO TO 728
1397        Z(8,21)=Z(8,21)+NCOMP*Y(COMP(Y9),16)
1398        GO TO 729
1399 728    FL=FL+1
1400        Y9=Y9+1
1401        IF(Y9 .GT. Z(8,7))Y9=1
1402        GO TO 723
1403 724    STOCK(COMP(Y9),COMP(Y9))=STOCK(COMP(Y9),COMP(Y9))-NCOMP
1404        Y(COMP(Y9),11)=Y(COMP(Y9),11)+NCOMP*Y(COMP(Y9),16)
1405 729    Y(J,42)=Y(J,42)+NCOMP*Y(COMP(Y9),16)
1406 720    Y(J,37)=Y(J,37)-Z(8,6)
1407 C      INVESTMENT IN NEW BUILDINGS
1408        IF(Y(J,22) .EQ. 1)GO TO 732
1409        D22=AMIN1(10.,1+((Y(J,11)/RPI(CLOCK))*0.001)-Y(J,36))
1410        IF(D5 .EQ. 3)THEN
1411        NBUILD=AMAX1(0.0,D22)
1412        ELSE
1413        ORIG=Y(J,36)
1414 726    Y13A=OUTP(J,Y,Z,X,TIME)
1415        Y(J,36)=Y(J,36)+1
1416      . Y13=(OUTP(J,Y,Z,X,TIME)-Y13A)*(Y(J,16)*(1-Y(J,20)))
1417        IF(Y13 .LE. (M(1))*(1.1**(1+NBUILD))*REGFA(NINT(Y(J,1))) .OR. N
1418       &BUILD*REGFA(NINT(Y(J,1))) .GT. Y(J,49))GO TO 725
1419        IF(NBUILD .GT. 10)GO TO 725
1420        NBUILD=NBUILD+1
1421        GO TO 726
1422        END IF
1423 725    IF(NBUILD .EQ. 0)GO TO 727
1424        Y(J,36)=Y(J,36)-NBUILD
1425 C      NFAB(K)=NUMBER OF FACTORIES BEING BUILT BY I'TH FIRM
1426 C      FACB(I,J,K) J=1-> STAGE OF COMPLETION OF K'TH FACTORY FOR J'TH FIRM
1427 C                  J=2-> COST, J=3-> OWNER
1428        FL=0
1429        DO 734 K2=1,NBUILD
1430        IF(NFAB(Y10) .GE. 100)GO TO 734
1431        FL=FL+1
1432        NFAB(Y10)=NFAB(Y10)+1
1433        FACB(Y10,1,NFAB(Y10))=0.0
1434        FACB(Y10,2,NFAB(Y10))=0.0
1435        FACB(Y10,3,NFAB(Y10))=J
1436 734    CONTINUE
1437        IF(FL .GT. 0)Y(J,22)=1
1438 727    Y(J,36)=Y(J,36)-1
1439 732    STOK=STOK+STOCK(J,J)
1440 700    CONTINUE
1441        IF(YP .EQ. 1)PRINT *,'TOTAL OWN STOCKS =',STOK
1442 C
```

```
1443 C      SHOP'S DECISION MAKING PROCESS
1444        DO 350 J=1,65
1445        IF(Y(J,3) .NE. 3)GO TO 350
1446        IF(Y(J,34) .LT. 0)Y(J,17)=Y(J,17)*1.05
1447        DO 355 I=1,65
1448        IF(Y(I,3) .EQ. 3 .OR. Y(I,3) .EQ. 7 .OR. Y(I,3) .EQ. 0 .OR. Y(
1449       &I,3) .GE. 9)GO TO 355
1450        D14=2*SALE(J,I)
1451        IF(D14 .LT. Y(I,35)/2)D14=Y(I,35)/2
1452        IF(STOCK(J,I) .GE. D14)GO TO 355
1453        Y12=D14-STOCK(J,I)
1454        IF(Y12 .GT. STOCK(I,I))Y12=STOCK(I,I)
1455        Y(I,11)=Y(I,11)+Y12*Y(I,16)
1456        Y(J,50)=Y(J,50)+Y(I,16)*Y12
1457        STOCK(J,I)=STOCK(J,I)+Y12
1458        STOCK(I,I)=STOCK(I,I)-Y12
1459 355    CONTINUE
1460        CALL SKILEV(Y,EXEC,WC,SK,UNS,X,J)
1461 350    CONTINUE
1462 C
1463 C      FACTORIES DECISION MAKING PROCESS - PRODUCERS OF  ALL OTHER
1464 C      INDUSTRIES THAN SERVICES
1465 C
1466        DO 501 J=1,12
1467 501    Z(J,10)=0
1468        DO 500 J=1,65
1469        IF(Y(J,3) .EQ. 3 .OR. Y(J,3) .EQ. 0 .OR. Y(J,3) .EQ. 13)
1470       &GO TO 500
1471        D6=NINT(Y(J,3))
1472        IF(Y(J,3) .EQ. 7)GO TO 502
1473        IF(TIME .LE. 24)Y(J,47)=NINT(((Z(D6,22)*Y(J,19)/(M(18)*
1474       &Y(J,16)))**1.5)*Z(D6,12))
1475        IF(TIME .GT. 24)Y(J,47)=NINT(0.10*((Z(D6,22)*Y(J,19)/(M(18)
1476       &*Y.(J,16)))**1.5)*Z(D6,12))+0.90*Y(J,47)
1477        IF(Y(J,47) .GT. STOCK(J,J))Y(J,47)=STOCK(J,J)
1478        STOCK(J,J)=STOCK(J,J)-Y(J,47)
1479        Y(J,11)=Y(J,11)+Y(J,47)*Y(J,16)
1480        EXPT=EXPT+Y(J,47)*Y(J,16)
1481        Z(D6,23)=Z(D6,23)+Y(J,47)*Y(J,16)
1482 502    CALL SKILEV(Y,EXEC,WC,SK,UNS,X,J)
1483        DO 560 I=10,12
1484 560    STOCK1(J,I)=STOCK1(J,I)-Y(J,35)*Z(NINT(Y(J,3)),I-7)
1485        IF(STOCK1(J,10) .GE. 2*Y(J,35)*Z(D6,3) .OR. D6 .EQ. 10)
1486       &GO TO 562
1487        Y5=G05EYF(R5,X(10,7)+4)
1488        SALES=2*Y(J,35)*Z(D6,3)-STOCK1(J,10)
1489        Y(J,50)=Y(J,50)+((2*Y(J,35)*Z(D6,3)-STOCK1(J,10))*Y(MN(Y5),16))
1490        IF(SALES .LE. STOCK(MN(Y5),MN(Y5)))GO TO 561
1491        STOCK1(J,10)=2*Y(J,35)*Z(NINT(Y(J,3)),3)
1492        Z(10,21)=Z(10,21)+(SALES-STOCK(MN(Y5),MN(Y5)))*Y(MN(Y5),16)
1493        SALES=STOCK(MN(Y5),MN(Y5))
1494 561    Y(MN(Y5),11)=Y(MN(Y5),11)+SALES*Y(MN(Y5),16)
1495        STOCK(MN(Y5),MN(Y5))=STOCK(MN(Y5),MN(Y5))-SALES
1496        STOCK1(J,10)=2*Y(J,35)*Z(NINT(Y(J,3)),3)
1497 562    IF(STOCK1(J,11) .GE. 2*Y(J,35)*Z(D6,4) .OR. D6 .EQ. 11)
1498       &GO TO 564
```

```
1499        Y6=G05EYF(R6,Z(11,7)+4)
1500        SALES=2*Y(J,35)*Z(NINT(Y(J,3)),4)-STOCK1(J,11)
1501        Y(J,50)=Y(J,50)+((2*Y(J,35)*Z(NINT(Y(J,3)),4)-STOCK1(J,11))*Y(AG
1502       &R(Y6),16))
1503        IF(SALES .LE. STOCK(AGR(Y6),AGR(Y6)))GO TO 563
1504        STOCK1(J,11)=2*Y(J,35)*Z(NINT(Y(J,3)),4)
1505        Z(11,21)=Z(11,21)+(SALES-STOCK(AGR(Y6),AGR(Y6)))*Y(AGR(Y6),16)
1506        SALES=STOCK(AGR(Y6),AGR(Y6))
1507 563    STOCK(AGR(Y6),AGR(Y6))=STOCK(AGR(Y6),AGR(Y6))-SALES
1508        Y(AGR(Y6),11)=Y(AGR(Y6),11)+SALES*Y(AGR(Y6),16)
1509        STOCK1(J,11)=2*Y(J,35)*Z(D6,3)
1510 564    D14=2*Y(J,35)*Z(D6,5)
1511        IF(STOCK1(J,12) .GE. D14 .OR. D6 .EQ. 12)GO TO 499
1512        Y7=G05EYF(R7,Z(12,7)+4)
1513        SALES=D14-STOCK1(J,12)
1514        Y(J,50)=Y(J,50)+(D14-STOCK1(J,12))*Y(INM(Y7),16)
1515        STOCK1(J,12)=D14
1516        IF(SALES .LE. STOCK(INM(Y7),INM(Y7)))GO TO 565
1517        Z(12,21)=Z(12,21)+SALES*Y(INM(Y7),16)
1518        GO TO 499
1519 565    STOCK(INM(Y7),INM(Y7))=STOCK(INM(Y7),INM(Y7))-SALES
1520        Y(INM(Y7),11)=Y(INM(Y7),11)+SALES*Y(INM(Y7),16)
1521 499    Z(D6,10)=Z(D6,10)+Y(J,35)
1522 500    CONTINUE
1523 C
1524 C      CONSTRUCTION INDUSTRY
1525 C      CONSTFIRM=NUMBER OF CONSTRUCTION FIRMS
1526 C      I'TH COMPANY, NUMBER OF HOUSES OF TYPE J UNDER CONSTRUCTION, J=4
1527 C      INDICATES NUMBER OF FACTORIES UNDER CONSTRUCTION
1528 C      CONSN(I,J) NUMBER OF HOUSES OF TYPE J UNSOLD BY I'TH FIRM
1529 C      CONSAL(3,3,20)NUMBER OF HOUSE FOR SALE CONSTN FIRM HOLDS UNSOLD
1530 C      CONSTN1=IDENTITY OF FIRM, CONSTN2=STOCKS OF COMPLETED HOUSES, TYPE 1
1531 C      CONSTN3=STOCKS OF COMPLETED HOUSES OF TYPE 2, CONSTN3=STOCKS OF
1532 C      COMPLETED HOUSES OF TYPE 3
1533 C      HSEB(I,J,K)=STAGE OF COMPLETION OF K'TH HOUSE OF I COMPANY OF TYPE J
1534 C      HSEB(I,J+3,K)=CURRENT COSTS INCURRED IN BUILDING K'TH HOUSE OF I'TH
1535 C      COMPANY OF TYPE J.
1536 C      RANGES FROM 0.05 WHEN STARTS, TO 1 WHEN COMPLETED.
1537 C      NHSE(I)I=1,3 NUMBER OF HOUSES REGION I,I=4 TOTAL HOUSES BEING BUILT
1538 C      NHSB(I,J) I'TH FIRMS NUMBER OF HOUSES TYPE J UNDER CONSTRUCTION
1539        DO 1100 I=1,NINT(Z(7,7))
1540        I1=CONS(I)
1541        DO 1101 J=1,3
1542        IF(NHSB(I,J) .EQ. 0)GO TO 1135
1543        DO 1102 K=1,NHSB(I,J)
1544        HSEB(I,J,K)=HSEB(I,J,K)+(Y(I1,35)/(NHSB(I,1)+NHSB(I,2)*2+
1545       &NHSB(I,3)∘3+NFAB(I)/2.5))
1546        HSEB(I,J+3,K)=HSEB(I,J+3,K)+J*Y(I1,50)*(Y(I1,35)/(NHSB(I,1)+
1547       &2*NHSB(I,2)+3*NHSB(I,3)+NFAB(I)/2.5))
1548        IF(HSEB(I,J,K) .LT. 1)GO TO 1102
1549        IF(K .EQ. NHSB(I,J))GO TO 1107
1550        DO 1106 L=K,NHSB(I,J)-1
1551 1106   HSEB(I,J,L)=HSEB(I,J,L+1)
1552 1107   HSEB(I,J,NHSB(I,J))=0
1553        NHSB(I,J)=NHSB(I,J)-1
1554        NHSE(NINT(Y(I1,1)))=NHSE(NINT(Y(I1,1)))+1
```

```
1555        IF(DEMHS .EQ. 0)GO TO 1109
1556        D12=HSEBLN(DEMHS)
1557        DEMHS=DEMHS-1
1558        GO TO 1112
1559 1109   D12=NHSE(1)+NHSE(2)+NHSE(3)
1560 1112   HSE(D12,1)=-I
1561        HSE(D12,2)=1
1562        HSE(D12,3)=J
1563        HSE(D12,4)=2
1564        HSE(D12,5)=D12
1565        CONSN(I,J)=CONSN(I,J)+1
1566        CONSAL(I,J,CONSN(I,J))=D12
1567 1102   CONTINUE
1568        FL7=0
1569        DO 1103 J1=1,CONSN(I,J)
1570        D12=CONSAL(I,J,J1)
1571        D11=NINT(Y(I1,1))
1572        CALL HOUSE(D11,0.,REGHS,HSESAL,X,Y,BANK,HSE,I1,D12)
1573        IF(HSE(D12,4) .EQ. 1)GO TO 1103
1574        FL7=FL7+1
1575 1103   CONTINUE
1576        CONSN(I,J)=CONSN(I,J)-FL7
1577 C      NEW HOUSE STARTS
1578 1135   IF(NHSB(I,J) .GE. 10 .OR. CONSN(I,J) .GT. 0 .OR. NHSE(4)
1579      &  .GE. 1400)GO TO 1101
1580        NHSB(I,J)=NHSB(I,J)+1
1581        HSEB(I,J,NHSB(I,J))=0
1582        HSEB(I,J+3,NHSB(I,J))=0
1583        NHSE(4)=NHSE(4)+1
1584 1101   CONTINUE
1585 C      FACTORY CONSTRUCTION
1586        IF(NFAB(I) .EQ. 0)GO TO 1100
1587        DO 1108 J=1,NFAB(I)
1588         OLD=FACB(I,1,J)
1589        FACB(I,1,J)=FACB(I,1,J)+(Y(I1,35)/(NHSB(I,1)+NHSB(I,2)*2
1590      &+3*NHSB(I,3)+NFAB(I)/2.5))
1591        Y(NINT(FACB(I,3,J)),42)=Y(NINT(FACB(I,3,J)),42)+REGFA(NINT(
1592      &Y(I1,1)))*(FACB(I,1,J)-OLD)
1593        Y(54,42)=Y(54,42)+Y(NINT(FACB(I,3,J)),42)
1594        Y(I1,11)=Y(I1,11)+REGFA(NINT(Y(I1,1)))*(FACB(I,1,J)-OLD)
1595        IF(FACB(I,1,J) .LE. 1)GO TO 1108
1596        Y(NINT(FACB(I,3,J)),36)=Y(NINT(FACB(I,3,J)),36)+1
1597        Y(NINT(FACB(I,3,J)),22)=0
1598        IF(J .EQ. NFAB(I))GO TO 1110
1599        DO 1111 L=J,NFAB(I)-1
1600 1111   FACB(I,1,L)=FACB(I,1,L)+1
1601 1110   FACB(I,1,NFAB(I))=0
1602        NFAB(I)=NFAB(I)-1
1603 1108   CONTINUE
1604 1100   CONTINUE
1605        IF(YP .EQ. 1)PRINT *,'TOTAL INVESTMENT',Y(54,42)
1606 C
1607 C      INDUSTRY AND FIRMS PRICE
1608        DO 589 J=1,65
1609        D4=NINT(Y(J,3))
1610        IF(D4 .EQ. 3 .OR. D4 .EQ. 0 .OR. D4 .EQ. 13)GO TO 589
```

```
1611        Y(J,12)=Y(J,35)*(Z(D4,9)*Z(10,22))/(M(18)*10)
1612        IMPT=IMPT+Y(J,12)
1613 589    CONTINUE
1614        DO 581 J=1,12
1615        Z(J,8)=Z(J,11)
1616 581    Z(J,11)=0
1617        DO 585 J=1,65
1618        IF(Y(J,3) .EQ. 0 .OR. Y(J,3) .EQ. 13)GO TO 585
1619        IF(Y(J,3) .NE. 3)GO TO 582
1620        IF(Y(J,11) .EQ. 0)Y(J,40)=1
1621        IF(Y(J,11) .GT. 0)Y(J,40)=(Y(J,11)*(1+M(19)))/RPI(CLOCK)
1622        GO TO 585
1623 582    Y(J,40)=Y(J,11)/Y(J,16)
1624        STOCK(J,J)=STOCK(J,J)+Y(J,35)
1625        Y(J,4)=0.9*Y(J,4)+0.1*Y(J,35)
1626        STOK1=((STOCK(J,J)/Y(J,4))-3.0)
1627        IF(STOK1 .GT. 0.9)STOK1=0.9
1628        IF(Y(J,3) .EQ. 7)STOK1=0
1629        IF(STOK1 .GT. 0)Y(J,19)=Y(J,19)**0.9
1630        IF(STOK1 .LT. 0 .AND. Y(J,19) .LT. 1.5)Y(J,19)=Y(J,19)**1.1
1631 C      FIRM'S PRICE
1632 595    IF(Y(J,35) .EQ. 0)GO TO 566
1633        Y(J,16)=((Y(J,28)*Y(J,5)+Y(J,29)*Y(J,6)+Y(J,30)*Y(J,7)+Y(J,12)
1634        &+Y(J,50)
1635        &+Y(J,31)*Y(J,8)+Y(J,32)+(Y(J,10)*Z(9,8)+REGFA(NINT(Y(J,1)))*
1636        &Y(J,36)+Y(J,37)*Z(8,8))*(0.05+(1+M(30))**(1/12)-1))/Y(J,35))
1637        &*(1.65-STOK1/3)*0.25+0.75*Y(J,16)
1638        IF(Y(J,34) .LT. 0)Y(J,16)=Y(J,16)*1.1
1639 566    Z(NINT(Y(J,3)),11)=Z(NINT(Y(J,3)),11)+Y(J,16)*Y(J,35)/Z(NINT
1640        &(Y(J,3)),10)
1641 585    CONTINUE
1642 C        COMMON PRICE FOR FIRMS IN RAW MATERIAL AND INTERMEDIATE INDUSTRIES
1643        DO 591 J=1,65
1644        IF(Y(J,3) .EQ. 0 .OR. Y(J,3) .EQ. 13)GO TO 591
1645        IF(Z(NINT(Y(J,3)),11) .GT. 0 .AND. Y(J,16) .EQ. 0)Y(J,16)=
1646        &Z(NINT(Y(J,3)),11)
1647        IF(Y(J,35) .GT. 0)Y(J,20)=((Z(NINT(Y(J,3)),3)*Z(10,8)+Z(NINT
1648        &(Y(J,3)),4)*Z(11,8)+Z(NINT(Y(J,3)),5)*Z(12,8)+Z(NINT(Y(J,3
1649        &)),9)*Z(10,22))/(M(18)*100))/(Y(J,16))
1650        IF(Y(J,3) .LT. 10 .OR. Y(J,3) .GT. 12)GO TO 591
1651        Y(J,16)=Z(NINT(Y(J,3)),11)
1652 591    CONTINUE
1653        IF(YP .EQ. 1)PRINT *,'       PRICE            VOLUME OUTPUT'
1654 C      INDUSTRY IMPORT PRICE (ALSO DETERMINES EXPORTS)
1655 C      ALSO PRINT OUT OF INDUSTRY OUTPUTS
1656        GDP=0.0
1657        DO 586 J=1,12
1658        IF(YP .EQ. 1)PRINT *,IND(J),Z(J,11),Z(J,10),Z(J,21),Z(J,24)
1659        GDP=GDP+Z(J,10)*Z(J,11)
1660        Z(J,24)=0
1661        IF(J .EQ. 3 .OR. J .EQ. 7)GO TO 586
1662        Z(J,22)=Z(J,22)*1.005
1663        IF(TIME .EQ. 2)Z(J,22)=Z(J,11)
1664        IMPT=IMPT+Z(J,21)
1665 586    CONTINUE
1666 C      EXCHANGE RATE
```

```
1667        IF(YP .EQ. 1)PRINT *,'GDP',GDP
1668        IF(TIME .EQ. 1)EXW=RPI(1)
1669        M(18)=M(18)*(1+((EXPT-IMPT)/(1+(IMPT+EXPT)*15)))*0.6+0.4*
1670     &(EXW*1.005)/RPI(CLOCK)
1671        IF(YP .EQ. 1)PRINT *,'IMPS',IMPT,'EXPS',EXPT,'EXCH RATE',M(18)
1672 C
1673 C      THE LABOUR MARKET
1674        HIRE=0
1675        QUIT=0
1676        FIRE=0
1677 C      GOVERNMENT SECTOR VACANCIES
1678        DO 125 I=1,3
1679        DO 125 J=1,3
1680        DO 125 K=1,4
1681        IF(GOVW(J,K,I) .GE. GRR(I,K)*NCONA(J))GO TO 125
1682        VAC(50+I,J,K)=NINT(GRR(I,K)*NCONA(J)-GOVW(J,K,I))
1683        IF(VAC(50+I,J,K) .GT. 5)VAC(50+I,J,K)=5
1684        REG(J,K)=REG(J,K)+VAC(50+I,J,K)
1685        GVAC(J,K)=GVAC(J,K)+VAC(50+I,J,K)
1686 125    CONTINUE
1687 C
1688 C      PRIVATE SECTOR VACANCIES
1689        DO 950 J=1,65
1690        IF(Y(J,3) .EQ. 0 .OR. Y(J,3) .EQ. 13)GO TO 950
1691        DO 959 I=1,4
1692        VA=0
1693        VA1=Y(J,I+4)
1694        IF(Y(J,3) .EQ. 3 .AND. Y(J,35)/(Y(J,40)) .LT. 0.9
1695     &)GO TO 951
1696        IF(Y(J,3) .EQ. 3)GO TO 954
1697        IF(STOCK(J,J) .GT. Y(J,4)*2)GO TO 954
1698 951    Y11A=OUTP(J,Y,Z,X,TIME)
1699        Y(J,I+42)=Y(J,I+42)+M(20+I)
1700        Y(J,I+4)=Y(J,I+4)+1
1701        Y11=(OUTP(J,Y,Z,X,TIME)-Y11A)*(Y(J,16)*(1-Y(J,20)))
1702        IF(Y11 .LE. Y(J,I+27)*(1+((VA+1)/(1+Y(J,I+4)))*0.25))
1703     &GO TO 952
1704        IF(VA .GT. (1+VA1))GO TO 952
1705        VA=VA+1
1706        GO TO 951
1707 952    Y(J,I+42)=Y(J,I+42)-(VA+1)*M(20+I)
1708        Y(J,I+4)=Y(J,I+4)-VA-1
1709        VAC(J,NINT(Y(J,1)),I)=VA
1710        REG(NINT(Y(J,1)),I)=REG(NINT(Y(J,1)),I)+VA
1711 954    IF(Y(J,3) .EQ. 3 .AND. (Y(J,35)/Y(J,40)) .LT. 1.1
1712     &)GO TO 959
1713        IF(Y(J,3) .EQ. 3)GO TO 126
1714        IF(VA .GT. 0 .OR. Y(J,I+4) .LE. 1.0)GO TO 959
1715 126    Y11A=OUTP(J,Y,Z,X,TIME)
1716        Y(J,I+42)=Y(J,I+42)-M(20+I)
1717        Y(J,I+4)=Y(J,I+4)-1
1718        Y11=(Y11A-OUTP(J,Y,Z,X,TIME))*(Y(J,16)*(1-Y(J,20)))
1719        IF(Y11 .GE. 0.9*Y(J,27+I) .OR. Y(J,I+4) .LT. 1.9)GO TO 961
1720        Y(J,I+42)=Y(J,I+42)+M(20+I)
1721        Y(J,I+4)=Y(J,I+4)+1
1722        IF(I .EQ. 1)CALL FIRES(I,X,Y,EXEC,Y(J,I+4),J,UNE,REG)
```

```
1723          IF(I .EQ. 2)CALL FIRES(I,X,Y,WC,Y(J,I+4),J,UNE,REG)
1724          IF(I .EQ. 3)CALL FIRES(I,X,Y,SK,Y(J,I+4),J,UNE,REG)
1725          IF(I .EQ. 4)CALL FIRES(I,X,Y,UNS,Y(J,I+4),J,UNE,REG)
1726          FIRE=FIRE+1
1727          GO TO 954
1728 961      Y(J,I+42)=Y(J,I+42)+M(20+I)
1729          Y(J,I+4)=Y(J,I+4)+1
1730 959      CONTINUE
1731 950      CONTINUE
1732 C
1733 &        HIRES & RESERVATION WAGES
1734          DO 968 I=1,65
1735          IF(Y(I,3) .EQ. 0)GO TO 968
1736          D7=1
1737          DO 970 J=1,4
1738          IF(Y(I,J+4) .GE. 75)GO TO 970
1739          IF(I .LT. 51 .OR. I .GT. 53)D6=NINT(Y(I,1))
1740 588      IF(I .GE. 51 .AND. I .LE. 53)D6=D7
1741          IF(VAC(I,D6,J) .EQ. 0 .OR. REG(D6,J+4) .EQ. 0)GO TO 970
1742          J1=INT((REG(D6,J+4)/REG(D6,J))*VAC(I,D6,J))
1743          IF(J1 .LT. 1)J1=1
1744          DO 973 I1=1,J1
1745          IF(VAC(I,D6,J) .LT. 1 .OR. REG(D6,J+4) .LT. 1)GO TO 973
1746          K5=5+1.4*REG(D6,J+4)
1747          CALL G05EBF(1,REG(D6,J+4),R12,K5,IFAIL)
1748          J3=G05EYF(R12,K5)
1749          IF(UNE(J3,D6,J) .EQ. 0)GO TO 973
1750          X(UNE(J3,D6,J),2)=X(UNE(J3,D6,J),2)+0.2*(X(UNE(J3,D6,J),2)/
1751         &Y(54,28))*(Y(I,27+J)-X(UNE(J3,D6,J),2))
1752          IF(X(UNE(J3,D6,J),2) .GT. Y(I,27+J))GO TO 973
1753          X(UNE(J3,D6,J),7)=I
1754          REG(D6,J)=REG(D6,J)-1
1755          HIRE=HIRE+1
1756          REG(D6,J+4)=REG(D6,J+4)-1
1757          VAC(I,D6,J)=VAC(I,D6,J)-1
1758          IF(I .GE. 51 .AND. I .LE. 53)GVAC(D6,J)=GVAC(D6,J)-1
1759          X(UNE(J3,D6,J),2)=Y(I,27+J)
1760          X(UNE(J3,D6,J),35)=0
1761 963      Y(54,13)=Y(54,13)-1
1762          Y(I,J+4)=Y(I,J+4)+1
1763          Y(I,J+42)=Y(I,J+42)+X(UNE(J3,D6,J),29)
1764          IF(J .EQ. 1)EXEC(I,NINT(Y(I,5)))=UNE(J3,D6,J)
1765          IF(J .EQ. 2)WC(I,NINT(Y(I,6)))=UNE(J3,D6,J)
1766          IF(J .EQ. 3)SK(I,NINT(Y(I,7)))=UNE(J3,D6,J)
1767          IF(J .EQ. 4)UNS(I,NINT(Y(I,8)))=UNE(J3,D6,J)
1768          IF(J3 .EQ. REG(D6,J+4)+1)GO TO 587
1769          DO 977 J5=J3,REG(D6,J+4)
1770 977      UNE(J5,D6,J)=UNE(J5+1,D6,J)
1771 587      IF(I .LT. 51 .OR. I .GT. 53)GO TO 973
1772          GOVW(D6,J,I-50)=GOVW(D6,J,I-50)+1
1773          GOVW(D6,J+4,I-50)=GOVW(D6,J+4,I-50)+X(UNE(J3,D6,J),29)
1774          D7=D7+1
1775          IF(D7 .LE. 3)GO TO 588
1776          D7=1
1777 973      CONTINUE
1778 970      CONTINUE
```

```
1779 968    CONTINUE
1780 C       QUITS, AND COMPANY START UPS
1781         FL6=0
1782         DO 985 I=1,12
1783         IF(Z(I,24) .LE. FL6)GO TO 985
1784         FL6=Z(I,24)
1785         INDY=I
1786 985    CONTINUE
1787         DO 991 J=1,NCON
1788         IF(X(J,5) .EQ. 0 .OR. X(J,10) .EQ. 5 .OR. X(J,5) .GT. 660)
1789        &GO TO 991
1790         DUM=0
1791         IF(X(J,7) .EQ. 54)DUM=1
1792         D22=0.0001*X(J,29)*(1+DUM*2)
1793         D21=G05DZF(D22)
1794         IF(.NOT. D21)GO TO 748
1795 C       SETS UP A FIRM
1796         IF(FB .EQ. 0)GO TO 749
1797         NF=FIRB(FB)
1798         FB=FB-1
1799         GO TO 747
1800 749    NFIRM=NFIRM+1
1801         NF=NFIRM
1802 747    Y(NF,1)=X(J,8)
1803         Y(NF,2)=J
1804         Y(NF,3)=INDY
1805 748    IF(X(J,7) .EQ. 54 .OR. X(J,7) .EQ. 55 .OR. X(J,10) .EQ. 5
1806        & .OR. Y(54,13) .GE. 300)GO TO 991
1807         D7=NINT(X(J,8))
1808         D8=NINT(X(J,10))
1809         D9=NINT(X(J,7))
1810         IF(X(J,2) .GT. WAGE(D7,D8)*(0.9-Y(54,13)/1000))GO TO 991
1811         QUIT=QUIT+1
1812         IF(X(J,10) .EQ. 1)CALL QUITS(J,X,Y,EXEC,UNE,REG,D7,D8,D9)
1813         IF(X(J,10) .EQ. 2)CALL QUITS(J,X,Y,WC,UNE,REG,D7,D8,D9)
1814         IF(X(J,10) .EQ. 3)CALL QUITS(J,X,Y,SK,UNE,REG,D7,D8,D9)
1815         IF(X(J,10) .EQ. 4)CALL QUITS(J,X,Y,UNS,UNE,REG,D7,D8,D9)
1816         X(J,2)=REG(D7,D8+12)
1817 991    CONTINUE
1818 C
1819 C       FIRM'S WAGE RATES
1820         D6=0
1821         DO 989 I=1,65
1822         IF(Y(I,3) .EQ. 0. .OR. Y(I,3) .EQ. 13)GO TO 989
1823         D6=NINT(Y(I,1))
1824         DO 969 J=1,4
1825         D22=1+((REG(D6,J)-REG(D6,J+4)-GVAC(D6,J))/((1+REG(D6,J)+
1826        &REG(D6,J+4)-GVAC(D6,J))))
1827         IF(I .GT. 50 .AND. I .LE. 55)GO TO 969
1828         IF(VAC(I,D6,J) .EQ. 0. .AND. D22 .GE. 1)D22=1.
1829         IF(VAC(I,D6,J) .GT. 0)D22=D22*(1+VAC(I,D6,J)/((1+Y(I,J+4))*10))
1830         IF(TIME .LE. 36)Y(I,27+J)=Y(I,27+J)*(D22**0.2)
1831         D14=Y(I,27+J)
1832 988    IF(CLOCK .NE. Y(I,33) .OR. TIME .LE. 36)GO TO 969
1833         Y(I,27+J)=Y(I,27+J)*(D22**0.2)
1834 C       IF(TIME .GT. 120 .AND. Y(I,27+J) .LT. D14)Y(I,27+J)=D14
```

```
1835 969     CONTINUE
1836         Y(I,32)=Y(I,28)*1.2
1837 989     CONTINUE
1838 C
1839         IF(YP .EQ. 1)PRINT *,'WAGE VACANCIES UNEMPLOYMENT REGION SKILL'
1840         DO 980 I=1,4
1841         M(I+1)=0
1842         M(I+13)=0
1843         M(I+20)=0
1844         M(I+25)=0
1845         DO 980 J=1,3
1846         IF(YP .EQ. 1)PRINT *,WAGE(J,I),REG(J,I),REG(J,I+4),REGHS(J,5),
1847        &REGHS(J,6)
1848         REG(J,I+8)=0
1849 980     WAGE(J,I)=0
1850 C
1851         IF(YP .EQ. 1)PRINT *,'VACANCIES ',VACAN
1852         IF(YP .EQ. 1)PRINT *,'UNEMPLOYMENT ',Y(54,13)
1853         IF(YP .EQ. 1)PRINT *,'HIRES          ',HIRE
1854         IF(YP .EQ. 1)PRINT *,'QUITS          ',QUIT
1855         IF(YP .EQ. 1)PRINT *,'FIRES          ',FIRE
1856         IF(YP .EQ. 1)PRINT *,'UNEMPLOYMENT BENEFIT',Y(54,28)
1857         VACAN=0
1858 C
1859 C       INDIVIDUAL'S PORTFOLIO DECISIONS
1860 1204    BANK(8)=0
1861         PROFR=PROF/SHARET
1862         D14=AMAX1(2.5,2.5*(PROFR-M(30))/(M(30)+PROFR))
1863         IF(D14 .GT. 4.)D14=4.
1864         DO 1090 J=1,1200
1865         IF(X(J,5) .EQ. 0)GO TO 1090
1866         IF(X(J,1) .LT. (WEALT2/NCON)*D14 .AND. X(J,31) .EQ. 0)GO TO 1090
1867         IF(X(J,1) .GE. (WEALT2/NCON)*D14)GO TO 27
1868         DO 28 I=1,NFIRM
1869 28      SHARE1(I,NINT(X(J,31)),1)=SHARE(I,NINT(X(J,31)),1)
1870         GO TO 1090
1871 27      IF(X(J,31) .EQ. 0 .AND. SHRH .GE. 100)GO TO 1090
1872         IF(X(J,31) .GT. 0)GO TO 25
1873         SHRH=SHRH+1
1874         X(J,31)=SHRH
1875         DO 26 I=1,65
1876         IF(Y(I,3) .EQ. 0 .OR. Y(I,3) .EQ. 13 .OR. Y(I,18) .EQ. -1)
1877        &GO TO 26
1878         SHARE(I,SHRH,2)=J
1879 26      CONTINUE
1880 25      J3=NINT(X(J,31))
1881         IF(X(J,32) .LT. X(J,1)*(D14/16))GO TO 1092
1882         DO 1093 I=1,65
1883         IF(Y(I,18) .EQ. -1 .OR. Y(I,3) .EQ. 0 .OR. Y(I,3) .EQ. 13)
1884        &GO TO 1093
1885         SHARE1(I,J3,1)=AMAX1(0.0,SHARE(I,J3,1)-(X(J,1)*(D14/16.)/SHARET))
1886 1093    CONTINUE
1887 1092    IF(X(J,32) .GT. X(J,1)*(D14/16)*0.9)GO TO 1090
1888         DO 1094 I=1,65
1889         IF(Y(I,18) .EQ. -1 .OR. Y(I,3) .EQ. 0 .OR. Y(I,3) .EQ. 13)
1890        &GO TO 1094
```

```
1891        SHARE1(I,J3,2)=AMAX1(0.0,(X(J,1)*(D14/16.)/SHARET)-SHARE(I,J3,1))
1892        IF(SHARE1(I,J3,2) .GT. 0.5)SHARE1(I,J3,2)=0.5
1893 1094   CONTINUE
1894 1090   CONTINUE
1895 C
1896        BANK(2)=0
1897        BANK(10)=BANK(11)
1898 C      THE STOCK MARKET
1899 C      BUYING
1900        IF(SHRH .EQ. 0)GO TO 29
1901        DO 1083 J=1,SHRH
1902        DO 1080 I=1,65
1903        IF(Y(I,18) .EQ. -1 .OR. Y(I,3) .EQ. 0 .OR. Y(I,3) .EQ. 13)
1904        &GO TO 1080
1905        SELL=SELL+SHARE1(I,J,1)*Y(I,18)
1906        BUY=BUY+SHARE1(I,J,2)*Y(I,18)
1907        X(NINT(SHARE(I,J,2)),32)=0.0
1908 1080   CONTINUE
1909 1083   CONTINUE
1910        J=1
1911        DUMSE=0
1912 1084   DO 1081 I=1,65
1913        IF(Y(I,3) .EQ. 0 .OR. Y(I,3) .EQ. 13 .OR. Y(I,18) .EQ. -1)
1914        &GO TO 1081
1915        J4=SHARE(I,J,2)
1916        IF(SELL .EQ. 0 .OR. BUY .GT. SELL)D14=1.0
1917        IF(SELL .GT. BUY)D14=BUY/SELL
1918        IF(SELL .EQ. 0 .AND. BUY .EQ. 0)D14=0
1919        SHARE(I,J,1)=SHARE(I,J,1)-SHARE1(I,J,1)*D14
1920        X(J4,33)=X(J4,33)+SHARE1(I,J,1)*D14*Y(I,18)
1921 1082   IF(SHARE1(I,J,2) .EQ. 0)GO TO 1081
1922        IF(BUY .EQ. 0 .OR. BUY .LE. SELL)D14=1.0
1923        IF(BUY .GT. SELL)D14=SELL/BUY
1924        IF(BUY .EQ. 0 .AND. SELL .EQ. 0)D14=0
1925        SHARE(I,J,1)=SHARE(I,J,1)+SHARE1(I,J,2)*D14
1926        X(J4,33)=X(J4,33)-SHARE1(I,J,2)*D14*Y(I,18)
1927        IF(SHARE(I,J,1) .NE. 0)GO TO 1081
1928        I7=I
1929        J6=X(J4,31)
1930        DO 1086 J2=J6,SHRH-1
1931        SHARE(I,J2,1)=SHARE(I,J2+1,1)
1932        SHARE(I,J2,2)=SHARE(I,J2+1,2)
1933 1086   DUMSE=1
1934 1081   CONTINUE
1935        IF(DUMSE .EQ. 0)GO TO 1028
1936        DO 837 I=X(J4,31),SHRH-1
1937 837    X(NINT(SHARE(I7,I,2)),31)=I
1938        X(J4,31)=0
1939        SHRH=SHRH-1
1940        DUMSE=0
1941        IF(J .LE. SHRH)GO TO 1084
1942 1028   J=J+1
1943        IF(J .LE. SHRH)GO TO 1084
1944 958    D14=(BUY+1)/(SELL+1)
1945        IF(D14 .GT. 1.5)D14=1.5
1946        IF(D14 .LT. 0.5)D14=0.5
```

```
1947          SHARET=0
1948          DO 1085 J=1,65
1949          IF(Y(J,3) .EQ. 0 .OR. Y(J,3) .EQ. 13)GO TO 1085
1950          IF(Y(J,49) .GT. 0)BANK(2)=BANK(2)+Y(J,49)
1951          IF(Y(J,18) .EQ. -1)GO TO 1085
1952          IF(Y(J,34) .GT. 0)Y(J,18)=0.95*((Y(J,34)*12)/(M(1)+.2))+
1953         &0.05*Y(J,18)
1954          IF(Y(J,34) .LE. 0)Y(J,18)=Y(J,18)*0.85
1955          SHARET=SHARET+Y(J,18)
1956          DO 1088 J1=1,SHRH
1957 1088     X(NINT(SHARE(J,J1,2)),32)=SHARE(J,J1,1)*Y(J,18)
1958         &+X(NINT(SHARE(J,J1,2)),32)
1959 1085     CONTINUE
1960 29       IF(YP .EQ. 1)PRINT *,'SHARE INDEX',SHARET
1961          IF(YP .EQ. 1)PRINT *,'SHARES TO SELL',SELL
1962          IF(YP .EQ. 1)PRINT *,'SHARES TO BUY',BUY
1963          IF(YP .EQ. 1)PRINT *,'TOTAL DISTRIBUTED PROFITS',PROF
1964 C
1965 C        GOVERNMENT'S DECISIONS
1966          WEAL3=0
1967          WEAL4=0
1968          BANK(7)=BANK(7)+BANK(11)-BANK(10)
1969          Y(55,13)=0
1970          Y(54,13)=0
1971 C        DIRECT TAXATION
1972          DO 860 J=1,1200
1973          IF(X(J,7) .EQ. 0)GO TO 860
1974          IF(X(J,7) .EQ. 54)Y(54,13)=Y(54,13)+1
1975          IF(X(J,7) .EQ. 55)Y(55,13)=Y(55,13)+1
1976          IF(X(J,7) .NE. 55)M(20+NINT(X(J,10)))=M(20+NINT(X(J,10)))+X(J,29)
1977          IF(X(J,7) .NE. 55)M(25+NINT(X(J,10)))=M(25+NINT(X(J,10)))+1
1978          IF(X(J,7) .NE. 54 .AND. X(J,7) .NE. 55)
1979         &X(J,2)=Y(NINT(X(J,7)),NINT(X(J,10)))+27)
1980          IF(X(J,7) .EQ. 54 .OR. X(J,7) .EQ. 55)X(J,12)=Y(54,28)
1981          IF(X(J,33) .GT. 3*X(J,12))THEN
1982          GOV(3)=GOV(3)+(X(J,33)-3*X(J,12))*(M(1)/12)*M(10)
1983          BANK(7)=BANK(7)-(X(J,33)-3*X(J,12))*(M(1)/12)
1984          BANK(6)=BANK(6)+(X(J,33)-3*X(J,12))*(1+(M(1)/12)*(1-M(10)))+2*
1985         &X(J,12)
1986          X(J,33)=(X(J,33)-3*X(J,12))*(1+((M(1)/12)*(1-M(10))))+3*X(J,12)
1987          INCOME=INCOME+((((X(J,33)-3*X(J,12))*(M(1)/12))*(1-M(10)))
1988          ELSE
1989          BANK(6)=BANK(6)+X(J,33)
1990          END IF
1991          IF(X(J,7) .EQ. 54 .OR. X(J,7) .EQ. 55)GO TO 836
1992          IF(X(J,10) .EQ. 5.0)GO TO 831
1993          IF(X(J,7) .GT. 50 .AND. X(J,7) .LT. 56)GO TO 838
1994          M(NINT(X(J,10))+1)=M(NINT(X(J,10))+1)+X(J,2)
1995          M(13+NINT(X(J,10)))=M(13+NINT(X(J,10)))+1
1996 838      IF(X(J,2) .GT. 0)REG(NINT(X(J,8)),NINT(X(J,10))+8)=REG(NINT(X(J,8))
1997         &),NINT(X(J,10))+8)+1
1998          IF(X(J,2) .GT. 0)WAGE(NINT(X(J,8)),NINT(X(J,10)))=
1999         &WAGE(NINT(X(J,8)),NINT(X(J,10)))+ALOG(X(J,2))
2000 831      IF(X(J,2)*12 .GT. M(6))GO TO 830
2001          X(J,12)=X(J,2)
2002          GO TO 850
```

```
2003 830    IF(X(J,2)*12 .GT. M(7))GO TO 835
2004        X(J,12)=((X(J,2)*12-M(6))*(1-M(9))+M(6))/12
2005        GO TO 850
2006 835    IF(X(J,2)*12 .GT. M(8))GO TO 840
2007        X(J,12)=((X(J,2)*12-M(7))*(1-M(10))+(M(7)-M(6))*(1-M(9))+M(6))
2008    &/12
2009        GO TO 850
2010 840    X(J,12)=((X(J,2)*12-M(8))*(1-M(11))+((M(7)-M(6))*(1-M(9)
2011    &))+((M(8)-M(7))*(1-M(10)))+M(6))/12
2012 850    GOV(1)=GOV(1)+X(J,2)-X(J,12)
2013 836    X(J,33)=X(J,33)+X(J,12)
2014        X(J,1)=X(J,33)+X(J,32)
2015        WEAL3=WEAL3+X(J,33)
2016        WEAL4=WEAL4+X(J,32)
2017        IF(X(J,1) .GT. Y(54,28))GO TO 860
2018        X(J,33)=X(J,33)+Y(54,28)-X(J,1)
2019        BANK(6)=BANK(6)+Y(54,28)-X(J,1)
2020        BANK(2)=BANK(2)+X(J,33)
2021        X(J,1)=Y(54,28)
2022 860    CONTINUE
2023        GOV(7)=GOV(1)+GOV(2)+GOV(3)+GOV(4)
2024        IF(BANK(7) .GT. 0)GOV(7)=GOV(7)+BANK(7)
2025        IF(YP .EQ. 1)PRINT *,'GOV REV',GOV(1),GOV(2),GOV(3),GOV(4),BANK(7)
2026        DO 861 I=1,4
2027        DO 861 J=1,3
2028 861    GOV(9)=GOV(9)+Y(50+J,4+I)*Y(50+J,27+I)
2029        GOV(11)=Y(55,13)*Y(54,28)
2030        GOV(10)=Y(54,13)*Y(54,28)
2031        GOV(8)=GOV(9)+GOV(10)+GOV(11)
2032        GOV(6)=GOV(19)*M(1)/12
2033        IF(GOV(19) .LT. 0)GOV(7)=GOV(7)-GOV(6)
2034        GOV(12)=GOV(8)+GOV(5)
2035        IF(GOV(19) .GT. 0)GOV(12)=GOV(12)+GOV(6)
2036        GOV(20)=GOV(12)-GOV(7)
2037        GOV(19)=GOV(19)+GOV(20)
2038        IF(BANK(7) .LT. 0)GOV(12)=GOV(12)-BANK(7)
2039        IF(YP .EQ. 1)PRINT *,'GOV EXP',GOV(8),GOV(5),GOV(6)
2040        DO 869 J=1,4
2041        M(1+J)=M(1+J)/M(13+J)
2042 869    M(20+J)=M(20+J)/M(25+J)
2043        IF(TIME .LE. 20)D27=GOV(12)/GOV(7)
2044        D27=D27*0.9+0.1*GOV(12)/GOV(7)
2045        IF(CLOCK .NE. 4 .AND. TIME .GT. 60)GO TO 899
2046        M(11)=M(11)*D27
2047        IF(M(11) .GT. 0.95)M(11)=0.95
2048        M(10)=M(11)*0.75
2049        M(9)=M(11)*0.5
2050        M(19)=M(9)
2051        M(20)=M(10)
2052        FL=1000000
2053        DO 975 J=1,3
2054        DO 975 I=1,4
2055        WAGE(J,I)=EXP(WAGE(J,I)/REG(J,I+8))
2056        IF(FL .GT. WAGE(J,I))FL=WAGE(J,I)
2057 975    VACAN=VACAN+REG(J,I)
2058        Y(54,28)=FL*0.6
```

```
2059          M(6)=Y(54,28)*12
2060          M(7)=M(6)*3
2061          M(8)=M(6)*5
2062 C     51. EDUCATION, 52 HEALTH, 53 CENTRAL GOV
2063          DO 800 I=51,53
2064 C     WAGES OF GOVERNMENT EMPLOYEES
2065          CALL GOVWAG(Y,I,M,1.0)
2066 800   CONTINUE
2067 899   IF(YP .EQ. 1)PRINT *,'RATIO OF GOV EXPENDITURE TO REVENUE',D27
2068          IF(YP .EQ. 1)PRINT *,'WEALTH 33 & 34',WEAL3, WEAL4
2069 C
2070 C     HOUSE PRICE ADJUSTMENT
2071          DO 868 I=1,3
2072          DO 867 J=1,3
2073          IF(REGHS(I,4) .GT. 0)D14=REGHS(I,5)/REGHS(I,4)
2074          IF(D14 .GT. 1.1 .OR. REGHS(I,4) .EQ. 0)D14=1.1
2075          IF(D14 .LT. 0.9 .OR. REGHS(I,4) .GT. 70)D14=0.9
2076 867   REGHS(I,J)=Z(7,11)*J*D14*1.1
2077          REGFA(I)=REGHS(I,1)/2.5
2078 868   REGHS(I,6)=REGHS(I,4)
2079 C
2080 C     CALCULATING UNEMPLOYMENT BENEFIT. THIS IS A FIXED PROPORTION OF THE
2081 C     LOWEST WAGE PAID IN ANY INDUSTRY/REGION.
2082          IF(CLOCK .NE. 4 .AND. TIME .GT. 24)GO TO 866
2083          DO 865 I=28,32
2084 865   Y(54,I)=Y(54,28)
2085 866   DO 870 J=1,1200
2086          IF(X(J,7) .NE. 54 .AND. X(J,7) .NE. 55)GO TO 870
2087          X(J,12)=Y(54,28)
2088          X(J,2)=Y(54,28)
2089 870   CONTINUE
2090 C
2091 C     REINITIALISATION OF VARIABLES
2092          CALL REINT(GOV,NCONA,REG,VAC,Y,SALE,SHARE1,Z,BANK,TIME,M,INF,
2093         &GVAC,REGHS,YP)
2094          EXPT=0
2095          IMPT=0
2096          BUY=0
2097          SELL=0
2098          TIME=TIME+1
2099          IF(TIME .LT. 241)GO TO 301
2100          STOP
2101          END
2102 C          ********************************
2103 C          *    FUNCTIONS & SUBROUTINES   *
2104 C          ********************************
2105 C     FUNCTION OUTPUT
2106          FUNCTION OUTP(J,Y,Z,X,TIME)
2107          REAL Y(65,60),X(1200,36),Z(20,30),L1,L2,L3,L4,L51
2108          REAL LL1,LL2,LL3,LL4
2109          INTEGER TIME
2110          LL1=Y(J,43)
2111          LL2=Y(J,44)
2112          LL3=Y(J,45)
2113          LL4=Y(J,46)
2114          IF(Y(J,5) .LE. 0 .OR. Y(J,43) .LT. 0)LL1=0
```

```
2115        IF(Y(J,6) .LE. 0 .OR. Y(J,44) .LT. 0)LL2=0
2116        IF(Y(J,7) .LE. 0 .OR. Y(J,45) .LT. 0)LL3=0
2117        IF(Y(J,8) .LE. 0 .OR. Y(J,46) .LT. 0)LL4=0
2118        L1=LL1
2119        L2=LL2
2120        L3=LL3
2121        L4=LL4
2122        L51=X(NINT(Y(J,2)),29)
2123        L5=L51
2124        TOT=L1+L2+L3+L4+L51
2125        FLAG=0
2126        IF(LL1 .EQ. 0)FLAG=FLAG+1
2127        IF(LL2 .EQ. 0)FLAG=FLAG+1
2128        IF(LL3 .EQ. 0)FLAG=FLAG+1
2129        IF(LL4 .EQ. 0)FLAG=FLAG+1
2130        IF(L51 .EQ. 0)FLAG=FLAG+1
2131        IF(FLAG .EQ. 0)GO TO 875
2132        IF(L1 .GT. 0)L1=(LL1/Y(J,5))*(Y(J,5)-(FLAG/5))
2133        IF(L2 .GT. 0)L2=(LL2/Y(J,6))*(Y(J,6)-(FLAG/5))
2134        IF(L3 .GT. 0)L3=(LL3/Y(J,7))*(Y(J,7)-(FLAG/5))
2135        IF(L4 .GT. 0)L4=(LL4/Y(J,8))*(Y(J,8)-(FLAG/5))
2136        L5=L51*(1-FLAG/5)
2137        IF(L1 .EQ. 0)L1=(LL1+LL2+LL3+LL4+L51-L1-L2-L3
2138       &-L4-L5)/FLAG
2139        IF(L2 .EQ. 0)L2=(LL1+LL2+LL3+LL4+L51-L1-L2-L3
2140       &-L4-L5)/FLAG
2141        IF(L3 .EQ. 0)L3=(LL1+LL2+LL3+LL4+L51-L1-L2-L3
2142       &-L4-L5)/FLAG
2143        IF(L4 .EQ. 0)L4=(LL1+LL2+LL3+LL4+L51-L1-L2-L3
2144       &-L4-L5)/FLAG
2145        TOT=L1+L2+L3+L4+L51
2146  875   OUTP=1.7*Z(NINT(Y(J,3)),12)*(L1**Z(NINT(Y(J,3)),13))*(L2**Z(NINT
2147       &(Y(J,3)),14))*(L3**Z(NINT(Y(J,3)),15))*(L4**Z(NINT(Y(J,3)),16))
2148       &*(Y(J,10)**Z(NINT(Y(J,3)),18))*(L5**Z(NINT(Y
2149       &(J,3)),17))*(Y(J,37)**Z(NINT(Y(J,3)),19))*(Y(J,36)**
2150       &Z(NINT(Y(J,3)),20))/Y(J,19)
2151  C     IF(TIME .EQ. 120)Y(J,41)=OUTP/Y(J,36)
2152  C     IF(TIME .GT. 120 .AND. OUTP .GT. Y(J,36)*Y(J,41))OUTP=
2153  C    &Y(J,36)*Y(J,41)
2154        IF(OUTP .LE. 1)OUTP=1
2155        END
2156  C
2157  C     CHOOSING A RETAILER
2158        SUBROUTINE CHOICE(N2,MAKE,Y,X,M,WEAL,SHOP,J1,DUM,WEAL1)
2159        REAL Y(65,60),X(1200,36),M(30),WEAL,WEAl1
2160        INTEGER N2,MAKE,SHOP
2161        QUAL1=10000000
2162        DO 1000 J=1,65
2163        IF(Y(J,3) .NE. N2)GO TO 1000
2164        IF(ABS(Y(J,19)-X(J1,17)) .GT. QUAL1)GO TO 1000
2165        QUAL1=ABS(Y(J,19)-X(J1,17))
2166        MAKE=J
2167  1000  CONTINUE
2168        WEAL1=WEAL-Y(MAKE,16)*Y(SHOP,17)*(1+M(19))
2169        IF(WEAL1 .LE. 0)DUM=DUM+1
2170        IF(WEAL1 .LE. 0)X(J,36)=1
```

```
2171        END
2172 C
2173 C      SUBROUTINE SPEND
2174        SUBROUTINE SPEND(X,QF,QC,QD,QW,WEAL,EXPA,N6,J)
2175        REAL QF(5),QC(5),QD(5),QW(5),WEAL,EXPA,X(1200,36),D26
2176        INTEGER N6
2177        QF(N6)=QF(5)*WEAL/EXPA
2178        QC(N6)=QC(5)*WEAL/EXPA
2179        QD(N6)=QD(5)*WEAL/EXPA
2180        QW(N6)=QW(5)*WEAL/EXPA
2181        IF(QF(N6)+QC(N6)+QD(N6) .GT. X(J,12)*0.8 .AND. X(J,12) .GT. 0)
2182       &THEN
2183        D26=(X(J,12)*0.8)/(QF(N6)+QC(N6)+QD(N6))
2184        QF(N6)=QF(N6)*D26
2185        QC(N6)=QC(N6)*D26
2186        QD(N6)=QD(N6)*D26
2187        QW(N6)=WEAL-QF(N6)-QC(N6)-QD(N6)
2188        END IF
2189        END
2190 C
2191 C      GOVERNMENT'S SUBROUTINE TO CALCULATE PUBLIC SECTOR WAGES
2192 C      THESE ARE SET TO PRIVATE INDUSTRY AVERAGES FOR THAT CLASS OF WORKER
2193 C      MULTIPLIED BY A CERTAIN PROPORTION (LEEWAY)
2194        SUBROUTINE GOVWAG(Y,I1,M,LEEWAY)
2195        REAL Y(65,60),M(20),LEEWAY,GOV
2196        DO 24 J=2,5
2197 24     Y(I1,26+J)=M(J)*LEEWAY
2198        Y(I1,32)=Y(I1,28)*1.2
2199        END
2200 C
2201 C      FIRES SUBROUTINE
2202        SUBROUTINE FIRES(I2,X,Y,DUMA,RNUMB,J,UNE,REG)
2203        REAL X(1200,36),Y(65,60),RNUMB
2204        INTEGER UNE(200,3,4),REG(3,17)
2205        INTEGER DUMA(65,100),FLAG1,FLAG,I2
2206        FLAG=10000000
2207        DO 955 I=1,RNUMB
2208        IF(X(DUMA(J,I),29) .GT. FLAG)GO TO 955
2209        FLAG=X(DUMA(J,I),29)
2210        FLAG1=I
2211 955    CONTINUE
2212        X(DUMA(J,FLAG1),7)=54
2213        Y(J,42+I2)=Y(J,42+I2)-X(DUMA(J,FLAG1),29)
2214        REG(NINT(Y(J,1)),I2+4)=REG(NINT(Y(J,1)),I2+4)+1
2215        UNE(REG(NINT(Y(J,1)),I2+4),NINT(Y(J,1)),I2)=DUMA(J,FLAG1)
2216        Y(54,13)=Y(54,13)+1
2217        X(DUMA(J,FLAG1),35)=Y(54,13)
2218        Y(J,13)=Y(J,13)-1
2219        IF(FLAG1 .EQ. RNUMB)GO TO 957
2220        DO 956 I=FLAG1,RNUMB-1
2221 956    DUMA(J,I)=DUMA(J,I+1)
2222 957    RNUMB=RNUMB-1
2223        DUMA(J,NINT(RNUMB)+1)=0
2224        END
2225 C
2226 C      QUITS SUBROUTINE
```

```
2227          SUBROUTINE QUITS(J2,X,Y,DUMA1,UNE,REG,D7,D8,D9)
2228          REAL X(1200,36),Y(65,60)
2229          INTEGER UNE(200,3,4),REG(3,17),FL,DUMA1(65,100),D7,D8,D9
2230          FL=0
2231          IF(DUMA1(D9,NINT(Y(D9,D8+4))) .EQ. J2)GO TO 994
2232          DO 992 J1=1,NINT(Y(D9,D8+4))-1
2233          IF(DUMA1(D9,J1) .EQ. J2)FL=1
2234          IF(FL .EQ. 1)DUMA1(D9,J1)=DUMA1(D9,J1+1)
2235 992      CONTINUE
2236 994      Y(D9,D8+4)=Y(D9,D8+4)-1
2237          Y(D9,D8+42)=Y(D9,D8+42)-X(J2,29)
2238          Y(54,13)=Y(54,13)+1
2239          X(J2,35)=Y(54,13)
2240          X(J2,7)=54
2241          REG(D7,D8+4)=REG(D7,D8+4)+1
2242          UNE(REG(D7,D8+4),D7,D8)=J2
2243          END
2244 C
2245 C        LOSS SUBROUTINE TO ACCOUNT FOR FIRM'S NATURAL WASTAGE
2246          SUBROUTINE LOSS(DUMA1,X,Y,J)
2247          REAL X(1200,36),Y(65,60)
2248          INTEGER DUMA1(65,100),FL
2249          FL=0
2250          DO 1069 I=1,Y(NINT(X(J,7)),4+NINT(X(J,10)))-1
2251          IF(DUMA1(NINT(X(J,7)),I) .EQ. J)FL=1
2252          IF(FL .EQ. 1)DUMA1(NINT(X(J,7)),I)=DUMA1(NINT(X(J,7)),I+1)
2253 1069     CONTINUE
2254          Y(NINT(X(J,7)),43+NINT(X(J,10)))=Y(NINT(X(J,7)),43+NINT(X(J,10
2255         &)))-X(J,29)
2256          Y(NINT(X(J,7)),4+NINT(X(J,10)))=Y(NINT(X(J,7)),4+NINT(X(J,10
2257         &)))-1
2258          END
2259 C
2260 C        SUBROUTINE HOUSE
2261 C        I1=REGION,PR=PRICE OF HOUSE WANTS TO BUY
2262 C        I2=HOUSE SOLD, D5=SELLING PRICE FOR OLD HOME,
2263          SUBROUTINE HOUSE(I1,PR,REGHS,HSESAL,X,Y,BANK,HSE,J1,D23)
2264          REAL X(1200,36),Y(65,60),HSE(1400,5),PR,SPR,SPR1,DIFF,DIFF1
2265          REAL BANK(20)
2266          INTEGER REGHS(3,10),HSESAL(3,350),I1,J1,D23,D3,D24
2267          IF(D23 .EQ. 1)GO TO 1001
2268          IF(D23 .GT. 1)GO TO 1002
2269          REGHS(I1,5)=REGHS(I1,5)+1
2270          DIFF1=10000
2271          IF(PR .GT. REGHS(I1,3))PR=REGHS(I1,3)
2272          DO 995 J=1,REGHS(I1,4)
2273          SPR=HSE(HSESAL(I1,J),2)*REGHS(I1,NINT(HSE(HSESAL(I1,J),3)))
2274          IF(SPR .GT. 1.20*PR .OR. SPR .LT. 0.90*PR)GO TO 995
2275          DIFF=ABS(SPR-PR)
2276          IF(DIFF .GT. DIFF1)GO TO 995
2277          DIFF1=DIFF
2278          I2=J
2279 995      CONTINUE
2280          IF(DIFF1 .EQ. 10000)GO TO 999
2281          SPR1=HSE(HSESAL(I1,I2),2)*REGHS(I1,NINT(HSE(HSESAL(I1,I2),3)))
2282          D5=0
```

```
2283        D24=HSESAL(I1,I2)
2284        IF(X(J1,3) .EQ. 0)GO TO 996
2285        D3=X(J1,3)
2286        REGHS(I1,4)=REGHS(I1,4)+1
2287        HSESAL(I1,REGHS(I1,4))=X(J1,3)
2288        D5=HSE(D3,2)*REGHS(I1,NINT(HSE(D3,3)))
2289        BANK(11)=BANK(11)-D5*0.99
2290  996   DO 997 J=I2,REGHS(I1,4)-1
2291  997   HSESAL(I1,J)=HSESAL(I1,J+1)
2292  998   BANK(4)=BANK(4)+SPR1
2293        X(J1,3)=D24
2294        BANK(11)=BANK(11)+SPR1
2295        X(J1,4)=X(J1,4)+SPR1-D5*0.99
2296        REGHS(I1,4)=REGHS(I1,4)-1
2297        IF(HSE(D24,4) .EQ. 3)REGHS(I1,NINT(HSE(D24,3))+6)=REGHS(I1,NINT
2298       &(HSE(D24,3))+6)-1
2299        IF(HSE(D24,4) .EQ. 3)REGHS(I1,10)=REGHS(I1,10)-1
2300        HSE(D24,4)=0
2301        HSE(D24,1)=J1
2302        GO TO 999
2303 1001   REGHS(I1,4)=REGHS(I1,4)+1
2304        HSESAL(I1,REGHS(I1,4))=X(J1,3)
2305        D5=HSE(NINT(X(J1,3)),2)*REGHS(I1,NINT(HSE(NINT(X(J1,3)),3)))
2306        BANK(11)=BANK(11)-D5*0.99
2307        X(J1,1)=D5*0.99+X(J1,1)
2308        X(J1,33)=X(J1,33)+D5*0.99
2309        X(J1,3)=0
2310        GO TO 999
2311 1002   IF(REGHS(I1,NINT(HSE(D23,3))+6) .GT. 0.75*REGHS(I1,10)
2312       & .AND. REGHS(I1,NINT(HSE(D23,3))+6) .GT. 3)GO TO 999
2313        REGHS(I1,NINT(HSE(D23,3))+6)=REGHS(I1,NINT(HSE(D23,3))+6)+1
2314        HSE(D23,4)=3
2315        REGHS(I1,10)=REGHS(I1,10)+1
2316        REGHS(I1,4)=REGHS(I1,4)+1
2317        HSESAL(I1,REGHS(I1,4))=D23
2318        D5=REGHS(I1,NINT(HSE(D23,3)))
2319        BANK(11)=BANK(11)-D5*0.99
2320        Y(J1,11)=Y(J1,11)+D5*0.99
2321  999   CONTINUE
2322        END
2323 C
2324 C      REINITIALISATION OF VARIABLES + CENTRAL BANK SUBROUTINE
2325        SUBROUTINE REINT(GOV,NCONA,REG,VAC,Y,SALE,SHARE1,Z,BANK,TIME,M,
2326       &INF,GVAC,REGHS,YP)
2327        REAL GOV(20),Y(65,60),SHARE1(60,100,2),Z(20,30),M(30),BANK(20)
2328        REAL INF
2329        INTEGER REG(3,17),VAC(65,3,4),SALE(65,60),NCONA(3),TIME
2330        INTEGER GVAC(3,4),REGHS(3,10),YP
2331 C      CENTRAL BANK OPERATIONS
2332        BANK(1)=0
2333        IF(GOV(19) .GT. 0)BANK(1)=GOV(19)
2334        BANK(7)=-GOV(20)
2335        IF(BANK(1) .GT. 0)BANK(7)=BANK(7)+GOV(6)
2336        IF(TIME .EQ. 12)BANK(7)=0
2337        BANK(3)=BANK(3)*1.02
2338        IF(TIME .LE. 30)BANK(3)=(BANK(2)/3)-BANK(1)
```

```
2339        IF(BANK(3) .LT. 0)BANK(3)=0
2340        M(1)=M(1)*(BANK(2)/(BANK(3)+BANK(1)))/3
2341        IF(M(1) .LE. 0.03)M(1)=0.03
2342        IF(M(1) .GE. 0.6)M(1)=0.6
2343        M(30)=AMAX1(0.01,(M(1)-INF/100.))
2344        IF(M(14) .GT. 0)M(2)=M(2)/M(14)
2345        IF(M(15) .GT. 0)M(3)=M(3)/M(15)
2346        IF(M(16) .GT. 0)M(4)=M(4)/M(16)
2347        IF(M(17) .GT. 0)M(5)=M(5)/M(17)
2348        IF(YP .EQ. 1)PRINT *,'TOTAL BANK DEPOSITS',BANK(2)
2349        IF(YP .EQ. 1)PRINT *,'TREASURY BILLS',BANK(1)
2350        IF(YP .EQ. 1)PRINT *,'INTEREST RATE',M(1)
2351        IF(YP .EQ. 1)PRINT *,'GOVERNMENT DEBT',GOV(19)
2352        IF(YP .EQ. 1)PRINT *,'DIRECT TAX REVENUE',GOV(1)
2353   C
2354        BANK(2)=0
2355        GOV(20)=0
2356        DO 873 J=1,3
2357        NCONA(J)=0
2358        REGHS(J,5)=0
2359        DO 873 I=1,4
2360        REG(J,I)=0
2361        GVAC(J,I)=0
2362        DO 873 K=1,65
2363   873  VAC(K,J,I)=0
2364        DO 871 J=1,65
2365        DO 874 I=1,60
2366   874  SALE(J,I)=0
2367        IF(J .GT. 60)GO TO 871
2368        DO 876 I=1,100
2369        SHARE1(J,I,1)=0
2370   876  SHARE1(J,I,2)=0
2371   871  CONTINUE
2372        DO 872 J=1,12
2373        Z(J,21)=0
2374        Z(J,23)=0
2375        Z(J,24)=0
2376   872  GOV(J)=0.0
2377        Z(2,6)=Z(2,6)*1.015
2378        Z(4,6)=Z(4,6)*1.014
2379        Z(8,6)=Z(8,6)*1.02
2380   C    IF(TIME .GT. 120 .AND. TIME .LT. 133)Z(4,6)=Z(4,6)*1.5
2381        END
2382   C
2383   C    CALCULATE FIRMS SKILL LEVELS
2384        SUBROUTINE SKILEV(Y,EXEC,WC,SK,UNS,X,J)
2385        REAL X(1200,36),Y(65,60)
2386        INTEGER EXEC(65,100),WC(65,100),SK(65,100),UNS(65,100)
2387        DO 505 I=43,46
2388   505  Y(J,I)=0
2389        IF(Y(J,5) .EQ. 0)GO TO 401
2390        DO 400 I=1,Y(J,5)
2391   400  Y(J,43)=X(EXEC(J,I),29)+Y(J,43)
2392   401  IF(Y(J,6) .EQ. 0)GO TO 402
2393        DO 410 I=1,Y(J,6)
2394   410  Y(J,44)=X(WC(J,I),29)+Y(J,44)
```

```
2395 402    IF(Y(J,7) .EQ. 0)GO TO 403
2396        DO 420 I=1,Y(J,7)
2397 420    Y(J,45)=X(SK(J,I),29)+Y(J,45)
2398 403    IF(Y(J,8) .EQ. 0)GO TO 439
2399        DO 430 I=1,Y(J,8)
2400        Y(J,46)=X(UNS(J,I),29)+Y(J,46)
2401 430    CONTINUE
2402 439    CONTINUE
2403        END
2404 C      SUBROUTINE UPDATING CONSUMER MATRIX IF BUYS A CAR, CONSD, OR COMP
2405        SUBROUTINE CHSP(I2,J,X,M,Z,QW,I3,MAKE,SHOP,Y,GOOD,RPI,CLOCK,N7
2406       &,SALE,STOCK,TIME,I4,D20)
2407        LOGICAL D20
2408        REAL X(1200,36),M(30),Z(20,30),QW(5),Y(65,60),RPI(12),GOOD
2409        INTEGER CLOCK,N7,SHOP,MAKE,SALE(65,60),STOCK(65,65),TIME
2410        N7=I3
2411        IF(I2 .EQ. 2)X(J,36)=0
2412        IF(.NOT. D20 .AND. STOCK(SHOP,MAKE) .GE. 1)GO TO 315
2413        IF(.NOT. D20)GO TO 322
2414        IF(TIME .GT. 24)X(J,30)=X(J,30)*0.90
2415        QW(N7)=QW(N7)+(Y(MAKE,16)-Z(I2,22)/M(18))*Y(SHOP,17)*(1+M(19))
2416        IF(QW(N7) .LE. 0)GO TO 322
2417        X(J,I4)=Y(MAKE,19)*Z(I2,6)
2418        Y(SHOP,11)=Y(SHOP,11)+Z(I2,22)*Y(SHOP,17)/M(18)
2419        Y(SHOP,50)=Y(SHOP,50)+Z(I2,22)/M(18)
2420        GOOD=GOOD+Z(I2,22)*Y(SHOP,17)/M(18)
2421        Z(I2,21)=Z(I2,21)+Z(I2,22)/M(18)
2422        GO TO 321
2423 322    N7=4
2424        X(J,30)=X(J,30)*0.90
2425        GO TO 321
2426 315    X(J,I4)=Y(MAKE,19)*Z(I2,6)
2427        Y(SHOP,11)=Y(SHOP,11)+Y(MAKE,16)*Y(SHOP,17)
2428        GOOD=GOOD+Y(MAKE,16)*Y(SHOP,17)
2429        SALE(SHOP,MAKE)=SALE(SHOP,MAKE)+1
2430        STOCK(SHOP,MAKE)=STOCK(SHOP,MAKE)-1
2431        IF(TIME .GT. 24)X(J,30)=X(J,30)*1.05
2432 321    CONTINUE
2433        END
2434 C
2435 C      SUBROUTINE TO ALLOCATE GOVERNMENT EMPLOYEES TO DIFFERENT SECTORS
2436        SUBROUTINE GOVEMP(GOVW,Y,DUM,X,J1)
2437        REAL X(1200,36),Y(65,60),GOVW(3,8,3)
2438        INTEGER DUM(65,100)
2439        DO 802 K=1,3
2440        DO 802 J=1,NINT(Y(50+K,J1))
2441        GOVW(NINT(X(DUM(50+K,J),8)),J1-4,K)=GOVW(NINT(X(DUM(50+K,J),8))
2442       &,J1-4,K)+1
2443 802    GOVW(NINT(X(DUM(50+K,J),8)),J1,K)=GOVW(NINT(X(DUM(50+K,J),8))
2444       &,J1,K)+X(DUM(50+K,J),29)
2445        END
2446 C
2447 C      SUBROUTINE TO CALCULATE SALES OF FOOD CLOTHES AND DRINK TO SHOP
2448        SUBROUTINE SHSL(SHOP,MAKE,SALE,QQ,NQ,Y,M,STOCK,IMPT)
2449        REAL Y(65,60),QQ(5),M(30),IMPT
2450        INTEGER STOCK(65,65),SALE(65,60),SHOP,MAKE,NQ
```

```
2451        SALE(SHOP,MAKE)=SALE(SHOP,MAKE)+QQ(NQ)/(Y(SHOP,17)*Y(MAKE,16)
2452       &*(1+M(19)))
2453        STOCK(SHOP,MAKE)=STOCK(SHOP,MAKE)-QQ(NQ)/(Y(SHOP,17)*Y(MAKE
2454       &,16)*(1+M(19)))
2455        IF(STOCK(SHOP,MAKE) .GE. 0)GO TO 15
2456        IMPT=IMPT-STOCK(SHOP,MAKE)*Y(MAKE,16)
2457        Y(SHOP,50)=Y(SHOP,50)-STOCK(SHOP,MAKE)*Y(MAKE,16)
2458        STOCK(SHOP,MAKE)=0
2459 15     CONTINUE
2460        END
2461 C
2462 C      SUBROUTINE TO REMOVE BANKRUPT FIRMS FROM INDUSTRY MATRIX
2463        SUBROUTINE REMO(J,Y,Z,DUM)
2464        REAL Y(65,60),Z(20,30)
2465        INTEGER DUM(10)
2466        IF(NINT(Y(J,23)) .EQ. Z(NINT(Y(J,3)),7))GO TO 3001
2467        DO 3000 J1=NINT(Y(J,23)),NINT(Z(NINT(Y(J,3)),7))-1
2468        DUM(J1)=DUM(J1+1)
2469 3000   Y(DUM(J1),23)=J1
2470 3001   DUM(NINT(Z(NINT(Y(J,3)),7)))=0
2471        END
2472 C
2473 C      SUBROUTINE ADDS 1ST WORKER OF EACH SKILL TO FIRMS IN INITIALISATION
2474        SUBROUTINE INAL(X,J,Y,K,N)
2475        REAL X(1200,36),Y(65,60)
2476        X(K,7)=J
2477        IF(J .GT. 50)X(K,8)=3
2478        IF(J. LE. 50)X(K,8)=Y(J,1)
2479        X(K,10)=N
2480        END
```

Appendix 2: Nag Library Subroutines

This appendix provides a short guide to the Nag library subroutines used in the program.

GO5CBF(I): This sets the basic generator routine GO5CAF to a repeatable initial state. On entry I specifies a number from which the new internal generator is calculated. This basic generator routine is used by routine GO5DDF, GO5EYF and GO5DZF as described below.

GO5DDF(A,B): This provdes a pseudo-random real number from a normal, Gaussian, distribution with a given mean, A, and standard deviation, B. It is used in conjunction with GO5CBF which initialises the process.

GO5EBF(M,N,R,NR,IFAIL): This sets up a reference vector, R, for a discrete uniform distribution between two given numbers, M and N, inclusive. NR is the dimension of R. This reference vector is then used by GO5EYF as described below. For example in line 1747 it is used to set up a reference vector, R12, for a distribution between 1 and REG(D6,J + 4), the number of unemployed of occupation J + 4, in region D6.

GO5EXF(P,NP,IP,LP,R,NR,I,IFAIL): This sets up a reference vector R, of dimension NR, for a discrete distribution with a probability density function or cumulative density function P (dimension NP). It too is then used by GO5EYF as described below.

GO5EYF(R,NR): This provides a pseudo-random integer

from a discrete distribution which is defined by an initial reference vector, NR. For example in line 1748 a random unemployed individual is drawn from those in region D6 and occupation J + 4. This individual then has an 'interview' with the Ith firm.

GO5DZF(P): This provides a pseudo-random logical value —TRUE with probability P and FALSE with probability (1 − P). This is used, for example, in line 841 in programming births. The probability of a child being born to a parent of a suitable age is 0.009.

References

Adelman, I. and Adelman, F. (1959) 'The dynamic properties of the Klein–Goldberger-model', *Econometrica*, vol. 27, pp. 298–327.

Altman, E.I. (1983) *Corporate Financial Distress*, New York: John Wiley & Sons.

Arrow, K.J. (1959) 'Towards a theory of price adjustment', in Abramovitz, A. (ed.), *The Allocation of Economic Resources*, Stanford: Stanford University Press.

Arrow, K.J. and Debreu, G. (1954) 'Existence of an equilibrium for a competitive economy', *Econometrica*, vol. 22, pp. 265–90.

Balfour, A. and Marwick, D.H. (1979) *Programming in Standard Fortran 77*, London: Heinemann.

Ballard, C.L., Fullerton, D., Shoven, J.B. and Whalley, J. (1985) *A General Equilibrium Model for Tax Policy Evaluation*, Chicago: University of Chicago Press.

Barro, R.J. (1980a). 'A capital market in an equilibrium business cycle model', *Econometrica*, vol. 48, pp. 1393–417.

Barro, R.J. (1980b) 'The equilibrium approach to business cycles', in Barro, R.J. (ed.), *Money, Expectations and Business Cycles*, New York: Academic Press.

Barro, R.J. and Grossman, H.I. (1971) 'A general disequilibrium model of income and employment', *American Economic Review*, vol. 61, pp. 82–93.

Barro, R.J. and Grossman, H.I. (1976) *Money, Employment, and Inflation*, Cambridge: Cambridge University Press.

Barron, J.M., Bishop, J. and Dunkelberg, W.C. (1985) 'Employer search: the interviewing and hiring of new employees', *Review of Economics and Statistics*, vol. 67, pp. 43–52.

Berndt, E.R. (1976) 'Reconciling alternative estimates of the elasticity of substitution', *Review of Economics and Statistics*, vol. 58, pp. 59–68.

Beveridge, W.H. (1931) *Causes and Cures of Unemployment*, London: Longman Green.

Birmingham Community Development Project (1977) *Workers on the Scrapheap*, London and Oxford.

Bosworth, B.P. (1984) *Tax Incentives and Economic Growth*, Washington, D.C.: Brookings Institution.

Brenner, H. (1979) 'Estimating the social costs of national economic policy: Implications for mental and physical health and clinical aggression', Joint Economic Committee of the US Congress.

Brown, C.V. (1983) *Taxation and the Incentive to Work*, 2nd edition, Oxford: Oxford University Press.

Bulow, J. and Shoven, J. (1978) 'The bankruptcy decision', *The Bell Journal of Economics*, vol. 9, pp. 437–56.

Cannan, E. (1930) 'The problem of unemployment: A review of the *Post-War Economic Problem* by Henry Clay', *Economic Journal*, vol. 40, pp. 45–55.

Casson, M. (1983) *Economics of Unemployment*, Oxford: Martin Robertson.

Clark, K.B. and Summers, L.H. (1982) 'Labour force participation: Timing and persistence', *Review of Economic Studies*, vol. 49, pp. 825–44.

Classen, K.P. (1977) 'The effects of unemployment insurance on the duration of unemployment and subsequent earnings', *Industrial and Labour Relations Review*, vol. 30, pp. 438–44.

Clay, H. (1928) 'Unemployment and wage rates', *Economic Journal*, vol. 38, pp. 1–15.

Clay, H. (1929a) *The Post-War Unemployment Problem*, London: Macmillan.

Clay, H. (1929b) 'The public regulation of wages in Great Britain', *Economic Journal*, vol. 39, pp. 323–43.

Clower, R.W. (1965) 'The Keynesian counterrevolution: A theoretical appraisal', in Hahn, F.H. and Brechling, F. (eds), *The Theory of Interest Rates*, London: Macmillan.

Cork Committee (1982) *Insolvency Law and Practice, Report of the Review Committee*, Cmnd. 8558, London: HMSO.

Deaton, A.S. (1977) 'Involuntary saving through unanticipated inflation', *American Economic Revenue*, vol. 67, pp. 899–910.

Debreu, G. (1959) *Theory of Value*, New York: John Wiley.

Dixon, P., Parmenter, B., Sutton, J. and Orani, V.D. (1982) *A Multi-Sectoral Model of the Australian Economy*, Amsterdam: North-Holland.

Drazen, A. (1980) Recent developments in macroeconomic disequilibrium theory, *Econometrica*, vol. 48, pp. 283–306.

Ehrenberg, R.G. and Oaxaca, R.L. (1976) 'Unemployment insurance, duration of unemployment and subsequent gain', *The American Economic Review*, vol. 66, pp. 754–66.

Fair, R.C. (1979) 'An analysis of the accuracy of four macroeconomic models', *Journal of Political Economy*, vol. 87, pp. 701–18.

Feldstein, M. (1983a) *Capital Taxation*, Cambridge, Mass.: Harvard University Press.

Feldstein, M. (1983b) *Inflation, Tax Rules and Capital Formation*, Chicago: University of Chicago Press.

Fischer, S. (1977) 'Long-term contracts rational expectations and the optimal money supply', *Journal of Political Economy*, vol. 85, pp. 191–205.

Freeman, C., Clark, J. and Soete, L. (1982) *Unemployment and Technical Innovation*, London: Frances Pinter.

Friedman, M. (1957), *Theory of the Consumption Function*. Princeton, N.J.: Princeton University Press.

Friedman, M. (1968), 'The role of monetary policy', *American Economic Review*, vol. 58, pp. 1–17.

Friedman, M. (1977) 'Nobel lecture: Inflation and unemployment', *Journal of Political Economy*, vol. 85, pp. 451–72.

Gale, D. (1955) 'The law of supply and demand', *Mathematica Scandinavia*, vol. 3, pp. 155–69.

Giersch, H. (1979) 'Aspects of growth, structural change and employment—a Schumpeterian perspective', *Weltwirtschaftliches Archiv*, vol. 115, pp. 629–51.

Glaister, K.W., McGlone, A. and Ulph, D.T. (1979) 'Labour supply responses to tax changes—a simulation exercise for the UK', in Brown, C.V. (ed.), *Taxation and Labour Supply*, London: Institute for Fiscal Studies.

Goodhart, C. (1984) *Monetary Theory and Practice: The UK Experience*, London: Macmillan.

Hahn, F.H. (1976) 'Keynesian economics and general equilibrium theory', IMSSS Technical Report No. 219, Stanford: Stanford University.

Harberger, A.C. (1959) 'The corporation income tax: An empirical appraisal', *Tax Revision Compendium*, 1, in US Congress, House Committee on Ways and Means, Washington DC: Government Printing Office, pp. 231–50.

Harberger, A.C. (1962) 'The incidence of the corporation tax', *Journal of Political Economy*, vol. 70, pp. 215–40.

Harberger, A.C. (1966) 'Efficiency effects of taxes on income from capital', in Krzyzaniak, M. (ed.), *Effects of Corporation Income*

Tax, Symposium on Business Taxation, Wayne State University, Detroit: Wayne State University Press.

Harberger, A.C. (1974) *Taxation and Welfare*, Boston: Little, Brown and Company.

Hausman, J.A. (1981) 'Labour supply', in Aaron, H.J. and Pechman, J.A. (eds), *How Taxes Affect Economic Behavior*, Washington: Brookings Institution, pp. 27–83.

Helliwell, J., Sturm, P., Jarret, P. and Salou, G. (1985) 'Aggregate supply in interlink: Model specification and empirical results', OECD Department of Economics and Statistics Working Paper No. 26.

Holt, C.C. (1970) 'Job search, Phillips' wage relation and union influence: theory and evidence', in Phelps, E.S. *et al.*, *Microeconomic Foundations of Employment and Inflation Theory*, New York: W.W. Norton, pp. 224–56.

Hudson, J. (1982) *Inflation: A Theoretical Survey and Synthesis*, London: Allen and Unwin.

Hudson, J. (1984) *An Analysis of Company Liquidations in England and Wales*, University of Bath Working Paper 1284.

Hudson, J. (1986a) 'An analysis of company liquidations', *Applied Economics*, vol. 18, pp. 219-35.

Hudson, J. (1986b) 'Company births in Great Britain', unpublished paper.

Jaffee, D. and Modigliani, F. (1969) 'A theory and test of credit rationing', *American Economic Review*, vol. 59, pp. 850–72.

Jaffee, D. and Russell, F. (1976) 'Imperfect information and credit rationing', *Quarterly Journal of Economics*, vol. 90, pp. 651–66.

James, J. (1985) 'New developments in the application of general equilibrium models to economic history', in Piggot, J. and Whalley, J. (eds), *New Developments in Applied General Equilibrium Models*, Cambridge: Cambridge University Press, pp. 441–65.

Johansen, L. (1959) 'Substitution vs. fixed production coefficients in the theory of economic growth: a synthesis', *Econometrica*, vol. 27, pp. 157–75.

Jones, D.T. (1985) 'Vehicles', in Freeman, C. (ed.) *Technological Trends and Employment: 4 Engineering and Vehicles*, Aldershot: Gower, pp. 128–87.

Kasper, H. (1967) 'The asking price of labour and the duration of unemployment (in Minnesota)', *Review of Economics and Statistics*, vol. 49, pp. 165–72.

Keeton, W. (1979) *Equilibrium Credit Rationing*, New York: Garland Press.

Keynes, J.M. (1936) *The General Theory of Employment, Interest and Money*. London: Macmillan.

Kiefer, N. and Neumann, G. (1979) 'An empirical job search model with a test of the constant reservation wage hypothesis', *Journal of Political Economy*, vol. 87, pp. 89–108.

Klamer, A. (1984) *The New Classical Macroeconomics*, Brighton: Wheatsheaf Books.

Klein, L.R. and Goldberger, A.S. (1955) *An Econometric Model of the United States 1929–1952*, Amsterdam: North-Holland.

Knight, F.H. (1921) *Risk, Uncertainty and Profit*, Boston: Houghton-Mifflin.

Kondratief, N. (1925) 'The major economic cycles', *Voprosy Konjuntury*, vol. 1, pp. 28–9; English translation in *Review of Economic Statistics*, 18, (November 1935), pp. 105–15, reprinted in *Lloyds Bank Review*, no. 129, (1978).

Korliras, P.G. (1980) 'Disequilibrium theories and their policy implications: Towards a synthetic disequilibrium approach', *Kyklos*, vol. 33, pp. 449–74.

Kuhn, H.W. and MacKinnon, J.G. (1975), 'The sandwich method for finding fixed points', Dept. of Econ. and Math., Technical Report, Princeton University, N.J.

Kuznets, S. (1940) 'Schumpeter's business cycles', *American Economic Review*, vol. 30, pp. 257–71.

Laan, van der G. and Talman, A. J. (1979) 'A restart algorithm without an artificial level for computing fixed points on unbounded regions', in Petigen, H.O. and Walter, H.O. (eds) *Functional Differential Equations and Approximations of Fixed Points*, Heidleberg: Springer-Verlag.

Layard, R. (1981) 'Unemployment in Britian: Causes and cures', London: Centre for Labour Economics, London School of Economics.

Layard, R. and Nickell, S. (1985) 'The causes of British unemployment', *National Institute Economic Review*, February, pp. 62–85.

Leontief, W.W. (1941) *The Structure of the American Economy, 1919–1939*, New York: Oxford University Press.

Leontief, W.W. (1953) *Studies in the Structure of the American Economy*, New York: Oxford University Press.

Lippman, S.A. and McCall, J.J. (1976) 'The economics of job search: A survey', Part 1, *Economic Inquiry*, vol. 14, pp. 155–89.

Lloyd-Jones, R. and Le-Roux, A.A. (1982) 'Marshall and the birth and death of firms: The growth and size distribution of firms in the early nineteenth-century cotton industry', *British History*, vol. 14, pp. 141–55.

Lomax, K.S. (1954) 'Business failures, another example of the analysis of failure data', *Journal of the American Statistical Association*, vol. 49, pp. 847–52.

Lorenz, C. (1975) 'Balancing the Anglo-German investment equation', *Financial Times*, 4 September.

Lucas, R. (1972a) 'Econometric testing of the natural rate hypothesis', in Eckstein, O. (ed.) *The Economics of Price Determination Conference*, Washington: Board of Governors, Federal Reserve System, pp. 50–9.

Lucas, R. (1972b) 'Expectations and the neutrality of money', *Journal of Economic Theory*, vol. 4, pp. 103–24.

Lucas, R. (1975) 'An economic model of the business cycle', *Journal of Political Economy*, vol. 83, pp. 353–7.

Lucas, R. (1978) 'Unemployment policy', *American Economic Review*, papers and proceedings, vol. 68, pp. 353–7.

Lustig, R.J. (1985) 'The politics of shutdown: community, property, corporatism', *Journal of Economic Issues*, vol. 19, pp. 123–52.

Malinvaud, E. (1982) Wages and employment, *The Economic Journal*, vol. 92, pp. 1–12.

Marcus, M. (1967) 'Firms' exit rates and their determinants', *Journal of Industrial Economics*, vol. 16, pp. 10–22.

Massey, D. and Meegan, R.A. (1979) 'The geography of industrial reorganisation: The spatial effects of the restructuring of the electrical engineering sector under the Industrial Reorganisation Corporation', *Progress in Planning*, vol. 10, pp. 155–237.

Mathews, R.C.O. (1968) 'Why has Britain had full employment since the war?', *Economic Journal*, vol. 78, pp. 555–69.

Mellow, W. (1982) 'Employer size and wages', *Review of Economics and Statistics*, vol. 64, pp. 495–501.

Mensch, G. (1975) *Das Technologische Patt: Innovationen uberwinden die Depression*, Frankfurt, Umschau; English edition (1979), *Stalemate in Technology: Innovations overcome the Depression*, New York: Ballinger.

Merril, O.H. (1972) 'Applications and extensions of an algorithm that computes fixed points of certain upper semi-continuous point to set mappings', Ph.D. Dissertation, Dept. of Ind. Engin., University of Michigan.

METRIC (1981) *Une Modelisation de l'economie française*, Paris: INSEE.

Moffitt, R. (1985) 'Unemployment insurance and the distribution of unemployment spells', *Journal of Econometrics*, vol. 28, pp. 29–49.

Mortenson, D.T. (1970) 'Job search, the duration of unemployment and the Phillips curve', *American Economic Review*, vol. 60, pp. 847–62.

Muellbauer, J. and Portes, R. (1978) Macroeconomic models with quantity rationing, *Economic Journal*, vol. 88, pp. 788–821.

Muth, J.F. (1961) 'Rational expectations and the theory of price movements', *Econometrica*, vol. 29, pp. 315–35.

Narendranathan, W. and Nickell, S. (1985) 'Modelling the process of job search', *Journal of Econometrics*, vol. 28, pp. 29–49.

Nguyen, T. (1985) 'General equilibrium with price rigidities', in *New Developments in Applied General Equilibrium Models*, Piggot, J. and Whalley, J. (eds), Cambridge: Cambridge University Press, pp. 441–65.

Nickell, S. (1979) 'The effect of unemployment and related benefits on the duration of unemployment', *Economic Journal*, vol. 89, pp. 34–9.

Oi, W. (1983) 'Heterogeneous firms and the organisation of production', *Economic Inquiry*, vol. 21, pp. 147–71.

Parsons, D.O. (1973) 'Quit rates over time: a search and information approach', *American Economic Review*, vol. 63, pp. 390–401.

Patinkin, D. (1965) *Money, Interest and Prices*, 2nd edn, New York: Harper and Row.

Phelps, E.S. (1968) 'Money wage dynamics and labour market equilibrium', *Journal of Political Economy*, vol. 76, pp. 678–711.

Phelps, E.S. *et al.* (1970) *Microeconomic Foundations of Employment and Inflation Theory*, New York: W.W. Norton.

Phelps, E.S. and Taylor, J.B. (1977) 'Stabilising properties of monetary policy under rational expectations', *Journal of Political Economy*, vol. 84, pp. 163–90.

Piggott, J. and Whalley, J. (1985) *UK Tax Policy and Applied General Equilibrium Analysis*, Cambridge: Cambridge University Press.

Pigou, A.C. (1927a) 'Wage policy and unemployment', *Economic Journal*, vol. 37, pp. 355–68.

Pigou, A.C. (1927b) *Industrial Fluctuations*, London: Macmillan.

Pool, A.G. (1938) *Wage Policy in Relation to Industrial Fluctuations*, London: Macmillan.

Salop, S.C. (1973) 'Systematic job search and unemployment', *Review of Economic Studies*, vol. 40, pp. 191–201.

Sargent, T.J. (1973) 'Rational expectations, the real rate of interest and the natural rate of unemployment', *Brookings Papers on Economic Activity*, no. 2, pp. 429–72.

Sargent, T.J. (1976) 'A classical macroeconomic model for the United States', *Journal of Political Economy*, vol. 84, pp. 429–72.

Scarf, H.E. (1967) 'On the computation of equilibrium prices', in Fellner, W.M. *et al.*, (eds), *Ten Essays in Honour of Irving Fisher*, New York: Wiley, pp. 207–30.

Scarf, H.E. with the collaboration of T. Hansen (1973) *The Computation of Economic Equilibrium*, New Haven: Yale University Press.

Scherer, F.M. (1965) 'Firm size, market structure, opportunity and the output of patented inventions', *American Economic Review*, vol. 55, pp. 1097–125.

Schumpeter, J.A., (1911, 1951, 1952) *Theorie der Wirtschaftlichen Entwicklung, Eine Untersuchung über Unternehmergewinn, Kapital, Kredit, Zins und den Konjunkturzyklus* (5th edn, 1952). Berlin, Dunker & Humblot; English translation by R. Opie, *The Theory of Economic Development* (3rd end, 1951), Cambridge, Mass.: Harvard University Press.

Schumpeter, J.A. (1939) *Business Cycles: A Theoretical, Historical and Statistical Analysis of the Capitalist Process*, 2 vols, New York and London: McGraw Hill.

Schumpeter, J.A. (1943) *Capitalism, Socialism and Democracy*, New York: Harper and Row.

Scott, M. with Laslett, R.A. (1978) *Can't We Get Back to Full Employment?*, London: Macmillan.

Shoven, J.B. and Whalley, J. (1972) 'A general equilibrium calculation of the effects of different taxation of income from capital in the US', *Journal of Public Economics*, vol. 1, pp. 281–321.

Shoven, J.B. and Whalley, J. (1973) 'General equilibrium with taxes: A computational procedure and an existence proof', *The Review of Economic Studies*, vol. 40, pp. 475–89.

Shoven, J.B. and Whalley, J. (1974) 'On the computation of competitive equilibrium in international markets with tariffs', *Journal of International Economics*, vol. 4, pp. 341–54.

Shoven, J.B. and Whalley, J. (1984) 'Applied general-equilibrium models of taxation and international trade', *Journal of Economic Literature*, vol. 23, pp. 1007–51.

Sims, C.A. (1982) 'Policy analysis with econometric models', *Brookings Papers on Economic Activity*, pp. 107–64.

Sinai, A., Lin, A. and Robbins, A. (1983) 'Taxes, saving and investment: Some empirical evidence', *National Tax Journal*, vol. 36, pp. 321–45.

Slutsky, E. (1927) *The Summation of Random Causes as the Source of Cyclic Processes*, vol. III, no. 1, Moscow, Conjecture Institute (Russian with English summary).

Soete, L.L.G. (1979) 'Firm size and incentive activity: The evidence reconsidered', *European Economic Review*, vol. 12, pp. 319–40.

Stein, H. (1981) *Presidential Economics*, New York: Simon & Schuster.

Stephenson, S.P. Jnr (1976) 'The economics of youth job search behaviour', *Review of Economics and Statistics*, vol. 58, pp. 104–11.

Stigler, G.J. (1962) 'Information in the labour market', *Journal of Political Economy*, vol. 72, pp. 94–105.

Stiglitz, J.E. and Weiss, A. (1981) 'Credit rationing in markets with imperfect information', *American Economic Review*, vol. 71, pp. 393–410.

Telser, L.G. (1973) 'Searching for the lowest price', *American Economic Review*, vol. 63, pp. 40–9.

van Horne, J.C. (1976) 'Optimal initiation of bankruptcy proceedings by debt holders', *The Journal of Finance*, vol. 31, pp. 897–910.

Wilson Committee (1979) *Committee to Review the Functioning of Financial Institutions Interim Report: The Financing of Small Firms*, HMSO, London.

Index

Agent based model, 135–6,
  140–74, 186–8, 189–233
Aggregation problems, 2–3,
  40–1, 122–3
Altman, 84
Applied general equilibrium
  models, 123–8
Arrow, 19, 124
Aspiration (or reservation)
  wage, 23–6, 156–7

Balance of payments, 4–9
Ballard, 125
Bankruptcies, 31–3, 45–6, 48,
  55–7, 130–4, 155, 177
  age structure, 84–5, 86–92
Banks, 33, 80–-5
  secured loans, 79–80
Barro, 18, 19, 44
Barron, 24
Birmingham community
  project, 74
Bosworth, 41, 114
Brenner, 58
Brookings model, 121
Brown, 42
Bulow, 82
Business cycle, 17–22, 30–4
  the Kondratief, 29–34

Cannan, 10

Capital stock, 44–5, 47–55,
  68–74, 122, 128–9
Car industry, 61–2, 106–8
Casson, 10, 28
Clark, 19
Clarke, 32
Classen, 25
Classical theories, 9
Clay, 10, 28
Clower, 44
Compulsory liquidations,
  78–82, 86–90
Computer industry, 31–2,
  109–10, 115
Computer models 121–34,
  136–9, 140–74, 185–8,
  189–233
Cork report, 81–2, 99
Creditors' voluntary
  liquidations, 78–82,
  86–90

Debreu, 124
Disequilibrium, 2, 11–14,
  37–8, 40–1, 43–6
Dixon, 127
Drazen, 2, 43, 46
DRI model, 121

Effective demand, 44, 47–8,
  178–9

245

Effective supply, 47–8, 178–9
Ehrenberg, 25
Entrepreneurs, 30–2, 93–4, 97–9, 180
Equilibrium theories
  general , 16–22, 31–4, 36–8, 40–1, 44–6, 123–8
  partial, 9–10
Expectations, 11, 17–22

Fair, 18
Feldstein, 41
Fires, 158
Firms, 42–3, 144–6, 152–5, 180–1
  death of, 82–92
  new, 93–7
Fischer, 18
France, 15
Freeman, 32
Friedman, 15, 16, 17
Full employment, 12–15
Fullerton, 125

Gale, 124
Giersch, 30
Glaister, 41
Goldberger, 121
Goodhart, 85
Government policies
  balanced budget, 8, 181
  fiscal policy, 13–15, 113–14
  exchange rate, 9
  industrial, 114–16
  interest rate, 7–9
  targeting fiscal policies, 60–2
Government rescue of failed firms, 100–5
Grossman, 44
Grunberg, 17

Hahn, 45

Harberger, 124
Hausman, 41
Health and unemployment, 58, 100
Helliwell, 47
Hires, 158
Holt, 23
Hudson, 12, 27, 83

Inflation, 8–9, 12–13
Investment, 41–3, 61–2, 106–8, 129–34

Jaffee, 85
James, 126
Japan, 106–8, 114
Johansen, 49
Jones, 106

Kasper, 26
Keeton, 85
Kennedy, 14
Keynes, 11, 22, 36, 37, 39, 40, 116, 179
Keynesian theories, 11–15, 34–8, 60–2, 120–1
Keynes' law, 37, 74, 175
Kiefer, 26
Klamer, 19
Klein, 121
Knight, 11
Kondratief, 29
Korliras, 37
Kuhn, 125
Kuznets, 33

Layard, 29, 120
Lay-offs, 5–7
Leontief, 124
Le Roux, 84
Lin, 41
Lloyd-Jones, 84
Lomax, 84 ·

Lorenz, 73
Lucas, 17, 18, 21, 27, 119, 123

McGlone, 41
McKenzie, 124
MacKinnon, 125
Macroeconomic models, 121–3
Malinvaud, 44
Management buyouts, 105
Manufacturing industries, 4–8,
   56, 72–3
Marcus, 84
Massey, 73
Meegan, 73
Mellow, 25
Mensch, 32, 68
Merril, 125
METRIC, 47
Microeconomic approaches to
   macroeconomics, 22–7,
   40–1
Minford, 20
Mismatch unemployment, 157
Modigliani, 85
Moffit, 25
Monetarism, 15–17
Mortenson, 23
Muellbauer, 44
Muth, 17

Nag library subroutines,
   141–6, 148, 234–5
Narendranathan, 25
Neoclassical theories, 9–10,
   20–1, 27–9, 35
Neumann, 26
New classical theories, 17–22,
   35
Nguyen, 126
Nickell, 25, 120

Oaxaca, 25
Official reciever, 79

Oi, 25
OPEC price increases, 3–5,
   178–9

Parmenter, 127
Parsons, 27
Patinkin, 43, 44
Phelps, 18, 23, 27, 40
Phillips curve, 9, 16, 23, 71–2
Piggot, 127
Pigou, 10, 20, 28, 29
Pool, 28
Portes, 44
Preferential creditors, 76–82
Product cycle, 130–4

Quits, 157–8

Reagan Administration's
   economic policies tax
   cuts, 8, 41–2, 114
Receiver, 79–82
Reddaway Committee, 95
Robbins, 41
Russell, 85

Salop, 24
Sargent, 17, 18, 21
Say's law, 11, 37
Scarf, 71, 124
Scherer, 31
Search theories, 17, 22–27,
   156–8
   and unemplyment insurance,
   25–6
Schumpeter, 29, 30, 31, 35,
   102, 110
Schumpeterian analysis, 63–8,
   102–3
   creative destruction, 30–3,
   64
Secured creditors, 76–82
Shoven, 71, 82, 124, 125, 126
Sims, 123

Sinai, 41
Soete, 31, 32
Stein, 41
Stephenson, 26
Stigler, 23
Stiglitz, 85
Structuralist theories of
    unemployment, 27–34
Summers, 19
Supply side economics, 41–3
Sutton, 127

Taxes, 8, 14–5, 95–6, 114
Talman, 125
Taylor, 18
Telser, 24
Thatcher government's
    economic policies, 12,
    183–4
Townsend, 19, 20
Trade restrictions, 108–11,
    177–8
Trade unions, 10, 20, 120
Training, 27
    for entrepreneurs, 97–9
Treasury model, 122

Ulph, 41
Unemployment
    causes, 1–38, 120
    costs of, 58, 100–1, 104–5
    demand-deficient, 11–15,
    53–60
    frictional, 54–5
    natural rate of, 16
    and price surprises, 16–21
    and real wages, 10–1, 28–9,
    35–6, 111–12, 132–3

structural, 27–9, 55
supply-deficient, 53–60
and unemployment
    insurance, 10, 20, 25–6,
    28–9, 120
/vacancy curve, 71–2
United Kingdom
    corporate births, 94–6
    future policies, 98–111,
    114–18, 183–5
    insolvencies, 55–7, 86–90
    insolvency system, 78–82
    post-war policies, 12–13
    post-war unemployment,
    2–8
United States
    bankruptcies, 55–7, 90–2
    bankruptcy code, 76–8,
    91–2
    budget deficit, 8
    corporate births, 96–7
    Employment Act of 1946,
    14
    future policies, 98–111,
    114–18, 181–3
    post-war policies, 14–15
    post-war unemployment,
    2–9, 14–15
Unsecured creditors, 76–8

van der Laan, 125
van Horne, 83
Vincent, 127

Weiss, 85
Whalley, 124, 125, 126, 127
Wharton model, 122
Wilson Committee, 83